SQUARES

SQUARES

A Public Place Design Guide for Urbanists

Mark C. Childs

University of New Mexico Press   Albuquerque

10   09   08   07   06   05   04   1   2   3   4   5   6   7

LIBRARY OF CONGRESS CATALOGING-IN-PUBLICATION DATA

Childs, Mark C.
Squares : a public place design guide for urbanists / Mark C. Childs.— 1st ed.
p. cm.
Includes bibliographical references and index.
ISBN 0-8263-3003-7 (cloth : alk. paper)
1. Public spaces. 2. Architecture—Human factors. 3. City planning. I. Title.
NA9053.S6C49   2004
711'.55—DC22

2004015733

All photos by Mark Childs unless otherwise indicated.

Book design and type composition: Kathleen Sparkes

The text for this book was set in Utopia 9/13

The display type is Serlio and Univers

The display elements are Mini Pics Dohickies Too

IN MEMORY OF MY MOTHER—
DEDICATED TO THE FORCES OF PLENTY
ACKNOWLEDGING THE FORCES OF LOSS

CONTENTS

Part 2 ◪ Civitas

Part 3 ◉ Genius Loci

Part 4 ䷤ Urbanitas

TABLE OF QUERIES

Part 2 ◧ Civitas

Part 3 ◉ Genius Loci

Part 4 卐 Urbanitas

11 Walls, Floors, and Ceilings

12 Open Doors

TABLE OF FIGURES

part one

SCHOOLS OF THOUGHT

INTRODUCTION

The Joy of the Commons

*The city comes into existence, originating in the bare needs of life,
and continuing in existence for the sake of a good life.*

—*Aristotle*, Politics

As places of joyful celebration, heartbroken communion, civic discussion, and as places to exercise the rights of assembly and free speech, civic places are essential to participatory democracy and the good life. Vital civic places—squares, the post-office steps, farmers' markets—are the great advantage of life in town. The architecture of civic places can support or frustrate these convivial uses.

This book is intended to help designers, planners, public officials, students, developers, and community leaders understand the history and theories of public places, elicit community dialog and desires, respond to the natural and built environment, and design compelling places. It is intended to support the creation of convivial places.

The common meaning of *convivial* is "sociable and lively." Going to its roots, however, the word *convivial* is made from *com-*, meaning "together," and *-vivere*, meaning "to live," and comes from the Latin term *convivium* for 'banquet or feast'. Thus, conviviality may be used to speak of the enjoyment of festive society, as a means of living together.

Conviviality, in this meaning, is the vibrant sense of belonging to a settlement.

As a species, we are gregarious. Convivial places support our fondness for company. Of course, our desire to be with others varies from person to person and situation to situation. Privacy also is a human need and its provision a legitimate goal for urban design. Yet we gather as chess players in the square, citizens at political rallies, fraternities, book clubs, regulars at the bar, the early morning shift at the bus stop, parents sitting around a playground, pick-up football teams, schools of thought, Mardi Gras krewes, espresso cart queues, professional organizations, and in more ways than any one of us will ever know.

Love of landscape is a second component of conviviality, of the sense of belonging to a place. Just as we vary in our gregariousness, how we value the land varies from person to person and place to place. We are rose gardeners and wilderness hikers, dam builders and landscape painters, duck feeders and duck hunters, park strollers and freeway drivers.

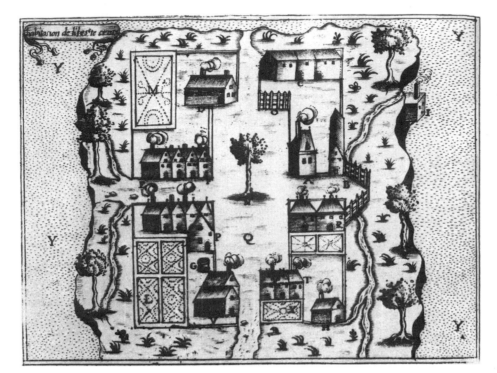

Figure 1.1.
View of Champlain's settlement on Sainte Croix Island, Maine, 1604. Note the central square. From a facsimile in H. P. Biggar, ed., The Works of Samuel de Champlain *(Toronto: Champlain Society, 1922).*

The Kaplans and other researchers have shown that access to nearby nature is highly cherished by urban citizens and has restorative value (Kaplan and Kaplan 1989; Kaplan et al. 1998). A review of real estate ads shows that a landscape view and adjacency to urban parks can have significant monetary value. Fredrick Law Olmstead, Jr., said in 1919, "it has been fully established that a well-located school and playground, or even the site for the same . . . adds to the value of all the remaining land in the territory to be served by the school more than the value of the land withdrawn for the purpose, just as a local park . . . adds more to the value of the remaining land in the residential area which it serves than the value of the land withdrawn to create it" (as cited in Weiss 1987). There have been numerous studies that support this claim. For example, a 1978 study found that properties adjacent to greenbelts in Boulder, Colorado, were on average worth 32 percent more than properties beyond average walking distance (Correll, Lillydahl, and Singell 1978).

The Latin root for conviviality, *convivium* ('banquet or feast'), holds within it the suggestion of both human community and the fruits of the land. In Italy the Slow Foods movement, dedicated to the enjoyment of local cuisine, gave birth to the Slow Cities movement, dedicated to the enjoyment of local communities. Perhaps the connection between the land and conviviality is most evident when we think as gardeners, cooks, and gourmets.

A third component of conviviality is identification with the built form of our dwellings, streets, and town. Being a New Yorker implies a deep knowledge of the built city, its forms and places. Miners in western towns carried with them a strong sense of the built form of "civilization" and created main streets with Victorian false fronts to house their sense of community (see Heath 1997).

Providing places to engage in our gregariousness, our love of landscape and of townscape is a critical function of our cities. Public gardens, plazas, bus shelters, and neighborhood mailbox clusters can all provide opportunities for enjoying a vibrant sense of belonging to a community and a landscape. In the conclusion of his book *The Ethical Function of Architecture,* Karsten Harries argues, "There is a continuing need for the creation of . . . places where individuals come together and affirm themselves as members of the community, as they join in public reenactments of the essential: celebrations of those central aspects of our life that maintain and give meaning to existence. The highest function of architecture remains what it has always been: to invite such festivals" (Harries 1997: 365).

Conviviality, to some, excludes emotions other than lightheartedness or frivolity. Understood simply as liking to party, the concept of conviviality does offer a basis for urban design; Las Vegas and Cancún provide examples. The gambling town and theme park trade on engendering such emotions, and indeed, indulging in a lighthearted sense of play may be beneficial. Nevertheless, the danger of confounding conviviality with frivolity is that it renders public life as simply entertainment. Frivolity is not the only flavor of conviviality.

Funerals may provide mourners with a profound sense of belonging to a community and a place. In the wake of the September 11, 2001, terrorist attacks, New Yorkers took to the squares. Henry Stern, New York parks commissioner, observed that the gatherings and collective artworks that appeared in the squares are part of a deep tradition: "It's an ancient concept. You go to a square, to the marketplace. Not to anyone's house—to *everyone's* house" (*New York Times Magazine,* Oct. 7, 2001, 51). These gatherings were one manifestation of the power of civic places.

When there is misunderstanding between the government and those governed, squares and town greens serve as places of discussion, gathering grounds, and stages for protest. The student uprising that unfolded in China's Tiananmen Square, like protests at other times in other squares across the world, illustrates the role civic places can play in expressing the consent, or lack thereof, of the governed.

There are, however, dangers in the promotion of conviviality. Noble goals can be twisted to other ends. An emphasis on conviviality can also be conflated with a concentration on clan or social organization. Although typically cloaked in terms of neighborliness, the impetus behind walled subdivi-

sions is, I suspect, often more about keeping people out than building community within. Likewise, we all can remember high school cliques defined by who was not a member rather than by camaraderie or love of an activity, and we know of many instances of attempts to build community self-pride on anger or hatred toward outsiders. This misidentification of conviviality with antagonistic chauvinism directs attention away from the center and toward guarding the borders. Conviviality does not require that you be among friends and family; you can feel conviviality among people whom you do not know. Tolerance for, and indeed delight in, the strangeness of fellow strangers is a central component of cosmopolitan conviviality. The sense of delight in belonging to a place and a community is one of the joys of watching a game in Yankee Stadium, going to concerts at the zoo, and strolling down a crowded street.

A darker problem is that a political program of spectacle and grandeur may be used to create a sense of belonging crafted to subsume and overwhelm individuals. The Nazis, for example, were masters of mass events in public places. Joseph Goebbels wrote, "The Statesman is an artist too. For him the people is neither more nor less than what stone is for the sculptor" (Goebbels 1929). Ivan Illich, in his book *Tools for Conviviality,* defines conviviality in a manner that resists its use to disguise mob-making. He sees it as an intrinsic ethical value: "individual freedom realized in personal interdependence" (Illich 1973). A convivial crowd supports and enjoys creative individuality—dancers playing off each other elaborate the dance. A mob suppresses the individual—each must march in lock step.

The architecture of civic places can support or frustrate conviviality; just as game boards frame games and stage sets support and are evocative of certain kinds of scenes. It is difficult (though not impossible) to play chess without a chessboard or to have the balcony scene without the spatial essence of a balcony. Likewise, running into acquaintances in the plaza during lunch is difficult if there is no readily accessible and attractive central civic place. Moreover, the means of gathering the resources to design, make, remake, maintain, and use a civic place is itself an organizing of community. The main street parade is the choreography of the town's citizens and government. The town

Figure 1.2. *A quiet interlude in a public place,
New York City, 1999.*

rose garden provides the members of the rose society an excuse to meet, share a passion, and give something to the larger community. A teenagers' Hacky-Sac game can be a locus of civic life.

How then can we build our squares and other civic places to support an enriching and democratic conviviality? The underlying contention of this book is that places built to support conviviality are part of a long discussion representing schools of thought about the nature of the commons and are rooted in a deep understanding of the local traditions of *civitas, genius loci,* and *urbanitas.* That is, a designer must understand the best ways in which the community gathers *(civitas),* the nature of the community's love of its landscape *(genius loci),* and its traditions of built form *(urbanitas).* Thus, the book is organized into four parts: (1) Schools of Thought, (2) *Civitas,* (3) *Genius Loci,* and (4) *Urbanitas.*

Schools of Thought

The discussion of the nature of the commons has taken place in text and in built form. A large number of disciplines, including architecture, economics, law, linguistics, politics, philosophy, and sociology, have taken up the debate. The designers, planners, managers, funders, and members of a commons bring to a design project knowledge and beliefs informed by various threads of this dialog.

These threads are often in conflict and frequently assume divergent goals. For example, in 1968 the ecologist Garrett Hardin wrote an influential article, "The Tragedy of the Commons," in which he presented a rhetorical argument for the elimination of the economic commons. He feared that ecological harm inevitably results from the use of resources held in common. U.S. Supreme Court Justice O'Connor, on the other hand, sought to defend a broad application of the concept of the public forum in a 1992 case: "The liberties protected by our [public forum] doctrine . . . are essential to a functioning democracy. . . . Public places are of necessity the locus for discussion of public issues, as well as protest against arbitrary government action." These two arguments seemingly are, and actually may be, in conflict. However, they are also addressing different goals, types, and aspects of the commons.

To increase the chances of a clear and fruitful dialog about the design of a specific square, town park, forecourt, or courtyard, the designers and other stakeholders should have at least an overview of the theories (see chapter 2 for texts and chapter 3 for built types). Designers must also build a common language to speak clearly about ecological concerns, human rights, architectural traditions, or other issues.

Civitas

In order to design a plaza, town dock, or town rose garden, the designers must anchor this debate about the nature of our commons in a specific community. The second section of the book addresses the question: how can designers elicit and understand the complex and often poorly articulated desires of a particular community for a set of civic places?

What are the theories, questions, practices, and desires of the community? Where and in what forms do they gather now and for what reasons? Who is the community; what groups and interests are represented? Can multiple goals, needs, and desires be quilted together? When and how is it desirable to draw people out, provide them with a place to socialize and maybe even to contemplate and discuss life, the universe, and everything? The challenge for the organizers, planners, and designers is to create a process that fruitfully asks these questions and suggests answers (see chapter 4).

This process will not end when design begins or even when construction ends. The built place will illuminate conflicts and opportunities and suggest new questions. Thus the design should proceed in increments that are complete in themselves but that suggest or allow additions or reinterpretations (see chapter 5).

Moreover, unintended consequences arise. A bus stop, for example, may be built in such a way as to create a prime opportunity for pickpockets, a group may attempt to dominate the commons and exclude others, or a farmers' market overburdens the trash system. There is risk in any enterprise. Anticipating types of risk and establishing an ongoing program of incremental adjustments can help minimize the effects of unintended consequences (see chapter 6).

Genius Loci

The third part of this book examines architectural responses to our species' love of inhabited landscape. We take meaning from being a desert dweller, living in the town by the bay or the windy city. Conviviality rests on both how we dwell together and on how we dwell on the land. For this reason, this book focuses on outdoor or semi-outdoor commons rather than deeply interior gathering places such as the tavern or the opera. How can designers anchor their design in a specific place? How can we build an urban place that is immersed in the landscape? (See chapter 7.)

Humanity has the propensity to encounter and respond to the landscape in ways that are exquisitely inventive and mindful. Outdoor places can orient us to a city's place in the landscape and create a legible framework of the city. The Japanese gardening concept of "capturing alive" (evoking the sense of a place seen in a view, for example pine trees framing the view of a pine-covered mountain in order

to give the sense of being on the mountain) and the Roman concept of *genius loci* (the spirit of the place) both suggest ways to design a place to engage its landscape. The materials we use and the tectonics of how we use them to build the floors, the walls, and the furniture of our civic rooms also evoke a sense of place (see chapter 9).

Outdoor public places are generally most used when they provide pleasant moderate climates. Yet crowds gather at ice-sculpture festivals, people leave their air-conditioned homes to sit in the heat near pools and fountains, and windy knolls are prized for flying kites. Crafting how a civic place responds to the weather, moderating or celebrating the local climate, is a critical component of our sense of place (see chapter 8).

It is the job of the designers of a civic place to uncover, foster, and give place to a sustained and evolving dialog between a community and its landscape.

Urbanitas

The final portion of the book will discuss architectural principles that support conviviality. How can we make great places to hang out, to contemplate our place in the city and the landscape, and to gather? This line of inquiry uncovers a number of underlying questions.

How can urban commons help compose the framework of a settlement? Squares and other civic rooms are not made simply of leftover space between buildings and parking lots. Rather they are strong organizing places about which buildings and other parts of the city take form. Good civic places are clearly legible figural spaces about which the town's fabric of building gathers. They are strategically located, inviting, and adaptable rooms of the city (see chapter 10).

What are the basic compositional components of a civic place and what are their roles in making the place? Outdoor rooms, just like indoor rooms, have floors, walls, and ceilings (see chapter 11). The architects of adjacent buildings, however, often make the walls, while tree canopies, strings of lights, or the height of the enclosing buildings imply the ceiling. Within these basic elements there are critical smaller pieces.

Good public places are visually, socially, psychologically, and physically accessible, and thus their entrances and gateways are critical (see chapter 12). Like living rooms, public places often have edges full of places to sit, and open centers. People sit and hang out around the edges, and dance, ice-skate, or hold protest rallies in the center (see chapter 13). How should we best shape these gateways, frames, and fields, and how should they relate to each other?

In my book *Parking Spaces,* I suggested that Americans have adapted parking lots as civic places despite their design (Childs 1999). Tailgate parties, Girl Scout cookie sales, RV camping in Wal-Mart parking lots, and parking-lot hockey games are common community uses of these otherwise mono-utilitarian landscapes. Just as the commons has begun to invade the parking lot, automobiles have invaded and often dominated pedestrian public places throughout the world. A discussion of twenty-first-century commons must address means to regain the public realm of the city from the automobile (see chapter 14).

The urban and architectural design of commons has long been in dialog with public art. In addition to their roles as social, political, experiential, and formal "speech," artworks may play a number of different architectural roles within a civic place. In Seattle, Pike Place Market's brass pig serves as a meeting place, and other works may serve as landmarks, pathways, or other way-finding devices. They may frame entrances, provide enclosure or shelter, provide iconographic identity, alter the microclimate, shape the character of light or sound, foster play, and provide what William Whyte called "triangulation" (i.e., an excuse for strangers to converse). All of these roles may, in response to the site, help create a distinct and engaging place. What might be the architectural and urban design roles of public art (see chapter 15)?

Components of the Book

This book includes three different elements: discussion of theory and principles, design queries, and mini–case studies. I concentrate on theory in section 1, "Schools of Thought." The remaining chapters present design queries, and the case studies and thought pieces are encapsulated in excursions throughout the book. These excursions, written by a constellation of experts, are intended to give brief overviews of issues and portraits of places.

The design queries are the core of the book. The idea of design patterns has a long and varied history. Work describing ideal and actual designs for housing appeared in sixteenth-century publications such as Jacques Androuet Du Cerceau's *Livre d'Architecture* (1559) (Dennis 1992: 7). Numerous houses in railroad towns throughout the United States were built from pattern books offered by Sears Roebuck Company and others. In 1977 Christopher Alexander and his coauthors published *A Pattern Language.* This work articulated and clarified the use of design patterns in architecture. They characterized the design pattern as describing a problem that frequently occurs, and then describing an essential approach to solving the problem "in such a way that you can use this solution a million times over, without ever doing it the same way twice" (Alexander et al. 1977: x).

Numerous design books have followed Alexander's lead. For example, *The Next American Metropolis* by Peter Calthorpe presents a set of urban design patterns, and *With People In Mind* by Rachel and Steven Kaplan and Robert L. Ryan offers patterns for landscape design. Donlyn Lyndon and Charles Moore's *Chambers for a Memory Palace* is composed of an interesting variation of the pattern book. Each of their patterns has a title consisting "of elements (nouns) and actions (verbs)," followed by an exchange of letters between the authors about places that exhibit the characteristics of the pattern. They too insist on the flexibility of their patterns: "The Chambers are not intended to limit or confine, but rather to nurture sparks in the designer's consciousness. These Memory Chambers then are starting points, aids to the imagination, not recipes for design" (Lyndon and Moore 1994: xiii).

I attempt to follow this lead for the queries in this book. The following queries are not presented as rules, but rather as prompts to the mind's eye. To emphasize this point, I have formulated the patterns as questions followed by discussion of approaches to the question. I have borrowed and adapted the practice of queries from the Religious Society of Friends (a.k.a. Quakers). The Friends use sets of questions, usually unadorned by commentary, to prompt contemplation about practices and beliefs. The table of queries summarizes them for quick reference. In discussions of civic space design there is a tendency to focus on European examples and short-change the American heritage of places. For this reason, and because of the scope of my experience, most of the examples I discuss are from North America. Question the questions; add new ones; disregard my discussion of the questions and ask them anew. My aim is to prompt contemplation about the physical design of commons.

Any given civic square or courtyard is a collection of answers to the queries—for example, a clock tower, a pavement, and arcaded walls working together to create a place. Not all of the queries will apply to all design projects.

The character and nature of our civic squares, courtyards, and other commons—our places of conviviality—are formed by the interactions of our community relationships *(civitas)*, our love of the land *(genius loci)*, and architectural and urban design *(urbanitas)*. A sense of conviviality is one of the prime experiences that town and city have to offer, and thus is a critical component for creating attractive, pedestrian-based, sustainable towns. Convivial towns can offer solace in disaster, solidarity in protest, and quiet everyday delight in urban life.

In an age of internet newsgroups and live journals, of FedEx and faxes, of telecommuting and mass migrations, the idea of physical civic commons may seem to some as quaint or quixotic. The opposite is true. The need and desire for vital civic places is both perennial and current, and the means are at hand. The question is what resources, skills, wisdom, and joy we will bring to the task. Creating and revitalizing places that foster conviviality is essential to the good life.

THEORIES OF THE COMMONS

What is common in community is not shared values or common understanding so much as the fact that members of a community are engaged in the same argument, the same raisonnement, the same Rede, the same discourse, in which alternative strategies, misunderstandings, conflicting goals and values are threshed out.

*—David Sabean, Power in the Blood, 29;
Reprinted with the permission of Cambridge University Press.*

ields of study have arisen from the collective life of classic public spaces. Economics is the study of the transactions of the *market*. Game theory may be seen as a latter-day analysis of how the activities of the game board or *arena* model life. Political, social, and legal theories have their roots in the soil of the *forum*. In turn, scholars of these fields have developed critical theories of the commons. Political and social theorists contemplate "the public realm." Game theorists examine "strategic cooperation." Economists study "common pool resources," and jurists debate the meaning and application of "public forums."

Following is a brief overview of critical thought about civic commons from the fields of political and social theory, game theory, economics, and the decisions of the United States Supreme Court. Just as the architect of a school building is informed by society's various concepts of education, the designer of a civic square should be conversant with theories of the commons. There is a breadth and depth of theory about the commons sufficient to fill a small library. The following overview is not by any means a definitive synopsis of the field. It is meant to (1) give a taste of various perspectives that clients, community groups, and critics may bring to a design; (2) introduce terms and concepts; and (3) help illustrate the complex roles that commons play in our settlements.

The Public Sphere and Public Realm

The commons can be defined from the point of view of social convention and political power. This viewpoint can be thought of as arising from the commons as agora.

In his foundational work, *The Structural Transformation of the Public Sphere,* Jürgen Habermas described the rise and fall of what he terms the bourgeois public sphere. "The [European] bourgeois public sphere may be conceived above all as the sphere of private people come together as a public;

Figure 2.1. *Emperor Caracalla declaiming in the market place, Laudica,* A.D. *214. Courtesy of the Ashmolean Museum, Oxford.*

influence power waned as the powers of bureaucracies and corporations waxed. Habermas argues that the transformation of our streets and squares from public space to arterials and parking lots echoes this change in values. "The resulting configuration [of modern cities] does not afford a spatially protected private sphere, nor does it create free space for public contacts and communication that could bring private people together to form a public" (1989: 158). We lost places to gather in private—the salon or front room in the house, the front porch near the sidewalk—and effective places to gather in public—the square.

This theme of decline and impoverishment of the public realm has been a concern for a number of social critics since World War II, such as John Kenneth Galbraith (*The Affluent Society,* 1958), Richard Sennett (*The Fall of Public Man,* 1977, and *The Conscience of the Eye,* 1990), Sharon Zukin (*Landscapes of Power,* 1991), and Michael Sorkin (*Variations on a Theme Park,* 1992). More recent work, such as Robert D. Putnam's *Bowling Alone* (2000), examines the rise, fall, and potential reawakening of the public realm. From the viewpoint of those who believe we live in a time of a fundamentally degraded public realm, the activity of designing and building plazas or other traditional public spaces may be skeptically examined as potentially naively nostalgic, part of the economics of tourism, or an attempt to manipulate the masses with the sign but not the power of the public realm.

Habermas's public realm has been criticized as a poor ideal (for example, see Stevenson 1998). Many people—women, minorities, the poor—were excluded from the bourgeois public realm. More subtly, while the Habermasian public realm is based on the ideal of objective discourse, the norms of what is considered objective may mask embedded social power. For example, in political discussions about the design of streets, codified and measurable professional street design standards often trump neighborhoods concerns about pedestrian safety, aesthetics, off-street impacts, and non-vehicular use of the street. These standards that traffic engineers have adopted are based on automobile-centered assumptions about the proper use and character of the right-of-way.

In her book *The Public Realm,* sociologist Lyn H. Lofland offers a sociological definition of the public realm that is independent of Habermas's or others' political and

they soon claimed the public sphere regulated from above against the public authorities themselves, to engage them in a debate over the general rules governing . . . commodity exchange and social labor. The medium of this political confrontation was peculiar and without historical precedent: people's public use of their reason" (1989: 27). Habermas argues that the rise in Europe of the public press, cafés, salons, and other discussion societies established a new basis of political power that replaced the royal courts, and that, *in the ideal,* this power was vested in the reasoned arguments of all citizens—the collective discussion.

Habermas then traces the fall of the bourgeois culture-debating public sphere into the modern world of a culture-consuming public. He argues that the bourgeois public sphere was invaded both by an enlarged scope of action by government and by increased powers of private corporations. The ability of the public debate to determine or economic relationships. "The public realm is constituted of *those areas of urban settlements in which individuals in copresence tend to be personally unknown or only categorically known to one another*" (Lofland 1998: 9). She contrasts the public realm (what I call the civic commons) with the private realm and the parochial realm of friends and neighbors (e.g., neighborhood commons or a "third place" such as a neighborhood bar). Moreover, based on the pioneering empiric studies of how people behave in public, by Gregory Stone (1954), Jane Jacobs (1961), Erving Goffman (1959, 1963, 1971, 1983), and William H. Whyte (1980, 1988), as well as an extensive bibliography of more current work, Lofland presents a case for the value of this public realm.

We must learn to nurture the advantages offered by cities and their public realms or risk creating the tribalized concrete jungles many fear. "The public realm offers a rich environment for learning, provides needed respites and refreshments, operates as a center of communication, allows for the 'practice' of politics, is the stage for the enactment of social arrangements and social conflict, and assists in the creation of cosmopolitans" (Lofland 1998: 231–32). The pleasures of the public realm include people-watching, public sociability, the freedom to try on roles (e.g., a college sophomore dressing as a business person or vice versa), public solitude (e.g., purposely being alone in a crowd), experiencing juxtapositions and layerings of history, and seeing the built complexity of a city.

In addition to this argument about the value of places to participate in a community of strangers, Lofland offers five principles of how strangers fruitfully interact in North America. These civic behaviors include:

(1) Cooperative motility—the complex set of cooperative behaviors between pedestrians, roller skaters, wheelchair users, etc., that choreograph their fluid movement. The British convention of standing on the right of an escalator to allow people to pass on the left is a rule of cooperative motility that Americans haven't adopted.

(2) Civic inattention—"What seems to be involved [in the practice of civic inattention] is that one gives to another enough visual notice to demonstrate that one appreciates that the other is present . . . while at the next moment withdrawing one's attention

from him so as to express that he does not constitute a target of special curiosity or design" (Erving Goffman, as quoted in Lofland 1998: 30). Civic inattention acknowledges the right for others to be present without attempting to bring them into one's orbit of friendship. The ability to adjust the position of one's chair to turn slightly away from a newcomer allows the expression of civic inattention. People in line at an ATM also practice civic inattention.

(3) Audience role prominence—All the world (i.e., public realm) is a stage. Typically we act as audience, but at any time we may become actors. Places that provide a stage and house such as the ice rink and balconies of Rockefeller Center support this public realm practice.

(4) Restrained helpfulness—"I wouldn't give him the time of day!" is an expression of utter disrespect. Giving directions, offering limited advice (you'll have to run to catch the bus), and other minor assistance is an accepted part of public manners.

(5) Civility toward diversity—Green-haired punks and blue-haired old ladies get the same service by the hotdog vendor.

Summarizing the value of the public realm, Lofland strongly agrees with and quotes William H. Whyte: "[T]he center is the place for news and gossip, for the creation of ideas, for marketing them and swiping them, for hatching deals, for starting parades . . . . [T]his human congress is the genius of the place, its reason for being, its great marginal edge. This is the engine, the city's true export. Whatever makes this congress easier, more spontaneous, more enjoyable is not at all a frill" (Whyte 1988: 341).

Strategic Cooperation: Game Theory Commons

The commons can be seen as a framework of rules shared by the players. People in a poker game share the rules and goals of poker. Vendors in a town market share laws, conventions, and marketing skills. Whereas most ordinary games are based on creating a winner, games, like life, can also have more complex outcomes where multiple players gain or lose. Studying carefully constructed games can help illuminate complex group behavior.

The classic game for cooperation theorists is the Prisoner's Dilemma. In the core version of the Prisoner's Dilemma game, there are two players. On each turn both players have the choice to cooperate or defect. Neither player knows what the other player will decide to do. Defecting will, on any single turn, give a player more points than cooperating, no matter what the other player does. If both players defect both will do worse than if they cooperated.

The points for defecting when the other cooperates are called the Temptation Score (T). The Sucker Score (S) is given to the player who cooperates when the other defects. If both cooperate they receive the Reward Score (R) and if both defect they receive the Punishment Score (P). The point system is structured from greatest to least as follows: temptation, reward, punishment, sucker (T>R>P>S). Also, players would receive more points if they always both cooperated (R) than if they took turns being the sucker (R>(T+S)/2).

The dilemma presented by this game is that on any given turn, fearing that they might get the Sucker Score, it is in each player's interest to defect, and thus receive the Punishment Score. However, if they both cooperated they would both receive the higher reward score. This paradox has occupied philosophers and game theorists for decades because it suggests that it is impossible for rational creatures to cooperate and thus raises fundamental issues in ethics and political philosophy. It also appears to be a good model for a number of real-world situations. Researchers have used the game to model interactions including the separate interrogation of partners in crime (from which the game gets its name), the deal-making of senators, informal truces in World War I, and the life of bacteria.

Robert Axelrod, a professor of political science, game theorist, and complexity scholar, has used Prisoner's Dilemma computer tournaments and evolutionary computer models in which the players can adapt their strategies to study the contexts in which cooperation emerges despite the dilemma presented by the game. In his book *The Evolution of Cooperation*, Axelrod makes a set of recommendations on how to promote cooperation:

- "As long as the interaction is not iterated, cooperation is very difficult. That is why an important way to promote cooperation is to arrange that the same two individuals will meet each other again. . . . This continuing interaction is what makes it possible for cooperation based on reciprocity to be stable" (1984: 125)
- Create more durable or more frequent interactions
- Change the payoffs and tip the scales toward cooperation
- Teach people to care about each other. "In game theory terms, this means that the adults try to shape the values of children so that the preferences of the new citizens will incorporate not only their own individual welfare, but to some degree at least, the welfare of others. Without doubt, a society of such caring people will have an easier time attaining cooperation among its members, even when caught in an iterated Prisoner's Dilemma" (134)
- Teach reciprocity
- Improve people's ability to identify and analyze other players and their actions

These recommendations evoke questions about the program and design of civic squares, forecourts, and courtyards. In what ways can civic places help induce durable interactions? Can civic places embody or promote a social norm of cooperation and care? In what ways does the game board frame the interactions of the game?

Axelrod's recommendations also apply to the process of planning and design with multiple players. One technique he suggests is to break the decisions into small steps, thus creating more frequent interactions and more possibility for cooperation. A designer of a civic place working with a complex set of clients and public groups may suggest incremental changes or even construct a series of temporary installations. The designer should also create discrete increments or portions of the total design to limit difficult trade-offs to the smallest possible portion of the design. Avoid all-or-nothing decisions. The process of design can also be a process of community building.

Game theory can raise valuable questions. Designers should take care not to apply the lessons of a game too literally. Models all have a set of simplifying assumptions. In practice not all of the assumptions may be valid. For example, one of the assumptions of the core version of the Prisoner's Dilemma is that there is no way to know in advance what the other player will do on a given move. Thus a player can't decide to do what the other player does. Good communication, third-party-enforced contracts, and reputations can all alter this rule of the game.

Nevertheless, even simple models can yield strong insight. "Agent-based modeling is a way of doing thought experiments. Although the assumptions may be simple, the consequences may not be at all obvious. . . . The large-scale effects of locally interacting agents are called 'emergent properties' of the system" (Axelrod 1997: 4). Cooperation is an "emergent property" of the evolutionary Prisoner's Dilemma tournaments Axelrod described. Evolutionary agent-based models suggest strategies to help create emergent properties such as conviviality.

In my paper "Civic Ecosystems" (Childs 2001), I argue that the models developed by scholars of complexity can illuminate the complex multi-player and multi-generation cooperation that creates great works such as the cities of Venice or San Francisco, and suggest attitudes toward design that help make great cities. For urban designers, the civic ecosystem trope suggests a move away from static master planning and single-use zoning to the development of historically and politically informed and evolving pattern languages, and a concentration on creating symbiotic links among built forms. For the designer of civic places, the concept of civic ecosystems suggests that squares and courtyards should (1) fit the initial intentions that called for their creation, and (2) become adaptable places that add to the life of the immediate surroundings, neighborhood, district, settlement, region, and world.

In the humid Gulf heat, people line up to play on a life-size chessboard in a small plaza along the main street of Galveston, Texas. In the snowstorms of the North, friends come to cheer hockey players chasing pucks. Even without game theory, playing and discussing games can teach us about the commons.

Common Pool Resources: Economic Commons

The public market provides another definition of the commons. What resources do we share and how do we share them?

"Ruin is the destination toward which all men rush, each pursuing his own best interest in a society that believes in the freedom of the commons," Garrett Hardin wrote in his influential 1968 article "The Tragedy of the Commons" (1244). To describe the structure of the tragedy, Hardin describes a pasture open to all. Each herdsman gets all the value from his cattle but shares the cost (the quality of the pasture) with all other herdsmen. Thus it appears to be the rational choice for each herdsman to add cattle even though the pasture will be overgrazed.

Hardin presented this thought experiment as a counter to a "dominant tendency of thought" based on Adam Smith's concept of "the invisible hand." In *The Wealth of Nations* (1776), a foundational text of modern economics, Adam Smith argued that under certain economic conditions each individual who "intends only his own gain" is, at it were, "led by an invisible hand to promote . . . the public interest." Hardin, in effect, was arguing that Smith's model of classic economic theory isn't accurate in the case of what are now called common pool resources.

Economists define "common pool resources," like the pasture of his example, as a resource system in which it is costly but not impossible to exclude potential beneficiaries from obtaining the benefits from its use (e.g., it is hard to keep multiple people from listening to a talented street musician). For a renewable resource, there is a maximum rate at which the resource can be extracted without harming the future flow of the resource. Fishing grounds, recharging aquifers, and picnic spots are examples.

Hardin further argued that the only methods of avoiding the tragedy of the open commons are (1) to privatize the resource (each herder gets a share of the pasture), or (2) to regulate the resource through a government larger than the set of users (each herder is only allowed a certain number of cattle per acre, as in Western grazing rights). There is a large body of literature that illustrates cases of the tragedy of the commons.

Figure 2.2. *The harbor at Mousehole, United Kingdom (2000), provides an economic and spatial commons for the town.*

Just as Hardin was attempting to counter the overuse of Adam Smith's model, Elinor Ostrom, in *Governing the Commons* (1990), points out the overuse of Hardin's model. Ostrom examines a number of longstanding "self-organizing and self-governing forms of collective action" for the use of a common pool resource, such as an approximately five-hundred-year-old pasture commons in Switzerland, and slightly older irrigation institutions in southern Spain. She uses this empirical information to propose a set of organizational conditions under which the commons is successful. Some commons are successful not only in longevity but also in more direct economic terms. For example, a detailed comparison between self-regulated irrigation commons and national government irrigation systems in Nepal showed that, overall, self-governed systems resulted in better-maintained irrigation infrastructure, more water available to farmers, and higher agricultural yields (Lam 1998). Ostrom summarizes her findings of principles

illustrated by long-enduring common pool resource (CPR) institutions:

1. *Clearly defined boundaries*
   Individuals or households who have rights to withdraw resource units from the CPR must be clearly defined, as must be boundaries of the CPR itself.
2. *Congruence between appropriation and provision rules and local conditions*
   Appropriation rules restricting the time, place, technology, and/or quantity of resource units are related to local conditions and to provision rules requiring labor, material, and/or money.
3. *Collective-choice arrangements*
   Most individuals affected by the operational rules can participate in modifying the operational rules.
4. *Monitoring*
   Monitors, who actively audit CPR conditions and appropriator behavior, are accountable to the appropriators or are the appropriators.
5. *Graduated sanctions*
   Appropriators who violate operational rules are likely to be assessed graduated sanctions (depending on the seriousness and context of the offence) by other appropriators, by officials accountable to these appropriators, or by both.
6. *Conflict-resolution mechanisms*
   Appropriators and their officials have rapid access to low-cost local arenas to resolve conflicts among appropriators or between appropriators and officials.
7. *Minimal recognition of rights to organize*
   The rights of appropriators to devise their own institutions are not challenged by external governmental authorities.

—*Ostrom 1990: 90; Reprinted by permission of Cambridge University Press*

The existence of longstanding common pool resource institutions, and Ostrom's work in articulating the conditions for their success, is not simply an academic repartee to Hardin. We face significant common pool resource management issues such as global warming, cross-boundary aquifer use, and the nurturing of the quality of life in our cities and towns.

Knowledge of functional commons adds to privatization and governmental regulation a third category of solution to Hardin's tragedy—self-regulated commons.

Part of the problem presented by common pool resources is the frequent condition that the actions of one appropriator (e.g., herder) harm the resources of the others (e.g., use up the pasture). Economists call this a negative externality. It is also possible to have positive externalities. For example, the more people who come to a place to see and be seen, the better that place is for people-watching (at least up to a point).

Moreover, there may be emergent properties that require a diverse, complex, and fairly large system to come into existence. New York's theater scene requires a complex set of supportive interrelations between production companies, schools, the tourist industry, individual actors, and many others. The emergence of Seattle's coffee-cart street life was supported by and helped support the increasing residential density of downtown. Sir Peter Hall, in his book *Cities in Civilization,* argues that the great inventive flourishes of civilization, such as classical Athens or fin-de-siècle Vienna, come from the emergence of "creative milieus." Describing the theories of Swedish geographers Torsten Hägerstrand and Gunner Törnqvist, Sir Peter writes: "[Creative milieus] need communication between individuals and between different areas of competence; so there must be a certain density of communication, which seems to require a rich, old-fashioned, dense, even overcrowded traditional kind of city. . . . The synergy comes from variation and diversity among activities that are often small-scale" (Hall 1998: 18). This creative milieu could be understood as an emergent property of a commons based on positive externalities.

Public Forum: Legal Commons

The First Amendment to the U.S. Constitution reads, "Congress shall make no law respecting an establishment of religion, or prohibiting the free exercise thereof; or abridging the freedom of speech, or of the press; or the right of the people peaceably to assemble, and to petition the Government for

Figure 2.3. *Civic spaces provide a place for protest. (Quebec City, 2002.)*

a redress of grievances." Case law concerning the use of public commons has focused on protecting the exercise of First Amendment rights, particularly the freedom of speech and of peaceable assembly. Regulations addressed to activities such as selling goods, discharging firearms, or setting up public amusement booths "not in the nature of civil rights [may] doubtless . . . be regulated or prohibited as respects their enjoyment in parks" (*Davis* v. *Massachusetts* 167 U.S. 43).

The U.S. Supreme Court has ruled that freedom of speech includes a broad range of expressive activity, including pitching tents in a park to bring attention to problems of the homeless (*Clark* v. *Community for Creative Non-Violence* 488 U.S. 288 [1984]), and soliciting for funds (*Heffron* v. *International Society for Krishna Consciousness Inc.,* 452 U.S. 640 [1981]). On the other hand, the Court has also considered where, when, and in what manner civil rights may be regulated. "Wherever the title of streets and parks may rest, they have immemorially been held in trust for the use of the public and, time out of mind, have been used for purposes of assembly, communicating thoughts between citizens, and discussing public questions. Such use of the streets and public places has, from ancient times, been part of the privileges, immunities and liberties of citizens," wrote Justice Roberts in *Hague* v. *Committee for Industrial Organization* 307 U.S. 496 (1939), but the rights must be exercised "in subordination to the general comfort and convenience, and in consonance with peace and good order."

This formula has been the cornerstone on which the U.S. Supreme Court has developed its approach to defining public forums in the twentieth century. In the 1992 case *International Society for Krishna Consciousness Inc., et al.* v. *Lee, Superintendent of Port Authority Police* 505 U.S. 672, Chief Justice Rehnquist summarized the doctrine:

> it is also well settled that the government need not permit all forms of speech on property that it owns and controls. *Postal Service* v. *Council of Greenburgh Civic Assns.*, 453 U.S. 114, 129 (1981); *Greer* v. *Spock*, 424 U.S. 828 (1976). Where the government is acting as proprietor, managing its internal operations, rather than acting as lawmaker with the power to regulate or license, its actions will not be subjected to the heightened review to which its actions as a lawmaker may be subject. *Kokinda, supra*, at 725 (plurality opinion) (citing *Cafeteria & Restaurant Workers* v. *McElroy*, 367 U.S. 886, 896 (1961)). Thus, we have upheld a ban on political advertisements in city-operated transit vehicles, *Lehman* v. *Shaker Heights*, 418 U.S. 298 (1974), even though the city permitted other types of advertising on those vehicles. Similarly, we have permitted a school district to limit access to an internal mail system used to communicate with teachers employed by the district. *Perry Ed. Assn.* v. *Perry Local Educators' Assn.*, 460 U.S. 37 (1983).

Rehnquist goes on to define three categories of public property in relation to their use as a public forum. The most protected places are traditional forums such as town squares. The second category encompasses nontraditional places that the state "has opened for expressive activity by part or all of the public." Many of the cases attempt to clarify this class of places. Under what conditions does an airport, train station, or subway platform fall into this category? The final category includes all other public property. Freedom of speech and assembly may be limited on army bases, for example. However, this limitation cannot be based on the content of the speech. Rehnquist clarifies these categories and continues his summary:

> In *Cornelius* we noted that a traditional public forum is property that has as "a principal purpose . . . the free exchange of ideas." 473 U.S., at 800. Moreover, consistent with the notion that the government—like other property owners—"has power to preserve the property under its control for the use to which it is lawfully dedicated," *Greer*, 424 U.S., at 836, the government does not create a public forum by inaction. Nor is a public forum created "whenever members of the public are permitted freely to visit a place owned or operated by the Government." *Ibid.* The decision to create a public forum must instead be made "by intentionally opening a nontraditional forum for public discourse." *Cornelius, supra*, at 802.

Justice O'Connor, while concurring in the judgment of the case, offers a different analysis of the public forum. In particular, she disagrees with the formation of Rehnquist's second category.

> [The analysis presented in the majority decision] is flawed at its very beginning. It leaves the government with almost unlimited authority to restrict speech on its property by doing nothing more than articulating a non-speech-related purpose for the area, and it leaves almost no scope for the development of new public forums absent the rare approval of the government. The Court's error lies in its conclusion that the public forum status of public property depends on the government's defined purpose for the property, or on an explicit decision by the government to dedicate the property to expressive activity. In my view, the inquiry must be an objective one, based on the actual, physical characteristics and uses of the property. . . .

The Court's approach is contrary to the underlying purposes of the public forum doctrine. The liberties protected by our doctrine derive from the Assembly, as well as the Speech and Press Clauses of the First Amendment, and are essential to a functioning democracy. . . . Public places are of necessity the locus for discussion of public issues, as well as protest against arbitrary government action. At the heart of our jurisprudence lies the principle that in a free nation citizens must have the right to gather and speak with other persons in public places. . . .

If the objective, physical characteristics of the property at issue and the actual public access and uses that have been permitted by the government indicate that expressive activity would be appropriate and compatible with those uses, the property is a public forum. The most important considerations in this analysis are whether the property shares physical similarities with more traditional public forums, whether the government has permitted or acquiesced in broad public access to the property, and whether expressive activity would tend to interfere in a significant way with the uses to which the government has as a factual matter dedicated the property. . . .

To treat the class of such forums as closed by their description as "traditional," taking that word merely as a charter for examining the history of the particular public property claimed as a forum, has no warrant in a Constitution whose values are not to be left behind in the city streets that are no longer the only focus of our community life. If that were the line of our direction, we might as well abandon the public forum doctrine altogether.

This case summarizes the thinking of the Court in the twentieth century about public forums on government-owned property. Streets and squares are traditional forums in which the rights of free speech and assembly are highly protected. On other state property, these rights may be more strongly regulated in regards to time, place, and manner. The majority asserts that the government may designate or may choose not to designate a place as equivalent to a traditional forum. Justice O'Connor maintains that the physical properties and uses of the place should be used to determine if a state-owned place should not be treated as a traditional forum.

The Court has also decided cases that in some ways treat certain *private* property as public fora. The foundational case is *Marsh* v. *Alabama* 326 U.S. 501. A Jehovah's Witness was arrested for distributing literature without a license on a sidewalk of the company town of Chickasaw, Alabama. The Court found that "the town and its shopping district are accessible to and freely used by the public in general and there is nothing to distinguish them from any other town and shopping center except the fact that the title to the property belongs to a private corporation." In deciding that the streets of the town were a public forum, the Court stated the principle: "Ownership does not always mean absolute dominion. The more an owner, for his advantage, opens up his property for use by the public in general, the more do his rights become circumscribed by the statutory and constitutional rights of those who use it."

In *Amalgamated Food Employees Union Local 590 et al.* v. *Logan Valley Plaza, Inc. et al.* 391 U.S. 308 (1967), the Court applied this principle in deciding that the privately owned parking lot of a shopping center was a public forum for the peaceful picketing of a business. This case was overruled by *Hudgens* v. *National Labor Relations Board* 424 U.S. 507. The majority decided that private property becomes a public forum only if the owner performs "the full spectrum of municipal powers and [stands] in the shoes of the State."

Justice Marshall, dissenting from this decision, writes:

The underlying concern in Marsh was that traditional public channels of communication remain free, regardless of the incidence of ownership. Given that concern, the crucial fact in *Marsh* was that the company owned the traditional forums essential for effective communication; it was immaterial that the company also owned a sewer system and that its property in other respects resembled a town.

In *Logan Valley* we recognized what the Court today refuses to recognize—that the owner of the modern shopping center complex, by dedicating his property to public use as a business district, to some extent displaces the "State" from control of historical First Amendment forums, and may acquire a virtual monopoly of places suitable for effective communication. The roadways, parking lots, and walkways of the modern shopping center may be as essential for effective speech as the streets and sidewalks in the municipal or company-owned town.

The public forum doctrine has many subtleties not captured in the above quotations, and will certainly evolve in the twenty-first century. The Court's concern with civic rights embodied in the Constitution, and particularly in the First Amendment, and the questions of how ownership and physical design interact with these rights will certainly remain critical.

Some scholars believe that the public trust doctrine may play a vital role in the definition and defense of commons, particularly those based on a natural resource (see Dowie 2003). The doctrine was first codified in 528 C.E. by the Roman emperor Justinian; is part of English, Spanish, and, by extension, U.S. common law; and was incorporated into the constitutions of many states. The public trust doctrine holds that certain resources must be held in trust by the government for the continued use of the public. For example, the Pennsylvania state constitution reads:

> The people have a right to clean air, pure water, and to the preservation of the natural, scenic, historic and aesthetic values of the environment. Pennsylvania's public natural resources are the common property of all the people, including generations yet to come. As trustee of these resources the Commonwealth shall conserve and maintain them for the benefit of all the people. (as quoted in Dowie 2003)

How this doctrine may evolve, and if and how it could be applied to urban commons, are open questions.

Philadelphia's squares, for example, certainly have scenic, historic, and aesthetic value, in addition to providing places for assembly and speech. Perhaps, however, the article does not cover them because they are built, not natural, resources. How do we make the distinction between natural and built resources? Must Pennsylvania act as trustee of the squares and act to "conserve and maintain them for the benefit of all the people"?

Crosstalk

Clients, community members, regulators, lawyers, funders, architects, critics, and other commentators may evoke any of these various theories of the commons during the design or redesign of a civic place. Conflict may easily arise when participants use similar terms to refer to differing concepts, and when goals based on one theoretical base are not recognized, understood, or valued by those invested in other theories. Moreover, theories are frequently taken as predictive beyond their ken.

Nevertheless, the breadth of inquiry into the nature of the commons points to its potential power in defining who we are. If various viewpoints are clarified, the dialog between them may help bring rich nuance to the process and products of design, and also may help clarify the interactions between physical design and social form—between *urbanitas* and *civitas*.

"Knowledge . . . is not a series of self-consistent theories that converges toward an ideal view. . . . It is rather an ever increasing *ocean of mutually incompatible (and perhaps even incommensurable) alternatives,* each single theory, each fairy tale, each myth that is part of the collection forcing the others into greater articulation and contributing . . . to the development of our consciousness" (Feyerabend 1975: 30).

DREAMS OF A COMMON LANGUAGE

3

(after Adrienne Rich 1978)

"When I use a word," Humpty Dumpty said in rather a scornful tone,
"it means just what I choose it to mean—neither more nor less."
"The question is," said Alice, "whether you can make words
mean so many different things."
"The question is," said Humpty Dumpty, "which is to be master—that's all."

—Lewis Carroll, Through the Looking-Glass

English is a language rich with words to describe types of civic commons—for example, *plaza, square, place, green, town park, lawn, quad, promenade, pier, public garden, courtyard, commons.* Unfortunately, the words have lost useful precision. In Boston many otherwise unremarkable street intersections are labeled "so and so" square. There are an uncountable number of shopping centers called some variant of "town plaza." There is a cottage industry within academia fueled by arguments about the term *public space.*

This confusion of terms makes it difficult to think about or discuss civic place clearly. Moreover, as George Orwell argued, "the slovenliness of our language makes it easier for us to have foolish thoughts" (Orwell 1981: 157).

Thus, for the purposes of this book, I propose the following definitions. I have attempted to follow, as much as possible, common usage. Inevitably, many of my definitions will differ from those of one or more authorities. I have offered new terms where I believe they could prove useful. It is my hope that this lexicon might serve beyond the confines

of the book, although I recognize that language is an emergent form and thus I alone cannot shape it.

A. Types of Urban Commons

Social categories

"Commons" are physical places to which a group shares a set of rights. The group may consist of all citizens or some limited set of members. The rights shared could be all those enjoyed by citizens, or some specific right (such as grazing one's cattle after the harvest). The rights may be complexly distributed (and traditionally have been; see Neeson 1993), yet they are shared in some roughly equitable fashion and, to a significant degree, are subject to the will of the group. In some cases, the space is only a commons during the time that it is used as such. Thus, we may think of a parking lot as a commons while a political rally is being held there, but not

Social Definitions

Civic Commons
Neighborhood Commons
Membership Commons

Types of Civic Places

Civic Rooms or Chambers
Squares (plazas, places, etc.)
Civic Coves
Forecourts
Courtyards
Civic Lots

Civic Lands
Civic Grounds
Closes and Yards
Campus
Urban Frameworks

Urban Paths
Public Streets
Public Walks and Promenades
Malls

Indoor Commons
Third Places
Public Institutions

Figure 3.1. *Types of Urban Commons.*

when it is used for valet parking. The term may be stretched to cover non-place resources such as intellectual property (public domain).

"Civic Commons" are physical spaces that, in the ideal, are open to all people for the exercise of their rights. Many writers use the terms *public space* or *public place* for this type of commons. The rights enjoyed by citizens in the civic commons are roughly equal. The writer and cultural critic Lucy Lippard suggests that passive access is not sufficient to make a public

commons: "Places that are merely accessible to citizens, rather than controlled by them through use, are not truly public places" (Lippard 1997: 243). Observers and critics often use the degree of open access, control, and participation to measure the publicness of civic commons. The term *civic* emphasizes the relationship of the commons to the settlement as a whole and to the collective value of the commons.

"Community or Neighborhood Commons" differ from civic commons in the nature or degree of relationship between their typical users. Neighbors and acquaintances dominate a community commons. In contrast, fellow citizens who do not necessarily know each other dominate a public commons. In a community commons, the majority may treat the stranger as if she didn't belong, but in a public commons a cosmopolitan civility among strangers dominates. The distinction between a community and civic commons can, and perhaps should, be difficult to make. A place may serve as a neighborhood commons to the regulars and a civic commons to a broader public. The legendary small-town square where everyone knows everyone's business and conformity is enforced portrays the community commons at its least civic and most destructive.

"Private or Membership Commons" are physical spaces that are shared by a limited group, each of whom share roughly equitable rights. The pasture commons of French, Spanish, and English colonial villages gave very specific rights to specific households. Today, apartment dwellers may share very specific uses of a common swimming pool while non-residents have no rights to it. Shopping malls may effectively be thought of as membership commons where the price of admission is adherence to a set of behavioral rules. Various court cases have attempted to define the legitimate breadth of these rules (see chapter 2).

Architectural Categories—Civic Places

Civic Rooms or Chambers

▦ **"Squares"** are designed commons that are (1) outdoor places enclosed by the fabric of a town (i.e., not a meadow outside town, but a place made by the buildings of the town); (2) of a size and shape that allow members of the public to interact as a social group (one index may be that people can see and recognize each other across the length of the space); and (3) intended as a public commons and regulated and designed to support this role. They have walls that provide a sense of enclosure. I am using the term *square* as a general term to discuss English squares, Spanish plazas, *piazzas*, *places d'armes*, and other central civic rooms. When a specific tradition is discussed the more specific term should be used.

Squares may be joined into a suite or ensemble of civic rooms. San Marco piazza in Venice, Italy, can be seen as a joined pair of rooms.

- "**Civic coves**" are smaller, often less formal, and sometimes more tenuously enclosed and defined civic rooms. Bus shelters and the sidewalks connected to them may create a civic cove. Likewise, clusters of mailboxes, a generous streetcorner with a fountain and seating, a small park at the dead end of a street, or the post office's sidewalk awning may create civic coves.

- "**Forecourts**" are outdoor rooms that adjoin a street or other public access and serve as the entrance for a building. Often forecourts are designed primarily to frame or present the building and its owner. The forecourt serves as a transition and orientation zone. For example, groups entering a museum may meet in the forecourt and discuss their plans. When the building and forecourt are privately owned, the forecourts are mixing zones of public and private activity. The nature of private regulation of public behavior in these places varies from instance to instance. For example, owners may allow relatively unfettered access to people having lunch, but forbid political activities.

- "**Courtyards**" are generally intended for a membership commons. They are places enclosed by a building or a related set of buildings and walls. Thus, they tend to be accessed from within a building complex or through an enclosing wall. An office-park courtyard and a condominium's pool court are typical courtyards.

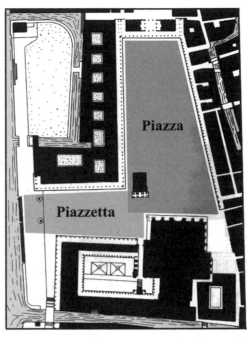

Figure 3.2. *Piazza San Marco in Venice, Italy, illustrating the overlapping rooms that form the ensemble.*

- "**Civic lots**" are civic rooms that have not been purposely designed to serve as a commons but have been used as such. The high school parking lot is frequently an example. Unbuilt lots in subdivisions often take on the role of informal neighborhood park and adventure playground.

Civic Lands

- "**Civic Grounds**" are designed public commons that are (1) figures in a ground of buildings and (2) larger than civic rooms. Central Park, Golden Gate Park, Tiananmen Square, and other imperial squares are of such a size and scale that people may only interact as a group of individuals in a corner of the square, or as a mass audience responding to a performance. Civic grounds are intended as civic commons open to the public.

- "**Closes**" or "**yards**" are membership commons that

are enclosed by a wall and, in turn, enclose a building or set of buildings. The grounds of a close or yard are typically composed as one design with subspaces and designs within it. Examples include Harvard Yard, many zoos, and some country clubs.

⊞ A **"campus"** is similar to a close but does not require an enclosing wall. Yet a campus, typically, has a well-defined edge separating the membership commons from the street.

⊞ **"Urban frameworks"** are landscapes or systems of infrastructure that shape edges or districts of a city. For example, greenbelts, waterways (bluebelts?), railroads, freeways, and power lines (greybelts?) provide structure to the form of a settlement. Often these frameworks can also provide a linked set of commons.

Urban Paths

⊞ **"Public Streets"** are paths that are (1) within the fabric of a town and lined by buildings that face and engage the street, (2) generally intended as public commons, and (3) dedicated in part to vehicular use. In contrast, roadways may not be lined by enfronting buildings or make significant allowance for non-vehicular use. As the percentage of space dedicated primarily to vehicular use increases, streets tend to transform into roads. This is not necessarily a function of the volume of traffic but of the care and space taken to support the pedestrian-based commons. See *Great Streets* by Allan Jacobs (1993) and *The Boulevard Book* by Jacobs, MacDonald, and Rofé (2001) for design analysis and recommendations.

⊞ **"Public Walks and Promenades"** are urban paths dedicated primarily to pedestrian use, generally enclosed by the built fabric and civic lands of the town and open to the public. Frequently, a walk may encircle civic grounds such as a lake, providing a frame to these large open fields.

⊞ **"Malls"** are pathways similar to public walks except that access and activities are regulated by a private owner rather than by community ownership. Malls have doorways that regulate entrance, and often

have roofs that signal singular ownership of the space. Airport terminals enclose malls. Because they are generally open to the public and take on roles similar to a public walk, they may not be considered purely private property. See the "Public Forum" section in chapter 2 for discussion of the legal nuances of the interaction between public access and private ownership.

Indoor Commons

⊞ **"Third Places"** are typically privately owned indoor places that are open to the public and support many of the functions of a community commons. Bars and coffeehouses are prime examples of third places. Ray Oldenburg coined this term in his book *The Great Good Place* (1989).

⊞ **"Public Institutions"** are buildings such as the public library, town meeting hall, or airport terminal that are held in common for defined public uses. Behavior is often regulated in these buildings if it interferes with the defined institutional purposes, but otherwise citizens have access and retain their general rights (see chapter 2, "Public Forum" section). For example, quiet may be enforced in a library, but people may not be removed for wearing a shirt that questions the wisdom of the president. Not all buildings owned by a government are public institutions. Military bases, for example, may regulate the rights of the general public.

B. Parts of a Civic Room

Figures 3.3 and 3.4 are idealized diagrams of a civic room showing the following parts:

⊞ **"District"** is the area surrounding the civic room that is architecturally and urbanistically associated with the room. Features of the district may include (1) a coherent architectural style (e.g., Spanish colonial) or set of building materials and typologies (e.g., brick townhouses with shops below), (2) formal composi-

Figure 3.3. *District and catchment. This diagram of Old Town in Albuquerque, New Mexico, shows a five-minute walking radius from the plaza and the set of blocks that constitute the Old Town district.*

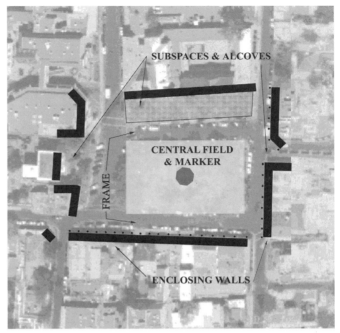

Figure 3.4. *Parts of a civic room. This diagram of Old Town in Albuquerque, New Mexico, shows the (a) central marker, in this case a gazebo; (b) central field; (c) subspaces; and (d) enclosing walls created by surrounding buildings.*

tional relationships (e.g., a street may run along a square, and the two may form a district), or (3) a set of uses concentrated around the room (e.g., the financial district or theater district). The definition and borders of a particular district will be an architectural judgment and may vary over time as buildings and streets evolve. Districts may be composed of multiple **quarters.** For example, many of the plazas in smaller New Mexico towns have both a town fabric and an agricultural landscape as critical parts of their immediate surround. Frequently there may be an inner ring and an outer ring of a district. The inner ring, for example, may be a set of multistory commercial and civic buildings and the outer ring a fabric of townhouses.

- ⊞ **"Catchment"** is the area from which most users of the civic room arrive. With the proper modifiers, this area can be objectively measured. (See chapter 10.)
- ⊞ **"Enclosing Walls"** are the set of building façades, tree lines, freestanding walls, arcades, and other vertical forms that surround the open portion of a civic room and provide the sense of enclosure. Rooms—particularly those in public institutions—within these walls that overlook or are accessed from the outdoor room should be thought of as an integral part of the ensemble. The central volume of the Pantheon, church naves, and public halls opening off public squares shown in the Nolli plan of Rome illustrate the conceptual relationship of these places (see fig. 3.5).
- ⊞ The **"floor"** of a civic room is the horizontal surface

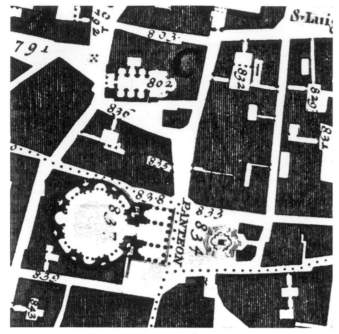

Figure 3.5. *Detail of the plan of Rome prepared by Giambattista Nolli in 1748, showing the Piazza della Rotunda (834 on the map) and the main volume of the interior of the Pantheon.*

the central field. This is the first place people sit, hang out, eat, and watch the activities in the central field. A frame can have multiple layers and small fields within it. The thickness of the frame can vary as chairs and tables are set out or removed, awnings are opened, bollards are removed, or other furniture is moved. At night, theatrical lighting can be used to establish a stage (central field) and seating (frame) and then vary the proportion and relationship between the two. Within the frame there may be **subspaces** or **alcoves** that provide a degree of enclosure but open to the larger space.

- The **"virtual ceiling"** is a sense of overhead enclosure. It may be suggested by a strong and consistent cornice line on the enclosing wall, a canopy of trees, the location of lights (e.g., a football field's flood lights), etc. Historically, designers have given considerable thought to the proportional relationship between the height of the virtual ceiling and the width of the floor.

C. A Patchwork Quilt of American Civic Places

The United States has multiple traditions of creating places dedicated to the commons. "We forget that Jamestown and Plymouth came before the pioneer farm and the log cabin in the forest, and that inter-dependence in America came before Independence" (Jackson 1985: 5). The following is not meant to be a history nor an exhaustive list of the American patchwork quilt of historic civic-place types, but rather to give a brief overview of some of the major traditions. These traditions both condition social practice and inform physical design. Some examples follow.

Native American Central Places

There are numerous Native American settlement design traditions in North America. Many of these included outdoor central community places. The documentation, study, and understanding of these places is sparse. Nonetheless, it

enclosed by the walls. It may be composed of a set of pavements such as asphalt driving lanes, a frame of planting beds, brick walkways, and a central pond.

- The **"central field"** is the portion of the floor that is compositionally centered in the room. It is typically an open field such as a lawn, a pond, or open pavement, but may have a statue, fountain, gazebo, or other **"central marker"** within it. Sometimes, the central field is not physically occupied by people but is a flower bed (for example, in many Savannah, Georgia, squares), a pond, or other feature. Frequently it is only used to pass through, as a sports field (e.g., Rockefeller Plaza's ice rink), or for events that draw large crowds (which at Market Park in Seattle includes lunch on a sunny day).
- The **"frame"** is the portion of the floor that surrounds

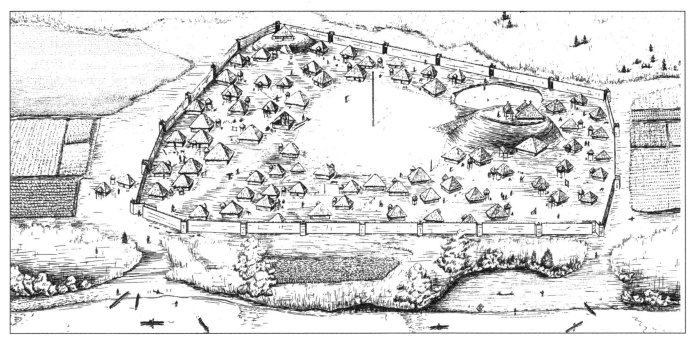

Figure 3.6. *Artist's reconstruction of Toqua, a proto-Cherokee town, c. 1500 A.D., in what is now a lake bottom in Tennessee. Note the central open area with a single standing pole (the swept area) and the ceremonial mound. From Richard R. Polhemus, Arthur E. Bogan, and Jefferson Chapman,* The Toqua Site, *(Tennessee Valley Authority, 1987) figure 13.4. Courtesy of the Frank H. McClung Museum, University of Tennessee.*

appears that, in varying form and meaning, the central town place was widespread across pre-Columbian America.

Italwa, the Creek word for town, implies "spiritual membership in and social responsibility for a civic ceremonial center with a square ground and, most important, its sacred fire" (Nabokov and Easton 1989: 109). Four buildings, open to the square and containing seating, surrounded the square ground. Town councils and ceremonies were held in the square ground. Creek towns also contained a "swept area." The "swept area" featured a manicured ground and a central pole that was used as goal post for a ritual game in which women formed one team and men another (fig. 3.6). This game and another called *chunkee* were sometimes played between towns as a means of settling disputes. The Creek retained their town-making principles despite their relocation and forced march to Oklahoma. There they built new "stomping grounds" and continued the rituals.

The *bu-ping-geh* (heart of the pueblo or earth) contains the literal center of the earth, and serves as the central community place for the Pueblo villages of the Southwest (Swentzell 1997). This place, also called a Pueblo Indian plaza, is central to daily life, community events, the spiritual world, and the landscape. The roofs of enclosing buildings typically serve as bleachers (or perhaps skyboxes) that overlook the activities of the center. Frequently, the enclosing buildings also frame views from this central place of notable aspects of the surrounding landscape, such as sacred mountains.

Many other Native American town design traditions exist, which include central outdoor places such as Algonquian village centers, Hawaiian *heiau*, Mandan ceremonial plazas, and the bays and beaches around which the Tlingit and other Northwest coast tribes built their villages. More study of these places could help dispel the notion that plazas and other civic rooms are primarily European phenomena, and enrich our understanding of how to create new civic places.

Native American central place designs influenced early European settlements and continue to serve as models. In the epilogue to *Anasazi Architecture,* the poet and architectural critic V. B. Price argues:

> Anasazi architecture has more to contribute to the health of the future than history lessons or Disney-esque imagineering. . . . [We need to] focus instead on functional and symbolic issues, on ecological utility and the social metaphors of form. . . . Architecture and urban design can reinforce humane values or disrupt them. [The Anasazi settlement] Chaco shows how useful it might be for American designers of the future to get beyond commercialism and deeply examine the metaphors and values of their own culture. (1997: 227–28)

Spanish Plazas

"The main plaza is to be the starting point for the town. . . . The plaza should be square or rectangular, in which case it should have at least one and a half its width for length inasmuch as this shape is best for fiestas in which horses are used and for any other fiestas that should be held": so read no. 112 of the Law of the Indies, the Spanish codification of town design principles for the New World. Thus, throughout the Spanish territories from South America to the Southwest United States, towns center on their *plaza mayor.* The Law of the Indies also specifies:

> 113: The size of the plaza shall be proportioned to the number of inhabitants. . . . [The plaza] shall not be less than two hundred feet wide and three hundred feet long, nor larger than eight hundred feet long and five hundred and thirty-two feet wide. A good proportion is six hundred feet long and four hundred wide.

> 115: Around the plaza as well as along the four principal streets which begin there, there shall be *portales*, for these are of considerable convenience to the merchants who generally gather there; . . .

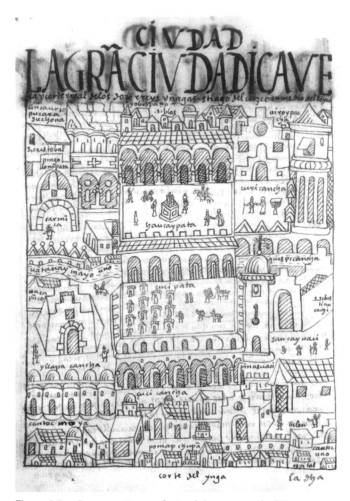

Figure 3.7a. *Guaman Poma de Ayala's portrayal of Cuzco, from his* Nueva corónica y buen gobierno de las Indias *(c. 1614). This drawing of the former Inca capital centers around the main ceremonial plaza, Haucaypata, and the market plaza, Cusipata. Courtesy of the Royal Library, Copenhagen.*

Figure 3.7b. *Guaman Poma de Ayala's portrayal of Santa Fe de Bogotá, from his* Nueva corónica y buen gobierno de las Indias *(c. 1614). Like most of his drawings of Spanish settlements, this view of Santa Fe de Bogotá is centered on the plaza and composed on an ideal model of the Heavenly City. Courtesy of the Royal Library, Copenhagen.*

124: The temple in inland places shall not be placed on the square but at a distance . . . (Crouch, Garr, and Mundigo 1982: 13–15)

In addition to the *plaza mayor*, the Law of the Indies prescribed smaller plazas (no. 118) for parish churches, and a pasture commons (nos. 90, 129, 130).

These laws were often applied with flexibility on the ground, and the features of these plazas evolved over time. Many plazas, like those in Taos and Los Angeles, were transformed from an open earthen field to a landscaped park when they became part of the United States.

These codified Spanish town patterns overlaid, and may have been informed by, pre-Columbian town-design traditions. The Inca, Maya, and Aztecs built towns with a range of types of central civic places. Mayan settlements had large ceremonial precincts, plazas, civic ball courts, and courtyards. Incan Cuzco (now in Peru) had a number of small "plazas" and a large central ceremonial place called *Haucaypata* that, after conquest, the Spanish divided into three squares. The *Zócalo* of Mexico City took the place of the central ceremonial complex of Aztec Tenochtitlán. Beyond the Spanish occupation and redesign of these sites, the degree to which they influenced subsequent Spanish design is a matter of debate.

English City Squares (and Circles and . . .)

The instructions given the founders of Jamestown in 1606 included a central market square. "And seeing that order is at the same price with confusion it shall be advisably done to set your houses even and by a line, that your streets may have a good breadth, and be carried square about your market place, and every street's end opening into it, that from thence with a few field pieces you may command every street throughout, which market place you may also fortify if you think it need full" (as quoted by Reps 1965: 90). This central square settlement form was used by the Massachusetts Bay Company for many of the early New England settlements and, with more elaborate fortifications, was also used by the Dutch for New Amsterdam.

William Penn and Thomas Holme's Philadelphia opened a new era of English town design by moving beyond the single

Figure 3.8a. *Perspective of Annapolis, Maryland's Public Circle and the State House. (From Werner Hegemann and Elbert Peets,* The American Vitruvius: An Architect's Handbook of Civic Art *(New York: The Architectural Book Publishing Company 1922), 237.*

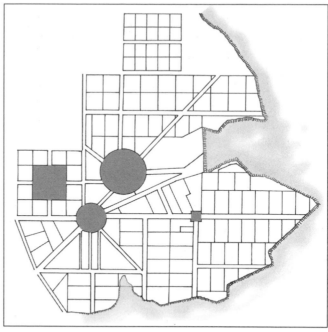

Figure 3.8b. *Diagram of the original plan of Annapolis, showing the major public spaces: Bloomsbury Square, the marketplace, Public Circle, and Church Circle.*

central place pattern. Philadelphia's central square of ten acres was reserved for public buildings, and in addition the plan called for four squares of eight acres each "to be for the like Uses, as the Moore-fields in London" (Reps 1965: 161). London's Moorfields was open to the general public, unlike the then-new squares of Bloomsbury and Covent Garden that were reserved for the use of the aristocrats who lived in the bordering houses.

In the following decade, the new capitols for Maryland (Annapolis) and Virginia (Williamsburg) were created under the governorship and likely the hand of Francis Nicholson (Reps 1965: 103–14). In Annapolis, Nicholson, who was familiar with English and Continental town design, created two *rond-points* (circular open spaces from which streets radiate) on the highest and most prominent ground. Saint Anne's

Church in Church Circle and The State House within State Circle thus are well placed as focal points of the town. The original design of Annapolis also included a Bloomsbury Square (named after the elegant square in London) and a smaller market place at the terminus of Market Street (figs. 3.8a and 3.8b). In contrast to Annapolis, where the composition focused on central outdoor rooms, the plan of Williamsburg relies on the long axes of Duke of Gloucester Street and the Palace Green. The capitol, the Governor's Palace, and the preexisting College of William and Mary terminate these axes, in good late Baroque style.

This precedent of formal town design was followed in the eighteenth century by Savannah, Georgia. The plan of the town that James Oglethorpe and the other Trustees for Establishing the Colony of Georgia established in 1733 is

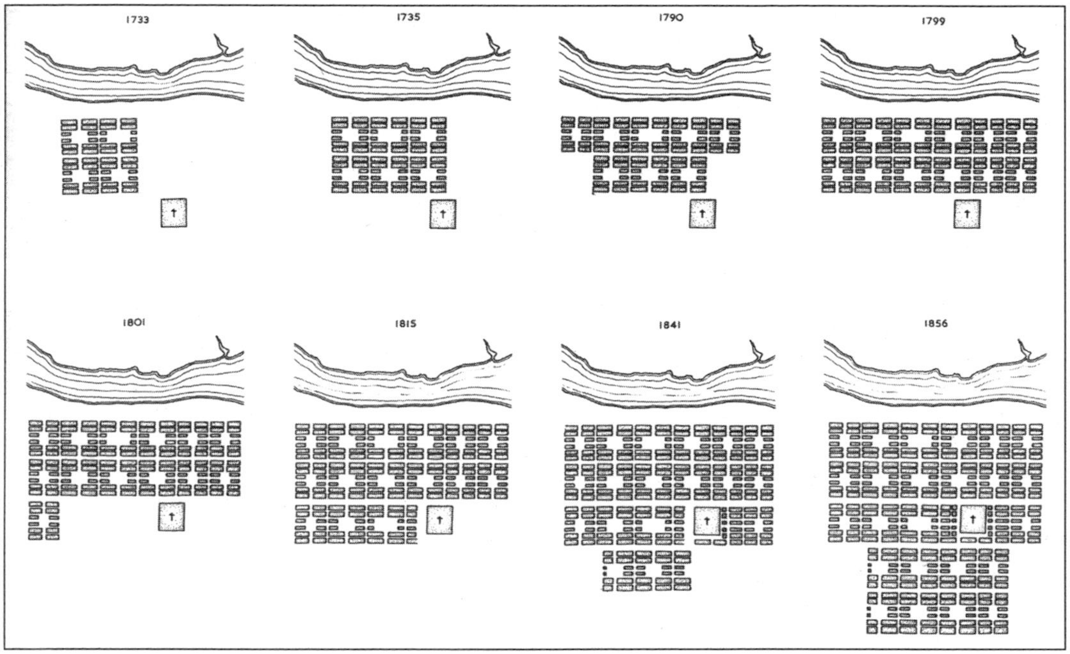

Figure 3.9.
*Diagram of the growth
of Savannah, Georgia,
1733–1856. From John W.
Reps,* The Making of
Urban America
*(Princeton, N.J.:
Princeton University
Press, 1965). The coher-
ence of this plan over
a century and a quarter
of growth is remarkable.
Used by permission of
John W. Reps.*

remarkable (see fig. 3.9). The original plan was composed of six wards. Each ward contained six blocks around a central square. The blocks on the east and west of the square were reserved for institutional and public buildings. This pattern provided generous public open space, a cohesive neighborhood unit, and an easily expandable town plan.

These four cities—Philadelphia, Annapolis, Williamsburg, and Savannah—gave British America some of the best-designed town plans within the British Empire.

New England Greens

The New England green, with its church, other institutional buildings, and wall of businesses, evolved from early colonial seeds. These original seeds often consisted of an acre or so of commons, a meetinghouse, and a burying ground. The commons was owned jointly by the original proprietors for pasturing livestock, echoing the ancient English tradition of the village commons (see Neeson 1993 for an analysis of the English common). Despite a short-lived (1635–1640) order

from the Massachusetts Bay General Court that houses must be built within a half-mile of the meeting house, farmsteads during the seventeenth and eighteenth centuries were widely scattered (Wood 1997). During their first century, the complex of meeting house and commons were typically more rural gathering spots than town centers.

After the Revolutionary War, when local manufacturing and commerce began to proliferate in New England, these seeds began to grow into compact and active village centers. "Across New England, stores and shops and offices, courthouses and academies, and residences of nonfarmers—all material manifestations of the maturing rural economy—were gathered about hundreds of meetinghouse lots" (Wood 1997: 102). The town centers we recognize today were formed during this Federalist period.

A century later, around the nation's centennial, town commons became village greens. Throughout New England, the unimproved collective pasture of the commons was cleared, leveled, fenced, and edged with elms or other trees and transformed into a green for strolling, socializing, and celebrating. "Victorian gazebos, bandstands, fountains, and sculptured flower beds, along with fences that kept traffic off the planting, enabled townspeople and villagers to use greens for endless community activities, carnivals, auctions, fairs, and patriotic celebrations . . ." (Webb 1990: 175).

French Places

Quebec City, Montreal, St. Louis, New Orleans, Mobile, and a number of smaller towns along the St. Lawrence and Mississippi valleys were established by the French. A central feature of most of these French colonial towns was the *place d'armes.* Unlike the Spanish plazas and the English squares, many of the *places* were set at the edge of the town, along the river as a kind of place of entry (and defense) for the settlement. The record is unclear, but it appears that this difference in conception can be seen in the transformation of St. Louis from a French to a Spanish settlement. The original French *place* appears to have been set along the river. Two decades later, under Spanish rule, the central square was inland and centrally placed in the grid of the town (Reps 1965: 75–77).

In many locations, French town design was strongly modified (as in St. Louis) or erased (as in the French settlement of Detroit). The strongest examples of French town planning come not from French settlements but from French influences and designers working for others. Pierre Charles L'Enfant's design for Washington, D.C., with its *rond points,* great mall, and diagonal boulevards terminating in monumental buildings is the prime example.

Courthouse Squares

A Square, the courthouse in its grove the center; quadrangular around it, the stores, two-storey, the offices of the lawyers and doctors and dentists, the lodge-rooms and auditoriums, above them; school and church and tavern and bank and jail each in its ordered place; the four broad diverging avenues straight as plumb-lines in the four directions, becoming the network of roads and by-roads . . . along which would flow the aggrandizement of harvest: the gold: the cotton and the grain;

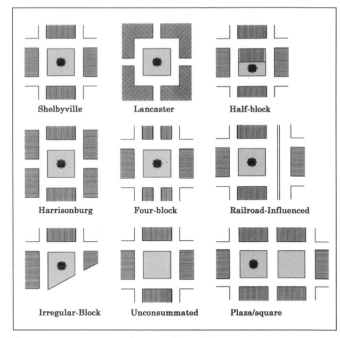

Figure 3.10. *Diagram of types of courthouse squares.*

But above all, the courthouse: the center, the focus, the hub; sitting looming in the center of the county's circumference . . . protector of the weak, judicator and curb of the passions and lusts, repository and guardian of the aspirations and hopes . . .

Thus William Faulkner described the square of the fictional Jefferson, based on the central courthouse squares that dominate county seats throughout the Middle West and South of the United States (Faulkner 1951: 34–35).

The geographer Edward T. Price wrote the classic study of the central courthouse square (Price 1968). He names four types of courthouse squares after the town he identifies as their source in the United States—Shelbyville, Lancaster, Harrisonburg, and Four-block Square. Robert E. Veselka, in his extensive study *The Courthouse Square in Texas* (2000), adds five more types: Plaza Square, Railroad-Influenced Square, Irregular Block, and Half- and Quarter-Block (fig. 3.10).

The urban researcher should be aware of one other type.

Figure 3.11.
The lawn at the University of Virginia from the enclosing colonnade, 1998.

As railroads and other developers platted towns throughout the South and into Texas and New Mexico, they frequently reserved a plot for the county courthouse they hoped to secure. Some of these towns, such as Elida, New Mexico, failed to become the county seat but the public square remained. These unconsummated courthouse squares are easily confused with other traditions.

Open Quadrangle, Campus, and Lawn

Following the example of medieval monasteries, colleges in Oxford and Cambridge, England, were built as a continuous wall around a central cloister or quadrangle. By the time of English colonial settlement in America, a revision of this pattern was in vogue in Cambridge: "open quadrangles" enclosed on three sides by multistory college buildings and on the fourth by a lower wall and gate. Harvard, the first English college in the colonies, had ties to these new Cambridge colleges.

Harvard, and soon thereafter The College of William and Mary in Virginia, followed the Cambridge precedent of the open quadrangle. Moreover, as these colleges grew and

evolved they further opened the quadrangle. By the mid-eighteenth century, instead of a single continuous building wrapping a quad, a set of three buildings framed a central space open on one side and at the corners. This open quad reflected the educational goals of a college engaged with, rather than apart from, its community.

The original 1753 plan of Princeton established a second American precedent in university design—the campus. The first building of Princeton (then the College of New Jersey) was set back from a rural road, creating a large four-and-a-half-acre green in a rural setting. Possibly the design echoed the New England village green, but it was an innovation in English college design. By the 1770s the word *campus* (Latin for 'field') designated Princeton's open green. Eventually, the word and the idea expanded to designate the open, bucolic grounds of a university.

A third type of commons arose from early American collegiate design. Thomas Jefferson designed the University of Virginia around a large linear lawn terracing down to an open view of the countryside (fig. 3.11). Continuous arcades line the long sides of the lawn connecting an alternating set

Where the Young Child May Play in Safety

THE interior block play area, of which a plan by Gardner S. Rogers is herewith reproduced, is particularly adapted to congested city areas, since it is reached by a gate from the back yard rather than by way of busy streets with their attendant traffic dangers. It is particularly adapted to the use of small children, since those older and more active and self-reliant find more entertainment on the larger playgrounds of the neighborhood.

Mr. Rogers is assistant manager of the Civic Development Department of the Chamber of Commerce of the United States, and is a city-planning engineer. His recently issued Playground Handbook for Chamber of Commerce Executives (see page 193) contains four suggested plans comprising a comprehensive community playground system. Of the interior block plan, as shown in the illustration below, he says:

"Such a development should be so de-

signed and planted with trees, shrubs and grass that (1) some shade is available all day, (2) there is an open area of grass suitable for active games, (3) provision is made for sand boxes, teeters and swings. If possible a shelter should also be provided, with seats and chairs for those superintending the activities, and from relief from extreme heat or in case of rain. While access to all of the private gardens in the block is desirable, it is not wise to provide any access to the street."

Figure 3.12.

A proposal for playgrounds in the interior of housing blocks. From The American City, *July 1928, p. 118.*

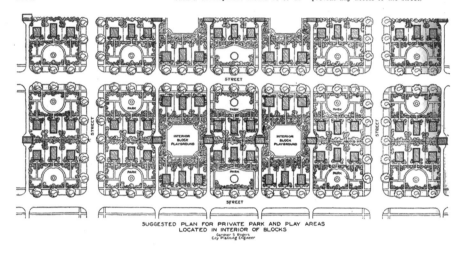

SUGGESTED PLAN FOR PRIVATE PARK AND PLAY AREAS
LOCATED IN INTERIOR OF BLOCKS
Gardner S. Rogers
City Planning Engineer

of two-story professors' pavilions (designed as house and classroom) and one-story students' dormitories. At the top of the lawn, replacing a chapel in the place of honor, sits the library rotunda. The University of Virginia Lawn remains one of the most graceful commons in the United States.

Playground

At the turn of the twentieth century, the playground movement in the United States embedded a new type of civic place into the American palette of town design. The arguments for creating these rooms and parks is summarized in an article by Herbert H. Weir, Field Secretary, Playground and Recreation Association of America, in the February 1911 issue of *The American City* magazine:

> Thinking people all over the United States have come to realize the importance of making some provision not only for the play of children, but also for the

recreation of the entire community. They realize that industrial work will be better done if the workers are more alive and better fitted to their tasks. They realize that the scientific study of juvenile delinquency made in Chicago has shown that recreation centers are one of the most powerful agents for reducing juvenile crime. . . . They realize that through festivals and other meetings . . . a community spirit is developed which insures better citizenship. . . . they realize that life is worth living for its own sake, and anything that gives people capacity for greater enjoyment, which enables them to live more keenly, is doing much for society.

In the early years of the movement, many of the playgrounds were retrofitted into existing town plans. By the 1920s numerous plans for new developments incorporated playgrounds as central features (fig. 3.12). Radburn, New Jersey,

Figure 3.13. *A proposal for a civic center for the city of Fall River, Massachusetts. From* The American City, *July 1928, p. 140.*

represents the apogee, with its paths and parkways that allowed children to walk from each home to their school without crossing a street.

Civic Centers

"The civic center was intended to be a beautiful ensemble, an architectonic triumph far more breathtaking than a single building. . . . Grouping public buildings around a park, square, or intersection of radial streets allowed the visual delights of perspectives, open spaces, and the contrast between the buildings and their umbrageous settings" (Wilson 1989: 92). Assembling a town's public buildings into an urban set piece was one tenet of the City Beautiful movement. At the turn of the last century, the members of the movement developed a number of plans, and, in a handful of cities such as San Francisco and Denver, managed to build

civic centers (fig. 3.13). Some of the unbuilt plans continue to inform new urban-design activities. In Seattle, for example, the unbuilt 1911 Virgil Bogue plan has inspired a number of recent proposals for the South Lake Union area.

D. Unsung Civic Places

Beyond the Spanish plaza and New England town green, there are traditional and emerging place types that fulfill the role of civic places but have not yet received much attention and analysis. The Mormons, for instance, built settlements with central civic places in Utah and the West (see Reps 1965 and Hamilton 1995). The Russians built settlements in Alaska. Shelikhov, the leader of Russian colonization in Alaska, instructed: "In plan and in actuality create squares for public gatherings and streets, though not very long ones, as they can be extended from the squares in several rows—but make them wide" (as quoted in Senkevitch 1979: 24). Certainly, other immigrant groups have brought and continue to bring their civic-place traditions.

In addition to immigrant groups, other forces have generated types of civic places. The railroads, for example, built stations that served as the civic hub for towns across the country. In the Southwest, the Santa Fe Railroad and the Fred Harvey Company built complexes with stations, hotels, and parks. Commuter rail lines, likewise, built stations and station forecourts for satellite towns.

Beyond these railroad forecourts, other transportation terminals can serve as civic rooms. In chapter 14, I argue that parking garages can support the life of a square just as railroad stations have in the past. Even large bicycle shelters can nourish civic coves. In Portsmouth, New Hampshire, groups of motorcyclists park their bikes along a side street, get pastries and coffee from the local shop, and hang out in the square. U.S. Supreme Court cases have examined the legal status of airport terminals as public forums (see chapter 2). Among the islands of the Alaska panhandle and the bayous of Louisiana, the town dock serves as a civic place (fig. 3.14). Bus stop shelters and subway stations could also be understood as small civic coves or rooms.

Figure 3.14. *The town dock of Thorne Bay, Alaska (2000), is the place of arrival and departure, the place where fishermen swap stories and neighbors meet on their way to work. Inset shows fishermen at the public fish-cleaning facility on the dock.*

Figure 3.15. *Even simple street furniture can serve as a "seed" or support for civic commons and sometimes may embody and engender political discourse. In the early 1900s the Oregon lumber baron Simon Benson wanted to discourage his workers from drinking alcohol in the middle of the day. As part of this campaign, Benson donated twenty four-spout fountains that were installed around Portland in 1912 and 1913. It is said that many were placed in front of taverns. Today the elegant fountains, designed by architect A. E. Doyle, are a cherished part of downtown Portland and one has been donated to Portland's sister city, Sapporo, Japan. Image from* The American City, *April 1916, p. 385.*

Other places may also be emerging as civic places. In some towns the recycling center includes places to exchange books and to hang out. Mailbox gazebos provide a structure and place that goes beyond the gang mailbox requirements of the U.S. Post Office and may serve as a small commons. Sidewalk canopies such as those in front of movie theaters or service stations may also serve as forecourts. Any publicly accessible place where people like to loiter may be the seed of a civic place—just add a sense of welcome (places to sit and watch other people, shade, access to food and water) and a sense of delight.

Excursion

THE ECONOMIC VALUE OF PARKS AND OPEN SPACE

Ted O. Harrison

Throughout the country, well-maintained and actively programmed parks have contributed extraordinary economic value to nearby residential properties and business districts. Parks, gardens, and trails are also frequently cited as community assets that inspire high levels of neighborhood awareness, civic engagement, and public safety. Furthermore, the recreational value of parks and open space supports improved measures of physical and psychological health for central city residents, especially among children and senior citizens.

In addition to attracting home buyers and increasing property values, parks and public spaces can also support significantly increased rates of local business ownership and community economic development. Indeed, culturally relevant, strategically located urban parks, gardens, and open space can be catalysts for community renewal by their contribution to increased levels of home ownership and enterprise development, and by enhancing opportunities for neighborhood engagement.

A Legacy of Place-making

The Trust for Public Land (TPL) was founded on the premise that strategically located, well-planned urban parks, community gardens, and playgrounds can enhance the quality of life and economic health of cities and towns. Throughout its thirty-year history, TPL has facilitated the acquisition and permanent protection of nearly fourteen hundred parks and open space properties, totaling over 1.5 million acres.

The organization's conservation and community-building portfolio includes a diverse array of projects and programs. TPL's intervention in New York City Mayor Giuliani's proposed sale of sixty-three well-loved and painstakingly cultivated community gardens exemplifies the organization's commitment to neighborhood green-space protection. In addition to our metropolitan area park-making efforts, TPL has also completed a large number of "landscape-scale" conservation projects. These include acquisitions of multi-thousand-acre wilderness tracts in northern Montana, as well as a recent 162,000-acre purchase in New Hampshire's "North Woods" to advance a unique mix of sustainable forestry and habitat protection.

The Parks and Open Space Value Proposition

In most cases, TPL's land work is advanced by policymakers, business leaders, and citizen activists who appreciate the powerful leverage achieved by matching strategic land-conservation objectives with sustainable economic-development goals. To inform an improved practice of policy setting and public-investment decision making, park professionals and academics are carefully evaluating the role of parks and open space as engines of wealth creation and anchors of neighborhood stability.

Enhancement Effects

A growing number of academic and private studies show a strong positive correlation between residential and commercial property values and access to parks and open space. The "enhancement effect" of well-located and well-maintained open space, trails, and plazas within U.S. metropolitan areas has been documented in a wide variety of cases employing diverse methodologies. Some of the more compelling findings include:

New York City, New York: As early as the 1850s, landscape architect Frederick Law Olmstead justified the purchase of New York's Central Park by noting that the rising value of adjacent property would produce enough in taxes to pay for the park. By 1864, Olmstead documented a $55,880 net return in annual taxes over what the city was paying in interest for land and improvements. By 1873, the park—which until then had cost approximately $14 million—was responsible for an extra $5.24 million in taxes each year (Fox 1990: 11–12).

Boulder, Colorado: In 1967, Boulder became the first U.S. city to pass a dedicated sales tax to fund the preservation of open space. Thirty-five years later, Boulder residents enjoy access to nearly forty-five thousand acres of foothill trails, working farmlands, and river parkways. An economic analysis of the city's land-protection program evidenced a robust positive relationship between park proximity and property value. In a typical case, one neighborhood realized an increase in property values of over $5.4 million after an adjoining "greenbelt" was acquired and improved with trails. The greenway acquisition generated over $500,000 per year in new property taxes—enough to recoup the cost of the greenway in less than three years (Correll et al. 1978).

San Francisco, California: Proximity to Golden Gate Park is broadly regarded as a guiding force for growing property values among residential and commercial neighborhoods within a quarter-mile distance of the facility. In 1993, the park's effect on nearby property values was estimated between $500 million and $1 billion—an enhancement effect that generated $5–10 million in new annual property taxes (California Assembly Committee 1993).

Seattle, Washington: Homes bordering the twelve-mile "Burke Gilman Trail" were found to sell for 6 percent more than homes of comparable size and quality in neighborhoods without easy access to the trail network. Similar home price premiums have been documented in Portland, Oregon, for properties located within a ten-minute walking distance of a trail or passive open space area (Brabec 1992: 2).

Chattanooga, Tennessee: After decades of decline and abandonment, business leaders and public officials committed over $365 million in public and private funds to effect a dramatic redevelopment of the city's historic downtown riverfront area. Among the improvements was the acquisition and development of an eight-mile greenway, the centerpiece of an emerging seventy-five-mile network of greenways and trails. In the eight years between 1988 and 1996, the number of businesses and full-time jobs in the district doubled, and assessed property values increased over $11 million—an increase of over 127 percent. Over the same period, the annual combined city and county property tax revenues went up $592,000, an increase of 99 percent (statistics from Chattanooga News Bureau and Hamilton County, Tennessee, tax assessor.)

Dallas, Texas: In a recent study by ERA, a highly regarded Washington, D.C., based economic and market feasibility consulting firm, lease rates for offices and residential units overlooking a proposed park near the center of the city's historic business district are forecast to be from 20 to 40 percent higher than comparable properties that lack views or easy access to "Commerce Garden." Additionally, ERA estimates that the Dallas County Appraisal District will collect at least $1.45 million in new annual property taxes from the acquisition and development of the proposed six-acre park (Hughes 2002).

While parks and open space can be powerful catalysts for new residential and commercial investment, the relative contribution of green space to quality of life and community redevelopment goals can vary tremendously, depending on a facility's mix of physical and social attributes. Accordingly, job creation, business investment, and property value improvements need to be carefully calibrated according to the type of park, quality of programming, and level of maintenance directed to public spaces.

In many communities, passive open space resources, community gardens, nature preserves, and trails inspire faster rates of job creation, higher levels of private investment, and greater increases in property values than active recreation facilities. Indeed, intensively developed parks—especially playing fields that include elaborate high-power lighting—can actually depress property values for adjoining homes and businesses. As a result, park planners and landscape architects should take special precaution in their design and programming work to limit the effects of noise and light pollution from active recreation uses (i.e., playing fields, tennis and basketball courts, and recreation facilities).

Leveraging Strategies

Private/public partnerships have proven effective in leveraging economic and social value from park and open space investments. Thoughtfully structured and flexibly implemented business and community partnerships have brought new financial and political resources to parks departments throughout the country. New York and Boston offer notable examples of this emerging practice.

Bryant Park, located beside the New York City Public Library, was redeveloped with $9 million in Business Improvement District (BID) financing. To ensure the park's sustained value to the midtown area, a private nonprofit organization assumed responsibility for the property's maintenance and programming. Today, with enthusiastic support from philanthropists and business owners, Bryant Park Restoration Corporation manages the facility with unbounded energy and exquisite attention to detail—aggressively marketing events and programs that enliven the park on summer evenings, as well as ensuring that core maintenance issues, such as bathroom cleaning and trash emptying, are tirelessly attended (Garvin and Berens 1996: 27).

Park at Post Office Square: For years, a two-acre parcel in the heart of Boston's financial district was home to an unsightly 500,000-square-foot parking structure. In the early 1980s, business leaders partnered with city leaders to reclaim the site—now known as the Park at Post Office Square—for use as an underground parking facility, along with a spreading lawn, polished granite walls, teak benches, and a 143-foot-long formal garden and sculpture fountain. According to *Boston Globe* architectural critic Robert Campbell, "The business district used to be an unfathomable maze of street and buildings without a center. The park provides that center. . . . It's as if the buildings were pulling up to the park like campers around a bonfire." With financing from a BID to underwrite the facility development and maintenance costs, the city now enjoys a substantial increase in tax revenues from employers and property owners who surround the site (Harnik 1997).

Beyond Quantification

Understandably, the *economic* value of parks and open spaces is but one factor in the complex calculus of "quality of life" equations. While this "excursion" has been devoted to economy and finance—often the foremost concerns of business leaders and public-policy advocates—the social, political, and biological values that flow from park creation and open space protection demand fuller consideration. Similarly, flood prevention—as well as initiatives to protect community water supplies and water quality—provide compelling justification for aggressive policymaking and targeted fiscal investment in park and open space protection. Indeed, for land conservation organizations such as TPL, matters of physical and emotional health can make a strong case for generous public investment in park creation and open space protection.

But perhaps most important is the inherently subjective and wonderfully intangible non-accounting of non-policymakers and non-economists regarding the value of re-creational, contemplative, spacious places. For the communities we serve, it is often the longing remembrance of an elder, the ecstatic laughter of a child, or the fleeting awareness of *belonging* that make parks and open space unarguably and fundamentally *essential* elements of our experience as a vital people and an engaged society. By this more poetic evaluative model, the economic value of parks and open space is merely icing on a marvelously delicious cake.

References

Brabec, Elizabeth. 1992. "On the Value of Open Spaces." *Scenic America,* Technical Information Series, vol. 1, no. 2. Washington, D.C.: Scenic America.

California Assembly Committee on Water, Parks, and Wildlife. 1993. Testimony, "The Value of Parks" (May 18).

Correll, Mark et al. 1978. "The Effects of Greenbelts on Residential Property Values: Some Findings on the Political Economy of Open Space." *Land Economics* (May).

Fox, Tom. 1990. "Urban Open Space: An Investment that Pays." New York: Neighborhood Open Space Coalition.

Garvin, Alexander, Gayle Berens, and Christopher B. Leinberger. 1997. "Urban Parks and Open Space." Urban Land Institute.

Harnik, Peter 1997. "The Park at Post Office Square." In "Urban Parks and Open Space," by Alexander Garvin, Gayle Berens, and Christopher B. Leinberger. Urban Land Institute.

Hughes, Ken. 2002. Presentation to the Dallas City Council, December 4.

Ted Harrison is a Senior Vice President with the Trust for Public Land (TPL). Mr. Harrison's seventeen-year career with TPL has included project management, regional management, and national program development responsibilities. Mr. Harrison holds degrees in anthropology and political science from the University of California at Berkeley, as well as a Masters of City and Regional Planning from the University of North Carolina at Chapel Hill.

part two

CIVITAS

Writing the Syllabus

It is not the private interests of the individual that create lasting fellowship among men, but rather the goals of humanity.

—I Ching, Hexagram 13 (Wilhelm 1950)

Civic places serve multiple purposes, from a quiet place to eat lunch to a site for political rallies. They are also the public face of the city or town and thus their symbolic content is of social and political importance. Furthermore, people's desires, uses, and perceptions of a place differ with age, gender, community membership, economic status, and time.

The process of generating funds and support, defining the purposes of the place, and managing change is complex and emergent. Rather than using the architectural term *programming* for this process, I suggest that the designers of civic places think about developing a syllabus.

A syllabus is an outline of a discourse or course of study. The root of the word is associated with the Greek term *sullam-banein,* 'to put together'. There is no single, simply defined client for a public commons, but rather, if the place is to come alive there is a welter of overlapping stakeholders. The uses that a public commons accommodates change over time, and are often a matter of discourse and dispute. The term *syllabus*

suggests that the process is one of dialog and ongoing study. "Programming" suggests a mechanical process of inputting needs and outputting a completed design.

A. Process

"Making public spaces just like the old ones can't bring back the old public life for which we have such nostalgia. They were part of a different ecology, one that has changed and we need to look at the new ecology that surrounds public life in our towns and cities, in search for new, appropriate forms" (Altman and Zube 1989: 25). No longer do we have public hangings in the town square. Rather, many of our public places are now home to car rallies, skateboarding, and espresso stands.

Some of these changing uses are like different plays on a stage—the props and costumes change, but the fundamental relationships of the stage stay the same from play to play.

However, other changes may be akin to the difference between a classic proscenium stage and theater in the round; the theater itself may need to be altered.

To discover the appropriate form of the stage and the nature of the props, the planners, designers, and managers of an urban commons need to immerse themselves in the fabric of the neighborhood, town, and region that the place will serve.

Finding Seeds

Are there places that people use as a civic place despite the physical setting? Can these places serve as a seed for the development of a robust place?

Have you found yourself talking to a neighbor or colleague for forty-five minutes in the post office or grocery store parking lot? Is there a farmers' market, poets' society, or curling club that needs a permanent home? Is there an old commercial block in the neighborhood in need of revitalization? Can the stream that once flowed through a neighborhood be taken out of its sewer pipe and turned into a linear park? Can the bus lines that serve a district be collected to meet along a short segment of street? Social, historic, landscape, and transportation seeds offer resources that can grow incrementally. Physical (re)design can offer support and dignity to social practices.

Pike Place Market in Seattle serves as a prime example. Begun in 1907 and expanded throughout the early part of the twentieth century, by the 1960s the market was deteriorating and partially abandoned. The city council had proposed tearing down the set of structures and selling the land for a hotel. A well-orchestrated public campaign defeated this attempt and in 1971 created a preservation and development authority to manage the market. The public rallied around the physical remnants, practices, and memory of the early market.

While continuing to operate as a farmers' market, Pike Place has also served as the catalyst for social services and redevelopment. The market operates a low-income medical clinic; a childcare center and preschool; a food bank; a senior center; housing for about five hundred people, mostly low-income seniors; a set of fourteen street-performer "stages"; and an annual festival. The market also serves as a business

Figure 4.1. *Piano player at Pike Place Market, Seattle, Washington, 1999.*

incubator (Starbucks started at the Pike Place Market), a tourist attraction, and an anchor for the redevelopment of the surrounding district (www.pikeplacemarket.org, April 2, 2002).

Community Built

How can the life of the community be strengthened by the planning, design, and use of a civic place?

"Direct participation in designing, building and managing environments has been found to increase user satisfaction in a variety of spaces including communities, the workplace and open spaces such as parks and playgrounds" (Wandersman 1981). To create a living commons, the community must take ownership of the place. Designers, planners, and others should take the role of consultants to the community. Thus designers and planners do not invite the community to participate, rather the community allows the designers to help.

"The community," of course, can be a complex ecosystem, including, by some definitions, at least the next six generations, visitors from the other side of the world, and the planet itself. Planners and designers may be relative outsiders or longstanding members of the community. Each situation will have its own dynamics. A consultant can begin to understand and listen to the community by:

(1) Providing notice of proposed projects in various venues such as signs on the site, local papers, and newsletters to aid self-identification of stakeholders (this should happen early, before the design work is begun);

(2) Developing tailored outreach to hear quiet or upstaged voices such as those of children. This may include holding small group meetings facilitated by members of the quiet groups, going to meetings these groups hold, providing means of input that are anonymous, or finding the means these people typically use to communicate;

(3) Finding advocates for those without a voice; and

(4) Developing methods that facilitate actual work by the community.

Community work projects, barn raisings if you will, can take place during the planning and design, during construction, and in the use and maintenance of the urban commons. Possibilities include:

⊞ Chautauquas—Holding a series of lectures, panel discussions, movies, reading groups, walking tours, etc., to help the community educate itself about its history, current architecture, nonprofit organizations, and whatever issues are part of the syllabus.

⊞ Conceptual and place-practices mapping—Kevin Lynch developed an approach to analyzing the structure of a city by asking people to draw quick maps (Lynch 1960). These maps help identify community members' concepts of landmarks, barriers, districts, and major pathways. Community-drawn maps of where people do things (e.g., street games, gossiping, parade routes) can supplement building-based maps. Understanding this conceptual landscape allows designers to work within it, placing civic rooms,

urban frameworks, and other civic places in appropriate places.

⊞ Constructing visual albums—In order to discuss design it is often useful to have a shared set of images as reference points. The images may be brought to the table by the designers and by the community. An exercise that many have used is to give the community disposable cameras and ask them to go on treasure hunts for good, or bad, images of their community. Community members can also scan magazines or the designer's collection of slides. These albums of images can be used simply as shared material for discussion on an ad-hoc basis, or they can serve as material for a more intensive process. Anton Nelessen has developed a technique he calls "visual preference surveys," in which people quickly rate a set of slides and he uses this data to make conclusions about the group's visual predilections. My own experience suggests that numerical rankings of images are best used as points of departure for discussions. These discussions often uncover a variety of concepts about the images and lead to more nuanced understandings of places (see Childs and Childs, 2000).

⊞ Architectural/planning sports—Architectural sports, like theater sports, are short intensive exercises that focus on a particular portion of the larger process. The open charrette is probably the most extensively used exercise. In a charrette, a group of designers and others work intensively for a day, two days, or up to a week on developing schematic designs. Charrettes come in a variety of flavors. The significant variables are the role of the public (e.g., as audience, kibitzers, or partners with the designers), the length of the process, the stage of design (e.g., is the point to initiate a discussion, develop alternatives for action, or develop *the* scheme for a project?), and the charrette's relationship to ongoing work. The American Institute of Architects has a longstanding charrette process called Rural-Urban Design Assistance Teams. There is also a recently formed National Charrette Institute (www.charretteinstitute.org). Other sports include visioning and community action planning (group

Figure 4.2.
Parade entry by children who sold their produce at the farmers' market. From The American City, *April 1916, p. 371.*

discussions to develop goals and guides for public actions), community study circles (a series of regular study and discussion meetings), and site design board games in which participants arrange buildings and spaces on a model. Henry Sanoff discusses many of these techniques in detail in his book *Community Participation Methods in Design and Planning* (2000).

▦ Test-marketing architecture—In addition to off-site visualization techniques such as models, doctored photographs, and classic drawings, other techniques such as chalk lines, surveying strings, or inflatable plastic models can be used to mock up buildings on site. On-site techniques have the advantage of being fully in context, and thus relationships that were previously not thought about may become apparent. Pushcarts, tents, and temporary public artwork installations can also be used to investigate permanent changes.

▦ Sweat equity—actual barn raisings in which the community does construction, planting, or other work. An interesting variant of on-site work is to have contributors design and construct a tile or other component off-site. The tiles are then assembled like a collage or quilt on-site.

▦ Dancing—Ceremonial groundbreakings, cornerstone settings, topping-off festivities, and dedications provide excuses for convivial events. Time and money should be budgeted for these activities—they are one of the major reasons to make good civic places.

Sustaining Nonprofits
Nonprofits are corporations organized for a public purpose. How can they support and be supported by civic places?

"We live in a society that has always depended on volunteers of different kinds," wrote Margaret Mead and Rhoda Metraux, in *Aspects of the Present*. "If you look closely you will see that almost anything that really matters to us, anything that embodies our deepest commitment to the way human life should be lived and cared for, depends on some form—more often many forms—of volunteerism" (1980). By charter and law, not-for-profit corporations have a defined interest in the common good. Thus they are natural clients, allies, or both in the creation of civic places.

The syllabus for a square should include discovering the needs and desires of nonprofits, neighborhood groups, clubs, and other groups that have an interest in the area. These groups can provide suggestions for activities, political support, maintenance support (e.g., the senior center may provide gardeners to take care of flower beds), and people who are vested in the life of the commons.

A not-for-profit organization may be created to manage the creation and use of a civic place. The Central Park Conservancy supports New York City's Central Park. A special preservation and development authority manages Pike Place Market in Seattle. This practice can have good and bad effects. The creation of a nonprofit for a civic room, park, or other civic grounds can help insulate the management of the place from the vagaries of municipal budgets, allow the collection of private donations, and focus decision making. It can also disconnect management from civic politics and allow an elite to control what should be a wider commons. Careful crafting of the not-for-profit's mission and selection of a board that represents a variety of interests can help keep the not-for-profit focused on an inclusive definition of the public good.

Not-for-profit organizations may also provide institutional infrastructure for local communities. For example, The Trust for Public Land in San Francisco has an awards program to honor the important role of volunteers in maintaining and improving public open space in the city of San Francisco.

The Structure of Costs
How should we measure the costs and benefits of a material or project?

There is no one correct way to measure the economic cost of a material or a design. Each method embodies different political values. Nevertheless, understanding different methods will help the designer understand and balance the motives, interests, and judgments of various stakeholders.

Silver City, New Mexico, was born in 1870 as a mining camp deep in Apache territory, near the sketchy border with Mexico. Unlike the inhabitants of many other western towns, the builders of Silver City were interested in more than the immediate riches of the silver mines. They took a longer economic view and set about building a "proper" city. Within a year, a brickworks was built, and buildings fit to current eastern tastes were erected. "Silver City is essentially an eastern

Figure 4.3. *Water tank, public viewing platform, and landmark in Volunteer Park, Seattle, Washington. In addition to serving a role as part of the water-system infrastructure, this building was conceived as a public work that can serve multiple roles and help create the public form of the city. The publicly accessible platform at its top provides a spectacular view of the city. The tower sits at the terminus of a road leading into the park, marking the entry into the park. Over the years the garden at its base has become part of the formal landscaping of the park. A cost-benefit analysis of this project based solely on its water storage function would not have justified the other improvements. Image from* The American City, *May 1915, p. 426.*

town, full of live energetic and intelligent men who have come here to stay" (*Las Cruces Borderer,* March 1871). When President Cleveland repealed the Silver Purchase Act in October of 1893, the silver market crashed, and Silver City's investment proved its value. "With its 'pretensions to architectural elegance,' the 'eastern-looking' town still served as a railroad terminus and the political seat and trade center for a county that covered at that time over nine thousand square miles" (Berry and Russell 1986: 36).

The most important step in an economic analysis is stating the goals and assumptions of the project. A brickworks was not a sensible investment for a settlement whose only goal was the extraction of silver, but for the creation of a permanent town it was an essential investment.

Economists often identify a number of different categories of expense such as:

⊞ Initial cost: This can be thought of as the purchase and installation price. One should be careful about the unit being analyzed. For example, taxpayers may compare the cost of a flat lot with that of a steep lot and think that they are getting a better deal on a steep lot. The unit of analysis should be the cost of the lot plus the cost of a foundation (and in some cases the cost of utilities, etc.). Of course, the steep lot may offer a view that justifies the added expense.

⊞ Life-cycle cost: The life-cycle cost is the initial cost plus maintenance, use, and disposal costs over the entire life of the material. In some cases, the cost of risk or insurance is also included. Using life-cycle cost rather than initial cost allows one to figure in durability and maintenance. The use of one method over the other is often a species of hidden politics. Do we care more about the current costs to those paying or the ongoing costs of those maintaining the place?

⊞ Sunk cost: Sunk costs are funds already spent that cannot easily be recovered. Let's say that the initial cost of a brick pavement is much less than a stone pavement. This does not mean that a brick floor is always less expensive. If at the time of a redesign a town square has a stone pavement that is in good

shape, it may be cheaper to preserve it than to put in a new brick one. (There are important subtleties: maybe we could sell the stones, or maybe the stones are leaching a polluting chemical).

Sunk costs are a kind of economic inertia that favors continuity. Once we have built a plaza it is often cheaper and easier to repair, revise, and reuse it than to build a new place. This is another reason to carefully consider the underlying framework of a design. For example, you may be asked to design a building for a specialty restaurant on a site bordering an emerging square. There is a natural desire to create a structure that fits and represents the unique aspects of the restaurant as closely as possible. The building, however, may well outlast the restaurant and the initial owners should be able to sell the building to people who want to open a different kind of restaurant or a bookstore. The building should both serve its birth use and be able to grow into other uses. This way the initial owner can recover some of the sunk cost.

⊞ Opportunity cost: One of the costs of building a design is the loss of the opportunity to build all the competing designs for the site. When there are many parties to a design this can be a very significant issue. The local Rose Society may, for example, wish to have a rose garden as part of a new or redesigned town park. The moment a fountain is built instead, the Rose Society has lost an opportunity.

⊞ External cost: A design may impose costs on neighbors that are not accounted for or even recognized by the builders. For example, a new building may block a neighbor's view. Many environmental costs are not well accounted for in the purchase or life-cycle cost of a material or design. The greenhouse gas emissions created by the manufacturing of various materials, for example, are external costs passed onto the planet as a whole. It is also possible to create external benefits. Publicly funded redevelopment projects such as new and renovated squares are often justified on the basis that the public investment in the public realm will catalyze private investment in the area. The bankable reality of the positive external benefits is attested to by the creation of private/public partnerships that have invested in the redesign of civic rooms such as Post Office Square in Boston or Bryant Park in New York.

A concept related to external costs is the idea of external sites. Building the floor of a square and its enclosing façades from a local stone implies the opening or enlargement of a quarry. The design of the quarry is, in effect, part of the design of the square. The external site may also shape the core site. The form of the highway and access routes limits the size of beams and other items built off-site.

A complete economic primer is, of course, beyond the scope of this book. Nonetheless, answering the political question of how to measure the costs and benefits of materials or of other design decisions is a critical component of the creation of a civic place.

B. A Taxonomy of Uses

Meeting the Hierarchy of Needs
What types of human needs and desires does the civic place help fulfill?

In the 1970s Abraham Maslow proposed a now influential typology of human motivations—Maslow's hierarchy of needs. Maslow suggests that ordinarily, needs lower on his pyramid take priority over higher needs (1970). The most basic needs are for air, drink, food, and warmth. Thus, normally, a person will slake his or her thirst before spending time listening to a concert.

Charting the services provided by a civic place against Maslow's hierarchy of needs may both illuminate the popularity of a space and point out potential oversights. William Whyte's observation, "If you want to seed a place with activity, put out food" (1980: 50), is consistent with Maslow's hierarchy, as is Oscar Newman's observation that places that don't feel secure are subsequently abandoned.

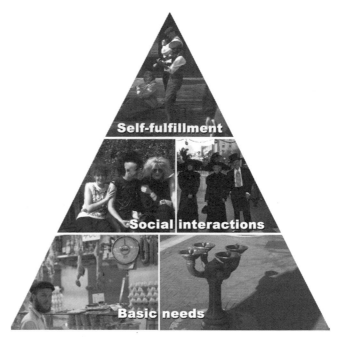

Figure 4.4. *Redrawing of Maslow's hierarchy of needs. Within basic needs, which his theory suggests we seek to fulfill first, Maslow identified a category of physiological needs such as food and drink, and a slightly less primary set of needs for safety and security. What this diagram titles social interactions, Maslow identifies as psychological needs, including a sense of belongingness and love, and esteem needs such as prestige and feelings of accomplishment.*

Of course, history is ripe with counterexamples to Maslow's hierarchy. Monks fast to aid enlightenment; athletes sacrifice companionship to achieve fame; lovers risk their safety and security to be together. Likewise, some squares may be dedicated to a narrow range of human aspirations ignoring more basic needs. The courtyard at the Salk Institute, for example, may be best dedicated to contemplation. The various ice and snow festivals of winter cities illustrate that, for a time, the pursuit of artistry, fun, and companionship can outweigh the desire for comfortable warmth.

However, careful consideration of the range of human needs may help enrich many public commons. For example, the provision of restrooms often presents a difficult problem in the design and management of a public square. Access to latrines, of course, serves a basic human need. It is nearly impossible to have a square full of successful food and drink vendors and not have access to toilet facilities. Unfortunately, public restrooms often create both a safety and a sanitation concern. Thus supervision and maintenance of these facilities are critical. The European solution is often to have a concierge whom one pays to enter the facility. The American solution is often to provide restrooms within adjacent commercial establishments.

Fulfilling basic needs may also aid in the fulfillment of higher needs. The cliché of the office drinking fountain being the center of sociability illustrates this principle. Likewise, farmers' markets are known for their sociability. Conducting business with city hall or the county brings people to a courthouse square, where they may also meet friends and associates.

Conversely, addressing higher needs may make the provision of basic needs more successful. Pam Roy, former market manager for the Santa Fe Farmers' Market, says that musicians, the shop-with-a-chef program, and multiple other social and aesthetic activities were essential to building the base of shoppers for the market (Roy 2002).

The mix and distribution of needs addressed by a civic place is critical to its character and success. Often the delight of a commons emerges from a complex interweaving of activities.

The Tree of Idleness
Does the urban commons invite people to idle?

In the town square of Bellapaix on the north coast of Cyprus there is an ancient mulberry tree. Lawrence Durrell made this tree and its lessons famous in *Bitter Lemons* (1957) and his collection of poems *The Tree of Idleness* (1955). This ancient tree, under which sit wooden chairs overlooking the town and sea, where wine may be ordered and the citizens of the town gather, "confers the gift of pure idleness on all who sit under it."

Any great urban commons will offer this gift.

Different Strokes
What might the demographics of the district suggest about the uses of a civic place?

At another level of refinement from Maslow's general categories, we can examine the needs and desires of different groups of people. The distribution of ages, genders, and cultural backgrounds, for example, can suggest types of activities that would be valued. Two significant caveats should be kept in mind when using demographic data. First, things change over time. New people move in and others move out. People age and children are born. Cultural views evolve. Secondly, demographic data are generalizations taken from samples. In a sense, demographic profiles can be more or less informed prejudices. Middle-aged white American males may be highly interested in professional sports, but I can't name more than four football teams. What demographic analysis can do is suggest:

- Lines of inquiry and engagement (e.g., there are many teenagers in the area. What would engage them in the life of a plaza?);
- The range and types of stakeholders that may exist;
- That there many be significant interests not represented by the majority (e.g., teenagers may wish to play group games such as Hacky-Sac in public while their elders have limited interest in such); and
- Questions about the assumptions that designers and planners bring to a project (such as those embodied in the patterns of this book).

A myriad of types of prejudices between groups have been and continue to be played out in public spaces. An examination of the range of types and means of bigotry exercised in the commons is beyond the scope of this book. However, in each place, designers should seek to be aware of how their designs may be used and interpreted. Differences between demographic groups, which a review of the research literature suggests are well documented, widespread, and persistent, include the following:

1. There is a deep history of women being constrained in their use of public commons—constrained by law, by threat of shame and violence, and by physical design and planning tailored more to the predilections of men. In classic Athens, women were not

permitted to enter the agora. This history continues to shape the use and perception of civic places. In her 1995 book *The Power of Place,* Dolores Hayden reports that in the 1980s only 4 percent of 299 landmarks in Los Angeles reflected the history of women. A 1981 U.S. study documented that women report significantly more fear of crime than men, and they concluded that fear and the actions taken due to fear significantly restrict women's freedom of movement in public places (Riger and Gordon 1981). A set of studies in San Francisco suggests that women tend to prefer public places or parts of public places that are oasislike (gardenlike, partially secluded, and designed as a refuge from the city), whereas men preferred places that offered publicness, social interaction, and activity (Marcus and Francis 1998: 26–27). Finally, a review of various studies led Karen Franck and Lynn Paxson to conclude: "we believe women are more likely to feel they need an observable reason or 'excuse' for being in a public space. This could be eating, shopping, talking with a friend, even sunbathing or reading. Not only may this make their presence more justifiable, it may also signal that they are not open to overtures" (1989: 130). They suggest (1) creating more commons within easy walking distance of residential areas; (2) creating squares, coves, and parks near or in places of shopping and childcare; (3) making civic places more accessible and enjoyable for people accompanying children; and (4) providing clear visual access into and out of public places to increase the sense of safety.

2. It is critical to reach out and involve teenagers in the life of the community. An English study examined the needs of teenagers and found that they had a similar set of needs to those of the general public—a feeling of safety, seating, a notice board of events, access to restrooms, and inclusion in decision making (Wooley et al. 1999). However, access to good community places is more critical to teenagers' attachment to a community than it is for other age groups (see Van Vleet 1983). Generally, teenagers have not chosen of their own accord the place where they live. Moreover,

teenagers' sense of community strongly centers on hanging out with friends and acquaintances. Thus, access to places where they can hang out is critical. Teenagers' buy-in (i.e., a sense of being part of a community) is thought to lower crime and vandalism rates, and to have a long-term effect on their social health.

Additionally, consideration of cultural background, income levels, employment patterns (lunchtime, for example, has significantly different characteristics for factory workers than office workers), education levels, and TV-viewing habits (you may wish to avoid scheduling events against Monday-night football) may uncover results particular to the place of study.

Tuesday Morning
Is the place delightful and commodious on a quiet Tuesday morning?

In *Life Between Buildings* Jan Gehl suggests that we divide everyday use of public places into three categories: (1) necessary (e.g., walking down the street to go to school or work), (2) optional (e.g., sunbathing, taking a stroll), and (3) social activities that depend on the presence of others in civic places (e.g., many children's games, gossiping) (1996: 11–14). Generating social activities from necessary and optional activities lies at the heart of creating strong civic places.

Can the room or cove be a supportive part of the trip to work? For example, is there a coffee shop and newsstand next to a bus stop? Is there a kiosk for public notices? Is there a shelter in which to wait comfortably for the bus and possibly talk to one's fellow riders?

Is the place on the route home from school? Are there good places to hang out and talk? Is it possible to play an active game such as Frisbee or basketball? Is there a way to involve the students in the design or care of the place, such as displaying their artwork or allowing student musicians to play in the afternoon? Again, is there access to food, water, and restrooms?

Is the square associated with public buildings—such as the post office, city hall, or motor vehicle department—

that draw people? Is it convenient to wait in the square for one's meeting in the public building? Does pedestrian traffic flow through the square, or do backdoors to parking lots short-circuit this flow?

Can the square serve as a delightful place for workday lunches? Are there good places for food vendors to set up shop? Is it possible to create a schedule of noon concerts, or provide a stage for street performers?

Can the middle-school war-game club hold its meetings in the square? Does the Master Gardeners Association tend the garden? Can the Tae Kwan Do club practice here?

On a summer afternoon, are there good places to read a book, to play a game of Go, or to watch your toddlers play? Do the folks from the retirement home have a good walking circuit with places to sit? Is the civic room a poetic place—a place to go simply to watch the world, and enjoy being?

Does the place serve the everyday needs of the community?

Anchors
Can an "anchor tenant" be found for an urban commons, or conversely can an existing highly trafficked institution serve as the seed for a new commons?

Throughout the southern United States, the commercial centers of many small towns are focused about a courthouse square. A major proposal of the City Beautiful movement at the turn of the twentieth century was the creation of civic centers with public institutions encircling a square. In Europe, churches and cathedrals frequently open onto "their" plazas. These "anchor tenants" are stable institutions that regularly attract people. This regular flow of people brings life to the urban commons, establishes a dependable market for stores, and makes the commons a likely place to run into others.

Potential anchors for an urban commons include post offices, city halls, schools, museums, libraries, movie theaters, stadiums, passenger railroad stations, ferry terminals, and subway entrances. Even a laundromat may serve as the anchor for a small square, as did the wash houses of past centuries (see Roddier 2003 for a beautiful set of French

examples). The commons, in turn, could serve as the focal point around which complementary uses could be organized. A greeting-card store, for example, may wish to be on the post-office square, or a café, bicycle rental shop, and tourist center could well sit on a ferry terminal plaza.

Current practice in the design of post offices tends to treat them as suburban retail stores with upfront parking and rear service access. This is a missed opportunity. In neighborhoods and small towns across the country, the post office, like the county courthouse in the courthouse square, could serve as the focus and anchor for an urban commons. New courthouse and post-office squares could help fulfill the 1962 Guiding Principles for Federal Architecture that stated that federal buildings should be designed to reflect "the dignity, enterprise, vigor, and stability of the American national government," and suggested that "special attention should be paid to the general ensemble of street and public places of which the Federal buildings will form a part" (Lee 2000: 291).

Permanent and Deployable Markets
What types of shops should we seek to have permanently around a square and what types can be set up on weekends or at an annual fair? How can conflicts between the two groups be managed?

On the streets of Shanghai, pushcart dentists tend to patrons' teeth. In Albuquerque, firewood, trees, and large landscape rocks are sold from the backs of pickups. Just about anything can be sold by temporary vendors. What types of shops should management seek to have in permanent buildings, and what, if any, restraints should be placed on street vendors?

Shops such as the laundromat near apartments, the pinball parlor near the college, and the bank that supports the everyday use of the plaza should have permanent homes. Additionally, it is useful to have an "anchor" or two. (See above.)

Temporary vendors can also serve as intermittent anchors. A Saturday-morning farmers' market can draw many people to a site at what otherwise may be a slow time. A street market may be more fluid and flexible than permanent shops and change with the seasons and the times. Permanent Christmas decoration shops certainly exist, but they have a significant overhead problem. Temporary vendors don't face the same problem.

Providing for farmers' and crafts markets may provide a range of other benefits. As low-overhead businesses they may provide opportunities for people to enter the world of business. They may also provide second incomes to families, practical experience to a teenager, or focus and income to support a retired person's hobby. Additionally, vendors have an immediate interest in the life of the street or square. They will watch for trouble and may be attentive to maintenance issues. Maybe a weekend vendor can be hired as a weekday site manager or gardener.

Not all temporary vendors are merchants. Master-gardener societies often have booths to provide information in civic places. Hospitals, public health agencies, and foundations may create health fairs. Other types of nonprofits may wish to display their services or engage in social marketing. Politicians and preachers may wish to plant their soapboxes where there is an audience.

To create a strong civic room, space and infrastructure should be designed for temporary vendors. Electrical outlets and access to water can be particularly critical. Likewise, management infrastructure must be created. What is the means of allocating vending spaces? What hours and days are available? How is electricity paid for? Are there limits on what can be sold or who can sell?

Designers and planners should work carefully to avoid potential conflicts between permanent stores and vendors. A weekend coffee cart in front of the coffee shop creates an obvious conflict. A temporary market that occupies parking spaces can upset storeowners who believe their clients will avoid their shop because of more difficult access. A musician in front of a shop playing the same songs all day long can be an irritant. Trash left after a market, unmaintained and intense use of restrooms, and any damage to the site create difficulties. If people live adjacent to the square, the early-morning arrival of vendors or late-evening performances are potential problems.

The solution to these and other problems will depend on the details of the site, ownership, and the management structure. Two general principles may be good to keep in mind. First, inform and involve stakeholders, and provide a mechanism to identify issues as early as possible. Secondly, build in features that help clarify territories and spheres of influence. Paving patterns that delineate the placement of vendors' stalls, bollards that define the area into which a storeowner may place chairs or sidewalk sales, or artworks that mark locations for street performers can all help set and maintain order.

Both permanent and temporary merchants can add to the life of a civic place.

C. Community Cultural Development

The town square and neighborhood plaza can provide counterbalances and complements to global media, protecting and nourishing local cultures and providing a venue for active, in-the-flesh participation. (See Adams and Goldbard.) Here is where emerging artists are immersed in their community. Here is where local heroes may be well honored, and local stories polished. These arts need not be poor and parochial. Mark Twain wrote with deep knowledge of the Mississippi and the people who lived along it, but he also spoke to a wider audience.

Storied Landscapes
How may the civic place inspire stories and other artwork that in return help enrich the life of the place?
Pike Place Market sponsors an annual design contest for a market poster. The poster artists have found inspiration from the layout of market stalls, the architecture, artworks, crowds, and street performers. In addition to advertising and presenting a means to view and enjoy the market, this collection of posters in turn informs the vendors, designers, and performers about how their displays are seen and valued.

Iconic artwork and architecture is often used as a backdrop for television news reports, televised political rallies, and local-flavor shows. This, in turn, entrusts the "local character" to the designers, managers and users of the place.

Places that provide the stage for public drama can inform poetry, prose, and film. Stuart Little's boat race takes place in the sailboat pond in Central Park. Sports fields from Yankee Stadium to the small-town ice rink serve as the venue

Figure 4.5. *Winning poster for the flower market at the Washington Monument in 1913. Image from* The American City, *April 1913, p. 390.*

Figure 4.6. *Television interview at the* Dickens on the Strand *festival in Galveston, Texas, 1993.*

for countless stories and movies. The swan boats of Boston Commons have plied through many poems, and somehow riding the boats is more deeply lyrical because of the literature. Town parks and squares host weddings, picnics, and festivals that engender both literature and everyday yarns.

Writing can go beyond highlighting the experience of a place. Public art may respond to stories about a place. For example, there is a statue of ducklings in Boston Commons celebrating the young-children's story *Make Way for Ducklings,* which takes place in the Commons (see fig. 4.7). Places may be restored or revitalized based on literature. Route 66 from Chicago through the Southwest to Santa Monica Pier echoes through songs and stories. This cultural resonance has provided a focus around which businesses and communities have built and rebuilt.

The art of place-making and the art of writing can inspire each other. The designer, developer, or planner of a square can encourage and benefit from this symbiosis in a number of ways.

Every place, whether an old plaza in need of revitalization or the site of a new square in a new development, has a history. A place history can be constructed by conducting oral interviews of neighbors and previous residents, gathering historic photographs and postcards, reviewing deeds and city records, hiring a geologist to describe the creation of the landform and soils, or interviewing a local ecologist to uncover the story of the local flora and fauna. Fictional histories such as *The Celebrated Jumping Frog of Calaveras County, Make Way for Ducklings, A Cricket in Times Square,* or *Midnight in the Garden of Good and Evil* (Savannah's squares) may also be associated with a place. In either case, the scope of the place investigated may be limited to the actual boundaries of the square or include the neighborhood, town, or region. These stories may then

Figure 4.7. *Statue in the Boston Public Gardens, 1999, of Mrs. Mallard and her eight ducklings, by Nancy Schön, based on* Make Way for Ducklings *by Robert McCloskey.*

inform the program of uses and the design of the architecture and public art.

Beyond gleaning stories from existing resources, active collaborations between designers and writers could be built to enliven both. A poetry or storytelling gathering could initiate the public planning for a civic place or be an annual event. The Welsh tradition of the *eisteddfod,* an annual competitive festival of poets and musicians, could provide festivity, history, and poetic fodder for architectural design. Perhaps a town square could have a poet or storyteller in residence who works with an urban artist to create a storied landscape.

This borrowing and play across media is an act of voluntary artistic collaboration. Overzealous insistence on intellectual property rights will kill or at least poison this play. Fostering borrowing and dialog, on the other hand, can launch a virtuous cycle of creative work that deepens the sense of place.

Dedications
With what name should we christen a square or other civic place? How might this name inform its design and use?

"Naming opportunities" are a significant and growing tool of fundraisers. For a significant donation, people may place their names on libraries, plazas, seats in a theater, bandstands, and other places. Something valuable is being sold.

The name of a civic room creates an association between the place and its activities and the person or concept embodied in the name. The name need not be sold to add value to the place. It is a means of honoring the person or concept and it can be a means of honoring and shaping the civic place. Iowa State University has a Plaza of Heroines and a web site that honors these women. This is clearly a means of social organizing and an action that conditions the meaning and use of the place. Calling a civic room "Georgia O'Keeffe," "Edward Hopper," or "Miles Davis" Square poses a set of design questions. How could we design "The Plaza of Lost Languages," "Hula-Hoop Garden," "Tranquility Base Square," or "Poet's Alley"?

Clearly there is a danger in having the name or concept become too dominant in the physical design. Can one play chess or hold a farmers' market in Cribbage Square if everything is a riff on cribbage boards? Civic places need to invite a broad range of uses that can evolve over time. However, a name can provide a means for coherence.

Games and Local Rituals
Do games or rituals rooted in the place exist, or can they be initiated?

"If, as a casual tourist to Barcelona, you happen to find yourself in front of the Cathedral on a Sunday afternoon, you will see ten musicians in dark suits arranging themselves and some unfamiliar wind instruments in ten chairs set out in two rows on a platform. As they take up their instruments, the people do not stand in front of them to look on, but begin to group themselves in circles, taking hands to make a ring and begin to dance a ritualistic dance" (www.sustance.com /catalan/catsardn.htm, November 5, 2003). The dance is called the *sardana,* and it is a symbol of Catalonia (the region

Figure 4.8. *Zucchini "box" car race in the street at Seattle's Pike Place Market, c. 1992.*

in Spain whose center is Barcelona). It is the dance of the cathedral plaza, the culture, and the region.

At Christmas time, neighborhoods in the Southwest work together to line streets and plazas with *luminarias* (paper sacks with candles inside). In the Colorado of my youth, some neighborhoods got together to decorate Christmas trees in local parks. Graduation rituals from high schools and universities include a number of activities in the public realm. These existing rituals must be discovered and integrated into the syllabus before a civic commons is remodeled.

All of these rituals had beginnings, and it may be possible to initiate new events. The Fremont neighborhood in Seattle regularly decorates the statue, *Waiting for the Interurban.* The Fremont Arts Council is a strong example of a neighborhood organization that has been able to create new place-based events and art such as summertime outdoor movies and the Fremont Troll (see www.fremontartscouncil .org). Similarly, the artist Rick Lowe has combined public art,

historic preservation, the provision of community services, and public celebration in reinhabiting a set of row houses in Houston (see www.projectrowhouses.org).

The Broccoli Queen
What roles can the public festival play in the twenty-first century?

Like many of these queries, the question of the potential roles of the festival deserves widespread debate, experimentation, and critical reflection. Clearly the public festival has wide and deep roots in the life of civic places and towns. Greek agoras, the plazas of Pueblo Indians, and courthouse squares across Texas are or were the place of festivities. Also clearly, many American festivals have become relics, quaint tourist attractions, or toothless fairy tales of past political/ economic dynamics. The broccoli queen, reigning over the broccoli capital, has not been deposed by the microchip manager or the call-center supervisor but continues as an ever fainter and less resonant echo.

Community festivals once performed a variety of roles. Teenagers and elders could be honored as part of the community. The political-economic structure of the town could be honored and, where incarnations of the jester held sway, also mocked. Festivals provided local artists with a venue, celebrated the harvest and the community, and engendered conviviality.

The dimming of the community theater-of-place reflects the globalization and mobility of our times. Americans move, on average, once every five years (Putnam 2000: 204). In his wide-ranging book about civic engagement, *Bowling Alone,* Robert D. Putnam argues that four factors contributed to the decline in civic engagement during the last half of the twentieth century: increased pressures of work, including the rise of two-career families, sprawl (the physical separation of communities), the rise of mass media as a competing source of entertainment, and a shift in values between the pre– and post–World War II generations. Putnam offers a series of challenges to reawaken civic engagement, including the creation of cultural activities "from group dancing to songfests to Community Theater to rap festivals" that Americans will "participate in (not merely consume or 'appreciate')" (2000: chapter 24; 411). There are multiple roots for this new theater-of-place:

- New life could be brought to old community festivals. For example, in 1986 Galveston, Texas, reestablished Mardi Gras after a forty-year hiatus.
- Community festivals can be created to serve as focal points for communities that previously did not have an active presence in the public realm. In her book *The Power of Place,* Dolores Hayden illustrates a number of activities in Los Angeles aimed at making public previously underrepresented histories (1995).
- Various public events such as *run for the 'X',* or a radio station's food drive can serve as seeds around which more multifaceted events could grow.
- Pure whimsy can inspire new events.

Critical to the success of any of these events as *community* festivals is the involvement of a wide spectrum of the community in the planning, preparation, and execution of the event. As a sketchy rule, potlucks are preferable to catered events to create a joint sense of ownership. Moreover, a sense of play is key.

Excursion

FARMERS' MARKETS

What Lies Beneath

Stanley Crawford

Most people probably think that farmers' markets just happen. Bingo, once or twice a week farmers and backyard growers drive up in their pickups and station wagons and vans and pick a good spot and unload their produce and homemade jams and ciders. They do this the way birds fly south in the autumn and north in the spring and arrive at just the right place. Something in the blood. In the season, the angle of the sun.

But farmers' markets don't just happen. Behind the informal order of their stalls and umbrellas and produce-laden counters and pickup trucks lie conflicts, planning efforts, and negotiations, and the endless jockeying for position. Quite a lot of this work is probably still going on in conversations held behind tarps or while leaning on front fenders of pickups, as the first early-morning customers begin ambling down the aisles, smiling at the miraculous way the market has seemed to drop out of the sky from nowhere, yet one more wonderful morning.

To begin with, take the parking lot or the city block closed off to traffic or the vacant lot. Inevitably these have private or public owners and eagle-eyed commercial and residential neighbors, who may have very definite ideas about the days and hours of operation, ideas often at variance with those of the farmers. Arrive too early? You wake up the neighbors. Stay too late? You interfere with adjoining storefronts. And someone will want insurance against accidents and promises that the trash barrels will be emptied and porta-potties carried away quickly or that public restrooms will be cleaned up afterward. And someone will actually have to do these things.

In my twenty-five years of experience with the Santa Fe Farmers' Market, as a farmer, a market board chair, and project director, toilet and hand-washing facilities have been a perennial issue. In the late 1980s we moved the market from one site to another in part because of problems with restroom access. In 1997, the "Bathroom Wars" erupted with various institutional and business neighbors. They will not have a peaceful resolution until the farmers' market finally obtains its own dedicated permanent facility in perhaps 2005. Shades of Northern Ireland or Palestine—in miniature.

Any successful market eventually attracts the attention of public health officials with their lists of regulations regarding how high off the ground produce must be displayed, at what temperatures cooked and uncooked meats and other processed foods must be kept, and the kitchen conditions under which they must be prepared. Eventually the state entomologist will wander in, wanting to inspect cut flowers and nursery stock for exotic pests.

Which leads to the question of just who runs the show. That Somebody can be a neighborhood activist, it can be a city employee, or it can be a paid or volunteer market manager under a nonprofit board. In any case, there are bound to be a lot of meetings concerning the market, particularly in the winter when things are slow or the market is not in session at all. Meetings? Lengthy and often acrimonious gatherings of farmers, boards, city officials, county ag bureaucrats, at which are argued the fee structure farmers should pay to sell at the market, and whether it should be a percentage of gross sales (and how do you police it?) or a flat daily or seasonal fee. And how to allocate spaces, how to allocate the *good* spaces—in the shade, in the sun, at the end of an aisle where most customers enter, close but not too close to the popular food concession, and not close at all to the porta-potties. And how to police farmers to make certain they're not selling produce imported from elsewhere or trying to pass off nonorganic for organic produce or products. And how to decide what is allowed and not allowed to be sold at farmers' markets. These contentious issues can take up hours at meetings, over the course of a generation, with no final resolution in sight. Add the usual business of electing boards and hiring and paying and firing staff. And what to do about the inevitable parking crisis.

And how to keep feuding among farmers and among market factions to a minimum, in order to avoid spoiling the wonderful upbeat mood of the market when the crowds start pouring in.

But contention is another face of competition. Good markets need to be competitive—which is to say they will also be contentious behind the scene. Every farmer or producer who has introduced a successful new crop or variety or created a new product or upgraded his display will watch his neighbors jump on the bandwagon, cut prices, improve packaging or display, sending out the restless message of markets everywhere: keep up, innovate, or die.

And far away from the market and all those meetings lie all those small and medium-sized farms scattered over hundreds and even thousands of square miles, little nodes of families working the earth with fanatical intensity to grow fruits and vegetables to take to market.

It seems miraculous that farmers' markets come together at all, appearing in their high-season glory as if they are models of productive harmony.

They are. But beneath the façades bubbling with excitement of these produce supermarkets for a day, there lies more planning, debate, dispute, negotiation, and maintenance than most people want to imagine.

Or need to, for that matter. What most customers want when they go to a farmers' market is to enjoy the sights and sounds and smells and tastes, inform themselves of what they are buying and where and how it was produced, and how is the family by the way, and go away with shopping bags laden and the sense that here at least, all is well in the world.

That's what makes the rest of it worth the bother.

Stanley Crawford is a farmer, market vendor, and the author of *A Garlic Testament: Seasons on a Small New Mexico Farm* (Albuquerque: University of New Mexico Press, 1998).

COLLECTIVE AND INCREMENTAL DESIGN

All minds quote. Old and new make the warp and woof of every moment.
There is no thread that is not a twist of these two strands. By necessity, by proclivity,
and by delight, we all quote. We quote not only books and proverbs, but arts,
sciences, religion, customs, and laws; nay, we quote temples and
houses, tables and chairs by imitation.

—*Ralph Waldo Emerson, from* Quotation and Originality

Squares and streets are, in Louis Kahn's words, "rooms of agreement." Multiple buildings must align, be of compatible heights, and share a set of ideas about how to make façades to create a strong street wall or enclose a plaza.

The dialog between designers does not require a strict conformity. For example, the main streets of small-town America typically offer a collection of building styles illustrating the dictates of fashion over the decades, yet still holding to a compelling coherence (see Francaviglia 1996). Until the rise of the automobile-dominated miracle mile and the shopping mall, Main Street was a dominant cultural agreement about how to construct business districts.

The walls are not the only elements of civic rooms that evolve over time. Santa Fe's plaza provides an example. It began as a dirt-floored space almost twice its current size. During their occupation of the city, Native Americans built in the eastern half of the original rectangular plaza. After the Spanish reconquest, the Spanish apparently accepted this reconfiguration and the plaza took on its present nearly square shape. In the 1860s, under American rule, the open plaza was planted with trees, a picket fence separated the central park from the streets, and a monument anchored the center. Thus the plaza-park was born. Gazebos, pavements, memorials, lighting systems, fences, and other features have been arranged and rearranged since then to create the current plaza (see Wilson 1997).

"Being part of the living organism of a city with its changing socioeconomic and technical condition, a square is never completed" (Zucher 1959: 5). Understanding that in its birth and over time a civic room is incrementally built by multiple designers, how can a designer help create a strong and compelling coherence?

A. Collective Work

The Design of Zoning

How can zoning and other regulations support the creation of vibrant civic places?

"The concept of the public welfare is broad and inclusive. The values it represents are spiritual as well as physical, aesthetic as well as monetary," wrote Justice Douglas in a case upholding the exercise of eminent domain for community development. "It is within the power of the legislature to determine that the community should be beautiful as well as healthy, spacious as well as clean, well-balanced as well as carefully patrolled" (*Berman* v. *Parker* [1954] 348 U.S. 26). This definition has since been cited in cases involving zoning and aesthetic regulation (see *Village of Belle Terre* v. *Boraas* [1974] 416 U.S. 1, 5–6, and *Metromedia, Inc.* v. *City of San Diego* 26 Cal. 3d 848).

Zoning is a restriction of people's use of their property. It is justified when the restriction is directly related to eliminating a public harm or creating a public good, and does so in a way that leaves the owner with reasonable use of the property. In many cases, the restriction directly benefits the landowner. This reciprocity of advantage may be seen, for example, in the coordination of the street network. Clearly such coordination restricts what a landowner may do, but just as clearly it is in the interests of the current and future landowners to have a legible and well-functioning street system. (See Ellickson and Tarlock 1981 or Wright and Wright 1985 for overviews of the legal history of zoning.)

As developed in the United States during the twentieth century, zoning has not been particularly supportive of the creation of civic spaces. The strong tendency for zoning to be based on the use rather than the form of buildings has limited the development of mixed-use districts that enliven many classic squares. The tendency to apply zones to blocks and to discuss cases based on parcel ownership, rather than developing and modifying zones around streets or other civic spaces, tends to create arterials as boundaries rather than promoting streets and squares as the centers of districts. Much of the justification for zoning has been centered around the elimination of public harms, and not as much

thought has been devoted to the creation of collective benefits such as the joint development of a plaza.

None of these practices is inherent to land-use regulation, and there is longstanding historical precedent for other zoning approaches. In 1899, for example, Washington, D.C., passed a regulation to restrict the height of buildings to preserve the prominence of the capitol dome. This was regulation based on building form, and designed to preserve the effect of a public building on its surrounding district. More recently, the "tout ensemble" doctrine has arisen from case law regarding historic district zones. Briefly, the doctrine holds that the character of the district is just as important as individual historic buildings, and thus new construction in a historic district may be made to conform to the requirements of the district (see *Maher* v. *City of New Orleans* 371 F. Supp. 653, 663 [E.D. La. 1974], and *A-S-P Associates* v. *City of Raleigh* 298 N.C. 207, 258 S.E. 2d 444 [1979]).

New Urbanist practitioners have developed architectural or form codes for a number of projects. Many of these have been implemented outside of municipal zoning through private covenants or other contracts. It may be possible to develop "square district zones" similar to historic districts around new or emerging civic rooms. These zones may have architectural codes that clearly and directly support the square such as a "build-to" line that requires adjacent buildings to help form the enclosure of the square, requirements that off-street parking be placed to the rear of lots, or other regulations developed from the patterns in this book.

In 1926 the United States Department of Commerce developed and promoted the Standard State Zoning Enabling Act that established many municipal practices. It may be time for a new national model that centers on the creation of vibrant civic spaces. To redesign our towns we need to redesign the rules of town making.

Embed and Catalyze
How can a civic room become the central place of a district?

First, planners and designers of a civic room should consider the placement of the room within the physical landscape. Does the site offer a view of defining features of the land and town? In what ways and from where is the site visible? Is it uphill or downhill from the area it serves? How do water and wind flow through the site? What is its microclimate? In what ways have previous designers understood and shaped the landscape? What features of the landscape have others celebrated? What features have they suppressed? Can the room be placed to center it in the landscape and provide a pleasant microclimate? Is it a natural place to gather?

Second, the urban landscape must be understood. The immediate catchment for a civic place encompasses a radius of about nine hundred feet to two thousand feet. People who live, work, and shop in this area will form the bulk of daily users (see "Catchments," chapter 10). The planners and designers of a civic room must understand the flow of people into and about this catchment. Can the subway or other terminals be incorporated into the plaza? The current and imminent activities and unmet desires of the people in the district should be understood. Will the room serve as the anchor to a commercial node, an oasis for office workers, or a playground for residents, or all three? Can the local radio or TV station be convinced to locate near the square and use it for in-the-street interviews? The shapers of the square should understand the evolution of the area, and look at adjacent districts to anticipate changes. Was there once a streetcar stop that created the commercial center? Is the university or other institution expanding into the district?

Third, what changes can be anticipated in response to the creation or revitalization of the civic room, and can these be shaped? If, for example, the plaza immediately overlooks an agricultural valley, one may foresee that the commercial success of the plaza will induce development of the farmland and suggest the purchase of development rights to preserve the view. Likewise, the activity of designing and constructing a square may help create a neighborhood or business association.

Finally, can the room and its artwork be placed in the mythic and poetic landscape of the district? What stories have happened here? What stories does the place suggest? (see "Storied Landscapes," chapter 4). The Fremont Troll in Seattle transformed the dirt wasteland under a bridge into a playground, festivity site, and tourist attraction. Tour buses pass by hourly, local stores feature trolls, and a community festival called Trolloween begins at the troll. I'm waiting for the neighborhood on the other side of the bridge to create a billy-goat gruff or other response.

Subsuming
How can designers both respect and reinforce the existing context and refine or develop the place?

The coherence of an ensemble rests on a concurrence between designers about what must be consistent and what should be variable among their creations. New designers who join an old conversation should not only honor their clients, the communities, and their own voice, but also the conversation.

The term *conversation* may be misleading as it evokes a group of people in face-to-face dialog. Perhaps e-mail discussions provide a better analogy to the built conversation of designers. E-mail discussions come in discrete parts, with variable increments of time between call and response. William Hubbard, in his book *Complicity and Conviction* (1980), proposed another model for fruitful time-delayed dialog—case law, the written decisions of judges.

Analyzing the means by which case law both presents a coherent tradition and reflects and responds to current conditions, Hubbard develops six approaches to subsuming earlier works:

1. **Swerving:** Following the earlier patterns up to the point that they went astray and then providing a more compelling next component. Suppose the buildings enclosing a town green have an arcaded base, an unelaborated middle, and a simple cornice. The new designer may add a penthouse as an elaboration of the cornice, with a porch that echoes the first floor arcade.

2. **Completion:** Showing that the previous patterns were not comprehensive or brought to their logical conclusion. For example, a claim of completion might be: "the plaza is waiting for a gazebo to balance the composition and provide a focal point for events."

3. **Focusing:** Demonstrating that the earlier work was too general. Maybe the first incarnation of a square

overlooks a view, but does little to frame or "capture" the view. A redesign can articulate the relationship between the square and the view.

4. **Self-limitation:** Picking only a single aspect of the earlier work to use in a new design. A designer may borrow the masonry techniques of the Anasazi, ignoring their building typologies and siting issues.

5. **Refilling:** Finding new meaning in old forms. Adaptive reuse, as when a parking lot is redesigned to accommodate a basketball court, is a kind of refilling (see fig. 5.1).

6. **Becoming the Essence:** The new work embodies the critical components of the earlier in a way that is more compelling, clear, or decisive. Modernism made this type of claim by stripping "decoration" away from earlier styles.

—Terms from Hubbard 1980,
used by permission

I would like to add two more architectural techniques for subsuming earlier work:

A. **Reflective counterpoint:** The new work takes on opposite qualities of the old work (frame v. mass wall, horizontal v. vertical composition, rustic v. polished) but reflects, frames, or is framed by the old work and corresponds to other aspects of the old work. For example, across the plaza from a dark, heavy, and closed library a community center may have an open glass façade. Both buildings, however, may front the plaza, share a scale, align on an axis of symmetry, and have an arcade.

B. **Flowering:** The new work may use a near copy of the old work as a base or framework out of which new elements emerge. For example, upon entering a square a line of simple lampposts may sprout banners, whirligigs, telephone booths, notice boards, benches, jukeboxes, or . . .

Undoubtedly there are other means of subsuming earlier work. Borromini designed Saint Agnese in Rome. His rival, Bernini, was the sculptor of the Circo Agonale Fountain in front of Saint Agnese. Bernini is reported to have said that a

Figure 5.1. *Jones Motor Company/Kelly's Brew Pub, Albuquerque, New Mexico. Like a hermit crab, the brew pub reused the abandoned shell of the gas station and car dealership. Remodel by Jorge de la Torre Architects. Upper photo c. 1930, courtesy of Kellys, lower photo 2004, Mark Childs.*

statue in the northwest portion of the fountain has his hands up "to shield his eyes from the façade of Saint Agnese" (Forbes 1899: 19). Even this response promotes a public dialog.

Public Record and Public Dialog
How can the dialog between designers be recorded so that others may enter the discussion at a later time?

The legal and medical professions have well-developed mechanisms to keep records of findings and judgments. These records allow multiple professionals to link their work together. Judges' decisions become part of the public record available to future lawyers, judges, and the public to cite in future cases. Similarly, medical charts allow multiple caregivers to share information now and in the future about both an individual patient and about the course of diseases. These records transform a set of individual actions into a body of knowledge.

The designers of a commons should create and publish a set of diagrams that records their thoughts on how their work fits within the previous work and possible ways they see future designers adding to and responding to their work. These diagrams could be attached to the construction set of documents to be filed with the local jurisdiction. Unlike working drawings that are explicit about detail, good diagrams have a level of generality that captures the overall intentions of design. Thus they are cogent about the major compositional issues *and* allow room for future interpretation of the development and details of the composition.

Like the decisions written by judges, these diagrams could be used by critics and others to further the public conversation about design. At the very least, individual architectural firms may wish to develop sets of diagrams in order to track and discuss the development of their own oeuvre.

B. Increments

Small Victories
What are the advantages of purposefully making incremental design moves?

The Project for Public Spaces (PPS), a nonprofit with decades of experience in helping revitalize civic places, recommends: "start with the petunias" (PPS 2000: 67). Small incremental changes can demonstrate progress, lend credibility to a project while larger plans are in the works, and offer a bit of delight early in the process. PPS describes setting up temporary markets and painting new crosswalk lines before installing new curbs as examples of starting with the petunias. Similarly, community block watch groups often kick off campaigns by holding neighborhood cleanups or street tree plantings.

Incremental steps can accommodate incremental budgets and sweat equity. Projects that would otherwise be unrealized due to unattainable funding may be created in

phases more suited to funding streams. Gothic cathedrals were built over generations partially because the towns did not have the resources to build them faster. Small projects may also be done with volunteer labor, particularly if the projects (1) don't have to be done on a fast timeline in order for the next contractor to begin work and (2) can be replaced if they prove faulty.

Foundational steps can also serve as a visual call to action. A set of trees planted in a lot planned to be a plaza may remind people to continue working on their common goal. Leveling a lot so that kids can play soccer may help establish the public use of a place that then attracts food vendors and provides an immediate reason to develop lighting and seating and . . .

Small projects can also provide a means to collect information, test-market an approach, or choose between alternatives. Is there a sufficient lunch crowd to support a sandwich shop? A vending cart can provide invaluable data. Will the public adopt a piece of public art? Perhaps a lease with a purchase option can be negotiated to try out the work, or maybe three projects can be installed for a year with the understanding that the local arts board can purchase one.

Finally, small steps can allow for contemplation and refinement of later steps. Unforeseen problems and opportunities can be addressed and new ideas have time to ripen. Few of us can see all the significant repercussions and implications of a large design project. Incremental steps give us time to learn and adapt.

Resonant Ensembles
How can each increment of design seem finished, yet also suggest future increments?

A New Theory of Urban Design by Alexander, Neis, Anninou, and Ling (1987) presents an approach to this question of how incremental steps can be both whole in themselves and suggest future growth. Among a nuanced set of seven rules, the authors suggest that each act of construction must respond to earlier acts, suggest forms larger than itself, and help create "coherent and well-shaped public space next to it" (66, e.g., courtyards, streets).

Axelrod explored the emergence of cooperation through multiple iterations of the Prisoner's Dilemma game (see chapter 2) and deduced rules to foster this emergence. Alexander et al. can be seen as attempting a similar task—developing rules to aid the emergence of profoundly coherent places and towns. In both models, the investigators suggest that dialog about the individual moves is critical, and that attention to the larger game must be fostered.

In his book *The Culture of Building* (1999), Howard Davis takes a more empirical approach than Axelrod or Alexander. Davis examines how various actual societies' rules, conventions, and habits of building have shaped the emergence of places. He then concludes with recommendations about how we may change *our* culture of building to create more humane cities and towns. In separate chapters, Davis suggests that our rules for making "incremental wholes" should rely on postindustrial craftsmanship ("detailed and unique shaping of the built world" (245) in response to local conditions using adaptable technology), culturally appropriate buildings (places that support the connection between people and their own pasts, the places they live, and the larger community), and human-based institutions (as opposed to corporations only beholden to the bottom line). For example, these recommendations suggest that rather than deploying a bank of corporate vending machines, a designer may create a well-crafted arcade for local farmers and chefs to set up shop, or adapt the vending machines to sell local artworks (see Artomat www.artomat.org). Either option might suggest a later project to provide a meeting room and workshop for the vendors.

Nested Types
How can we phase design and construction to allow incremental work by multiple designers?

There are two dominant approaches to phasing design and construction. The first is to complete areas one at a time, leaving future areas zoned, planned or designed for development, and as untouched as possible by construction. Unfortunately, this frequently leaves empty lots that have been graded and stripped of their native vegetation.

Temporary uses should be developed for these future development sites. Until the new building begins construction, the site can be left in its former use, or leased as a community garden, playground, sculpture park, farmers' market, or other civic place.

The second approach is the design and construction of "nested types." One of the most common examples of this is found in large urban buildings. One architectural firm will create the building shell and others will develop the tenant improvements. Residential subdivisions also frequently follow this pattern. One firm will design the site plan and others will design individual homes.

Following the nested-type approach, the design of a civic room could proceed as follows:

- An urban designer lays out the lot for a civic room, connecting streets and enclosing lots. The urbanist should develop a set of rules for each of these parts to ensure that they work together. For example, the enclosing buildings should form a strong street wall by being built to the sidewalk, having a common height, and being lined with an arcade.

- A civic-room designer and building designers each work on their projects within the rules developed by the urban designer. They meet frequently, particularly during initial design, to have discussions about how the parts work as an ensemble. They conceive of themselves as a jazz group, each with their solos but ultimately creating a collective work. These designers also leave projects and rules within their works for others. For example, the building designers create a façade system and set of rules that ensure that ground-floor tenants actively support the life of the sidewalk, and the civic-room designers develop a prospectus for an artist-made bus shelter, newsstand, or game-board tables.

- These later designers, as well as those before, systematically develop parts of their designs that can be adjusted, moved, or otherwise controlled by the people using the place (e.g., chairs, operable windows, awnings, hand-pump-operated fountains). They also include users and neighbors in creating parts of the constructions. For example, local school kids create

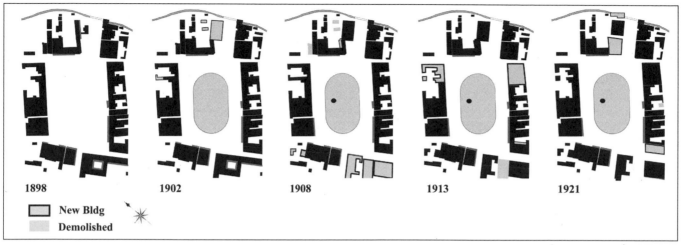

Figure 5.2. *Diagrams of morphological change in plaza of Las Vegas, New Mexico, from 1898 to 1921. Note that while buildings came and went, the shape of the plaza held. The plaza floor was elaborated over time with the addition of a park and then a gazebo. Drawn with information from Sanborn Insurance maps and historical photographs.*

tiles to surround the game boards, and the urban designer holds a poetry contest to name the streets and the square.

▦ Years later a building burns and a new designer immerses herself in the record left by the earlier designers of their deliberations and intentions and the actual life and adjustments of the ensemble. Just as a fusion band can bring new life to an earlier rock-and-roll riff, the new designer creates a new building that clearly respects the earlier work but also elaborates and refines it.

Variable Speed Adaptation
How can we balance the need for change and adaptation with the desire for permanence and continuity?

In *How Buildings Learn,* Stewart Brand (1994) observed that there are different frequencies at which we wish to change different parts of buildings. We may change furniture and other props on a frequent basis. The skin of a building, for example, or the façade of a store along Main Street, we

change as the theme (or ownership) of the store changes. The structure of the building should be the most durably built component.

These scales of change can be extended to the building blocks of a town. The footprint of the Santa Fe Plaza, for example, has changed once since being created in 1610, and that took the defeat of the Spanish in the Pueblo Revolt. The Palace of the Governors on the north side of the plaza has persisted as a continuous entity since its creation. Yet it also has had a number of significant restructurings and has changed its primary use once (from seat of government to museum). There have been at least three generations of fabric buildings lining the rest of the plaza, and the portals enclosing the plaza were removed for a generation and then reconstructed. In 1863, at the beginning of the American era, the plaza itself was changed from a multipurpose earthen yard to a park. The monument at its center and the grove of trees (not the individual trees but the set) have persisted to date; in contrast, the benches, walkways, gazebo, and other features of the park have changed at a frequency equivalent to similar parts within a building (see Wilson 1997).

The Italian theorist and architect Aldo Rossi explored

the persistence of form within town plans. For example, the footprint of a Roman amphitheater persists in the layout of streets in the Santa Croce district of Florence, Italy (Rossi 1982: 89). Others have also examined the morphogenesis of town forms (see Childs 1996b and 2001, Edwards and Howard 1997, Moudon 1986, Vance 1990, Warner 1962). From these works we can tentatively construct a spectrum of the speed with which parts of a city change, from most changeable to most durable: street and square furniture, noninstitutional buildings, lot patterns and building types, institutions (both buildings and civic rooms) and monuments, and finally the shape and size of blocks, streets, and squares.

Systems of infrastructure other than the street appear to be durable, but the record is less clear. The aqueducts and their fountain plazas have persisted through multiple empires in Rome. Hohokam Indian waterways structured the development of Phoenix, Arizona (Simon 2002). Public clocks persist in some places as quaint relics. Some rail lines have been transformed into paths while others have been energetically erased. Telephone lines have been placed underground, but I would place no bets one way or the other on the persistence of cell-phone towers.

The location, size, and proportion of a square are very long-term decisions. If the square serves as part of a passive storm-water system this may be an eon-spanning choice. The pattern and type of enclosing buildings lasts longer than individual buildings, and certainly the styles of the façades change much more rapidly. The selection of furnishings is a relatively short-term decision. Design decisions should take account of the probability that future designers will want to alter your work or change your context.

Designer in Residence
How can we set up a relationship so that a designer or team of designers can engage in a long-term set of incremental design moves?

The typical architectural contract assumes that design is not incremental. One hires an architect to come up with a set of blueprints, review construction, and then the contract is complete.

An undeveloped mode is to hire architects as designers-in-residence. All or a portion of their time can then be devoted to working with the community to help a square develop and mature. The tradition of artist-in-residence is longstanding and fairly widespread. The Sanitary Fill Company in San Francisco, for example, provides artists-in-residence with studio space, a stipend, exhibit space, and access to recycled materials. There are artist-in-residence programs in Roswell, New Mexico, in Seattle with City Power and Light, and at a number of universities. Architects and landscape architects sometimes fill these positions. However, the position of architect-in-residence, hired specifically to develop a place over time, is in need of development. Perhaps an enterprising university, city parks department, or a nonprofit can lead the way.

Maintenance as Incremental Design
Can we use maintenance as an opportunity to fine-tune a design?

Each spring in the traditional Spanish villages of New Mexico, each farmer of an *acequia* association sends a worker to the *mayordomo*. This team cleans and repairs the irrigation ditch, getting it ready for another farming season. In preparation for this work, the mayordomo inspects the ditch, remembering problems that arose last year and the years before. Thus as the crew works its way along the acequia, the mayordomo directs the work to reinforce a wall that broke away last year, to allow a sapling to grow, to move the ditch into a better relationship with a hillside, or to get a better flow of water through a flat spot. The ditch that emerges over generations of such adjustments is a work of man and of the landscape. The spring cleaning is both maintenance and crafting. Moreover, it is a rededication of the community formed by joint access to water, and upon its conclusion can be an excuse for a party (see Crawford 1988). All maintenance should aspire to be so productive.

Four practices may help us toward this goal:
- Include janitors as jury members: Include in the evaluation of initial and incremental designs those who will maintain a place.

- Host spring cleanings: Establish a regular work event, community meeting, and party to maintain the commons and the community.
- Contract for a commissioning period: No design will be perfect or perfectly understood on the day of the groundbreaking. Plan and budget for a period after occupancy begins during which the designer is available to refine the design.
- Develop a users' manual: In conjunction with design development and construction documents, prepare a manual that includes a maintenance plan. Document hidden conditions (e.g., photograph the waterlines before burying them), warranties, manufacturers' instructions, and operating instructions. Provide places for updates. This document may also include graphically clear emergency procedures and information that could be critical to firefighters (e.g., hazardous materials, gas shut-off locations).

Excursion

PUBLIC SPACE/URBAN BEACH

Lummus Park, South (Miami) Beach, Florida

Marilys R. Nepomechie

Featured in countless television shows and movies as an icon of the aesthetic vanguard, Lummus Park is the perfect setting for an exploration of the relationship between observer and observed that characterizes urban life in the traditional—and early modern—city. *Miami Vice, CSI Miami, Deco Drive,* and *Miami Rhapsody* are but a few of the films and broadcasts whose images and storylines are inextricably tied to their Ocean Drive setting. A character as vibrant as any of its human counterparts, Lummus Park is not simply the backdrop, but the provocateur of much of the action.

On the Atlantic shore of South Beach and at the heart of the city's Art Deco Historic District, the park comprises a unique cultural and physical context. It is a civic space that celebrates its subtropical setting, the cinematic quality of its provenance and marketing—as well as the process of its own making. The ten-block precinct fronts the Atlantic Ocean, stretching from Fifth Street at its southernmost boundary to Fifteenth Street along its northernmost edge. With its façade of colorful, decorative building fronts, elevated front porches, outdoor terraces, and waving palms, Lummus Park is the image indelibly associated with Miami Beach in the minds of tourists and dreamers the world over. One of only two public spaces in the city that incorporates the ocean, it serves as an active participant in—and barometer of—the life of its residents and visitors: it is an ideal place to study the physical design of buildings, the urban infrastructure that establishes their interrelation, and the unscripted theater of the street that this extraordinary setting makes possible.

Public Theater Is Unscripted but Conditioned by Urban "Stage Sets"

The *city as theater* is a metaphor with Renaissance origins and long resonance. It is the quintessential description of urban life: an acknowledgement that the density of city life inspires interactions that mold—and are, in turn, molded by—the physical form that circumscribes them. Historian A. Gray Read notes that in the early twentieth century, architects drew upon the traditions and techniques of the theater in order to design buildings and storefronts that would result in lively city streets. Through a manipulation of sectional relationships and the visual frame, the early modern city was self-consciously

Figure E.1.
Photographic series of the layers of Miami Beach from hotel façades to shoreline. Start in upper right, read right to left. Photos courtesy of Marilys Nepomechie.

theatrical, dramatizing physical and spatial associations among its citizen-actors. Comprised of urban stage sets that accentuated the spectacle of relationships between interior and exterior space, the early modern city that is identified with the Art Deco style found, in theater, an "intellectual framework for the social aspect of design" (Read 2003: 1).

A backdrop at once architectural, urban, and natural, Lummus Park/Ocean Drive is the archetypal frame for public performance: The front porches of district hotels, typically raised two to three feet above the level of the sidewalk, simultaneously harbor intimate conversations and become the stage for raucous public encounters. Both are witnessed—and interpreted—by legions of passers-by. Simultaneously, these porches are veritable box seats—the preferred vantage point for the unfolding, unscripted dramas of the city streets. In both conditions, the physical form of the city provides the perspectives of distance and location that transform quotidian events into real-life dramas.

Provenance and Marketing

At the close of the nineteenth century, Camillo Sitte gave prescriptive voice to a set of urban principles intended to document and generate the types of public spaces that successfully engender interaction—between actor and audience, between observer and observed. Significantly, the first decades of the twentieth century—years of early development in Miami Beach—also saw the publication of *The American Vitruvius: An Architect's Handbook of Civic Art,* written by Werner Hegemann and Elbert Peets. Drawing upon Sitte's work, the book proposed to guide the design of successful urban public/civic spaces in a rapidly growing America (Hegemann and Peets 1998 [1922]: 9–28).

Dating from the close of the nineteenth century and the early part of the twentieth, the development of Miami Beach paralleled these new advances in urban theory. Yet it is overwhelmingly a Depression-era city built along and around an oceanfront park bequeathed to the city of Miami Beach by its founders, John and James Lummus. Ocean Drive and Lummus Park were part of the inaugural 1912 plat of the new city. The point of highest ground on a barrier island covered almost entirely by underbrush and swampland, the park was the first point of urban development on the beach (see Lejeune and Shulman 2000: 8–37).

Allan Shulman writes that like many other Progressive-era cities, Miami Beach was conceived as an idyllic escape from the industrial areas of the northern United States. Its natural landscape of swamps and dense brush was radically altered by extensive dredge-and-fill operations to produce the invented resort city. Exotic plant material supplanted the native flora and became identified with the island. The tabula rasa condition of the new beachfront property resulted in a city that grew at an extraordinary rate, fueled by an interest in tourism that promised a slice of life in a year-round wonderland. Its developers fostered unique theatrical qualities in their creation—qualities commensurate with the narrative, scenographic demands of twentieth-century resort architecture.

Yet sequential layers of traditional American urbanism ultimately shaped the grid and defined the public spaces of Miami Beach (see Gelabert-Navia, Lejeune, and Shulman 2000). Organized by an orthogonal structure of broad north-south avenues and narrower east-west streets, the city was developed in 400-x-300-foot blocks, each subdivided into individual 50-x-145-foot lots. The blocks were typically platted with 15-foot mid-block (N-S) service easements, and oriented with their longer dimension facing either Ocean or Bay. The sole disturbance in the regular gridiron of the city occurs for a depth of two city blocks along a stretch that parallels the eastern coast of the island—precisely in the area occupied by Lummus Park. Here, the urban grid echoes the irregular Atlantic shoreline. This unique orientation underlines the significance of the park within the fabric of the city.

The early years of the twentieth century that produced Miami Beach also saw the shaping of a modern language of architecture. Competing historical and contemporary interpretations of its origins respectively locate the roots of Modernism in the heroic possibilities opened by technological revolution—or in the tradition of urban theater and marketplace. In counterpoint to canonical histories of modernism, A. Gray Read notes that architect Robert Mallet-Stevens, designing street fronts in 1920s Paris, argued for a "Modern Architecture [that] wears the mask of performance and plays in the public spaces of the city" emerging specifically in "popular Art Deco design [that] created vital city streets for urban life" (Read 2003: 1).

Modeled after Atlantic City, and contemporary to the construction of Rio de Janeiro's Copacabana Beach, Miami Beach embodies the cultural patterns and social norms of an early twentieth-century working class in pursuit of leisure. Self-consciously theatrical and openly catering to a resort crowd, the buildings along Ocean Drive were portrayed by their original owners through watercolor picture postcards that emphasized the façades of individual structures rather than their resulting assemblage. Yet Lummus Park is a prime example of the modern (Art Deco) city defined as a collection of stage sets. Both the language of its structures and the urban armature that organizes them are composed with a scenographic sensibility that supports public theater.

The Development of the District Is Akin to the Emergent Nature of Public Theater

Incrementally designed, constructed, and marketed over a half century, the structures that define Ocean Drive are at once the fabric and the monuments of the city (see Lejeune and Shulman 2000). Adopted urban patterns have resulted in a South Beach typology repeated throughout the midcentury: hotels—or mid-density housing—with elevated front porches and lobbies. The buildings are long, rectangular, double-loaded corridor structures, two to five stories in height, of concrete masonry and stucco construction. Their strip and corner windows are typically protected from sun and heat by the concrete eyebrows that characterize much of Deco architecture in this city. In mid-block locations, the structures are distinguished by centralized façades and plans. At block ends, they are asymmetrical celebrations of the streetcorner, employing vertical projections and exuberant signage. The hotels employ the technology and aesthetic of an emerging modernism: continuous bands of glass, wrap-around corner glazing, cantilevered concrete eyebrows, clean geometric lines and decorative motifs. Simultaneously, they retain many of the urban relationships that understand the city as theater: porches, manipulations of scale, street associations, and decorative façades. These oceanfront structures are the prime setting for public, civic, and social exchange.

Ocean Drive presents a collection of separate, highly articulate buildings designed and marketed as entirely independent creations. Yet the place of these structures within the regular grid of the city—as well as the customs and patterns of construction that developed in Miami Beach over time—work to regulate the nature of their interrelation. In effect, the development and form of the district are akin to the nature of public theater: Each building along Ocean Drive represents an individual action that adds with others to tell stories upon the stage of the city.

The Emergent Design Supports the Public Theater that Inspired It

Even people who disdained the tourist life of South Beach were seduced by this urban oasis. Then, as now, the heart of South Beach was the strip of Ocean Drive from Fifth Street to Fourteenth Street. Only the western side of the street was built up. To the east lay palmy Lummus Park, the wide white beach, the jewel-colored sea, and gorgeous

cumulus clouds hovering in the tropical sky. . . .
it was the only part of the Beach that had a kind of grandeur, or romance . . . the quality of a mystic Tahiti. It was totally different. (Armbruster 1995: 87)

The public domain of Lummus Park is an amalgam of privately owned building frontages, city infrastructure, and public space. Its cross section is a progression of thresholds that negotiate the relationship between city and beach. The sequence begins at the park's western boundary, defined by the array of two- to five-story, early twentieth-century hotels that form its urban façade—the face that the city turns to the Atlantic. These hotels, structures of approximately regular dimension and scale, feature emphatic corner elements, elegant signage, and decorative architectural motifs ranging from eyebrows to finials. Their elevated front porches accommodate seating for restaurants, bars, and, above all, people-watching. They abut sidewalks that are ten feet wide, filled beyond capacity with tables and chairs. Their patrons are amiably jostled and engaged in good-humored banter by waiters and passers-by alike.

Although metered parallel parking is allowed on both sides of the two-lane, two-way Ocean Drive, valet drop-off areas have sprouted along the length of the park in response to an acute parking shortage. Invariably so crowded as to impede substantive movement, at night the street is a frozen automotive parade of wheels, old and new. Windows (or convertible tops) down, air-conditioning running at full throttle, riders of the Drive converse gamely with pedestrians and one another as they crawl slowly through the ten-block spectacle, taking part in the sights and sounds of park and beach, and happily going nowhere.

A narrower, five-foot sidewalk, also paved in the city's signature red concrete, bounds the western edge of the park. Grassy, shaded by informal clusters of coconut palms, the park is home to the occasional public building. Some eighty years after its construction, the Oceanfront Auditorium, complete with cheerful, 1920s thermometer, still announces: "Welcome to Miami Beach! The Temperature Today is ___ degrees!" A base station for the lifeguard corps and a set of public restrooms are the only other structures within the park. Pedestrian walks meander through its tree-shaded areas, and lead to crowded benches, play structures, and a copious promenade for throngs of strollers, roller bladers, skateboarders, joggers, cyclists, and nighttime revelers that regularly parade the beach.

A low, undulating, coral stone wall of generous breadth borders the promenade and accommodates solitary musing, appreciative people-watching, or lively conversation. Allowing occasional passage to beachfront showers, volleyball sand courts, and planted dunes, the wall separates the world of shoes and hard surface from the world of sand and surf. Pierced by raised, wood-frame access routes, the dunes beyond the playing courts lead to an even broader expanse of glaring reflection: miles and miles of sandy shoreline. Erosion patterns produce a wildly changeable—and often unpredictable—coastline on Miami Beach. In response, the city regularly replenishes the sands of the island. Along the shore, a series of movable, eclectically designed lifeguard stands are the vertically prominent stage set for yet another set of daily theatrical exchanges—between lifeguards and sunbathers, lifeguards and swimmers, lifeguards and passers-by. Open in daylight and closed at night, tall enough to be discernable from the world of the city, these colorful pieces of urban furniture have become synonymous with South Beach. They dot the Atlantic shore, serving as the daytime focus of sunbathers, swimmers, and oglers alike.

In the course of the year, only the urban and natural armatures of the park remain constant: building façade, porch, street, lawn, promenade, and wall. A protective dune and mutable shoreline frame the ocean, describing a set of carefully calibrated spatial relationships nurtured by the designers. The city is the product of an early Modernism defined by narratives at once heroic and dramatic. In contrast and in complement, the props of a daily urban performance, much like its actors and audience, are ephemeral: the lifeguard stand, the volleyball net, and the flocks of flying kites are markers of daily and seasonal change. They are the everyday accoutrements of city life, at once public and private, familiar and strange. Self-consciously picturesque, the interrelation of armature and furniture defines the city as quintessentially theatrical, highlighting the negotiated, unscripted, and sometimes volatile terrain of exchange between place and inhabitant, between observer and observed. The form of the park mirrors and nurtures the public theater that inspired it: Here, in Lummus Park, a contemporary city of early modern origin can be interpreted as theater—the setting for both spectacle and event that are the hallmark of a vital urban experience.

Bibliography

Armbruster, Ann. 1995. *The Life and Times of Miami Beach.* New York: Alfred A. Knopf. (Ann Armbruster writes engagingly and in the first person about the history and character of Miami Beach.)

Gelabert-Navia, Jose, Jean-Francois Lejeune, and Allan Shulman. 2000. *Ciudad/City: Ocean Drive, Miami Beach, USA.* Babilonia/territorio para la innovacion, Publicación de Cultura Metropolitana, edición: ciudad 1, dossier 1. Navarra, España: Colegio Official de Arquitectos, Vasco-Navarro COAVAN. (Jose Gelabert-Navia gives a succinct history of the development of the Ocean Drive area as well as a pragmatic analysis of the development of the island's urban grid.)

Façade of Ocean Drive, Miami Beach, USA between Fifth and Sixteenth Streets/Fachada de Ocean Drive, Miami Beach, USA, entre calles quinto y quince: Ciudad/City: Ocean Drive, Miami Beach, USA. 2000. Babilonia/territorio para la innovación, Publicación de Cultura Metropolitana, edicion: ciudad 1, dossier 2. Navarra, España: Colegio Official de Arquitectos, Vasco-Navarro COAVAN.

Hegemann, Werner, and Elbert Peets. 1998 [1922]. *The American Vitruvius: An Architect's Handbook of Civic Art.* New York: Princeton Architectural Press.

Lejeune, Jean Francois and Allan T. Shulman. 2000. *The Making of Miami Beach, 1933–42: The Architecture of Lawrence Murray Dixon.* New York: Rizzoli. (Allan Shulman provides a provocative reading of the development of Miami Beach as a twentieth-century city responding to sequential layers of organization and interpretation at the hands of a succession of founders and developers.)

Read, Alice Gray. 2003. "Staging Architecture: Set Design and Modern Architecture in Paris Between the Wars." MS. (A. Gray Read makes a persuasive argument for an alternative reading of the origins of modernism, articulating the characteristics of a transitional, perhaps inaugural moment in twentieth-century urbanism.)

Longtime resident of Miami Beach, **Marilys R. Nepomechie**, AIA, NCARB, is an architect in private practice and Associate Professor of Architecture at the Florida International University School of Architecture. Her academic research focuses on issues of identity and architectural expression, and her office has won numerous regional and national design awards.

REASONABLE RISK

*Those who would give up essential Liberty, to purchase a little
temporary Safety, deserve neither Liberty nor Safety.*

—*Benjamin Franklin*

In the intervals between bursts of spray at the International Fountain in Seattle Center, children and adults repeatedly run to touch the fountain, trying more or less not to get soaked by a suddenly erupting nozzle. They risk getting wet to reach the goal of successfully touching the fountain. The facts that the goal is not inherently valuable, and that the danger is actually a benefit, provide a layer of tension and fun to the game. The more real danger of slipping and scraping a knee becomes an acceptable risk in light of the gain of fun. Moreover, I have watched innumerable children treat a minor fall with the same delight as when they receive an (un)expected soaking. Risk is a subtle matter.

Designers are charged with creating places that according to statute, the standards of practice, and good professional judgment do not impose "an *unreasonable risk* upon another which results in injury to that other" (emphasis in original, Emanuel 1979: c-12). Clearly, getting wet is a reasonable risk for those who venture into the realm of a fountain. The physical risk of slipping and falling in a fountain is also a reasonable risk as long as the designers don't place sharp objects in the area and otherwise look to minimize the conse-

quences of falling. Getting an infectious disease because the fountain's water is untreated is not a reasonable risk. The first two risks are apparent and thus consciously entered into by people running up to the fountain. These risks are also in proportion to the gain (some fun in public). The risk of disease from contaminated water is neither apparent, inherent in the situation, nor in proportion to the benefit.

Any designer, planner, or manager who hopes to support the emergence of a convivial place will design to allow users to calibrate their own social risk. Public commons are prime places for people to take social risks—talking to strangers, wearing outrageous clothes, trying on a social role, or simply being around people with different values. Still, each individual needs tools to signal how open they are to social risk.

Children, for example, may get unduly flustered by or angry at the fountain and risk losing face. The fact that the fountain pauses for a few minutes between shows allows them to quit with grace. Likewise, a thick edge zone around a dance floor allows people to sit out and watch without being wallflowers. Public commons should be safe places to take social risks.

Overlapping with social risk are the risks of being disturbed by disorderly people and crime against persons. For example, associated with the fear of talking to strangers are the fear of strangers barging into your conversations or begging for money and the fear of deceit, robbery, and assault. There is some evidence that physical design can moderate disorderly conduct and crime.

Thus there are three categories of risk that the planner, designer, and manager of a civic place should consider: physical hazards, social risk, and crime.

A. Physical Hazards

Beyond the physical hazards associated with all designs, are there issues that should particularly concern the designer of a civic place?

Wear and Tear
How can we minimize the production of hazards due to wear and tear?

Programs of inspection and maintenance need to clearly separate issues that are only cosmetic from those that pose hazards. This is not to dismiss the cosmetic issues but to prioritize addressing hazards. Eliminating a tripping hazard should be done before repainting a wall. (See, however, "Broken Window Theory," below, for a discussion of addressing vandalism.)

In addition to maintenance, a few strategies may be adopted to address wear and tear. Perhaps the most obvious and most beneficial method is to use durable materials and designs. Outdoor public spaces are subject to weather conditions and receive very heavy use. A second method is to understand the manner in which a material wears. Some surfaces are polished by foot traffic, while others avoid creating a slick surface by shedding material and maintaining a rough surface. An allied approach is to protect critical places from weathering. For example, steps, particularly in freezing climates, should be placed under shelter whenever possible.

Places of heavy use should have wearing surfaces that can be straightforwardly replaced, reapplied, or regrown. In all cases the rate of wear needs to be understood relative to the capacity to recreate the surface. Grass turf, for example, is a wonderfully self-repairing surface up to a certain level of use, when it fails and dirt paths are formed. Similarly, the rate of wear on paint can outstrip a community's financial capacity to repaint a surface.

Finally, care should be exercised in balancing good maintenance with letting a place record its history of use. The gentle curve in stone steps speaks of all those who have come before. Brass handrails, polished by use, provide evidence of how people hold a handrail and show that a place is well used.

Open Program
One of the delights of civic places is that their use is continually reinvented. How can the designer reduce the possibility that an inventive use creates a hazardous condition?

Kids climb on statues. Farmers' markets set up in parking lots. It is impossible to anticipate all inventive uses of a place. On the other hand, categories of reuse can be expected, and some general strategies of design may help reduce the creation of hazards.

First, almost any object in a civic place that can be sat upon will become a seat. Objects that are reasonably climbable will be climbed. Things that can be moved or adjusted will be, sometimes with excessive force. Players on a field will go out of bounds and pedestrians will cut corners or create shortcuts where there are not significant barriers. Designs should be tested against these uses.

Additionally, designs should be robust. Safety factors for unanticipated loads should be generous (kids may climb on just about anything). Controls should be highly legible, and everything should be designed to make repair simple. Once again, a regular inspection and maintenance plan should be established.

None of this is to imply that urban commons must feel like fortresses. Flower beds, for example, adorn innumerable squares. Just don't plant the tulips where people will sit.

Figure 6.1. *Car and horse wash, c. 1998. People reinvent the uses of even the most utilitarian structures.*

Miscues

Is the safe use of the design clearly legible?

A step in a flight of stairs that is a different height than the others can easily cause people to trip. A wheelstop that has been placed across the walking aisle of a parking space likewise is a tripping hazard. In both cases, reasonable expectations have been violated, creating a miscue for the user.

Tripping and slipping hazards are probably the most common miscues to be considered in the design of a civic space. Curbs, steps, and the effects of settlement, water, and ice should be carefully considered to eliminate miscues. Curbs and wheelstops can often be eliminated or replaced with bollards. Good soil engineering can reduce settlement, but settlement of pavements is, in the long run, inevitable. In addition to establishing a regular inspection and maintenance system to correct settlement problems, the pavement system itself should be designed to ease maintenance.

Finally, a pavement designer should seek to minimize the adverse impacts of water. In rainy and snowy climates, main pedestrian routes should be within arcades or covered by continuous awnings. Care should be taken to avoid introducing excess water from downspouts, gardens, or other sources. Drains and gutters should be placed as far away from main pathways as possible. Walkways should have a 1- to 2-percent slope to drain (so that even after a bit of settlement they still drain), and non-slip pavements are requisite.

Other typical miscues include the swing of doors and the right-of-way of pedestrians and vehicles. Recent research suggests that at unsignalized crossings, crosswalk stripes may give pedestrians undue confidence that automobiles will yield to them. Thus crosswalk stripes may effectively and counterintuitively make these crossings less safe (Kocpsell et al. 2002).

Novel designs may benefit from fewer assumptions in the public's mind and thus more careful attention about the proper use of the space. However, designers should review the design for the appropriateness of the cues embedded in the design. In some cases, it may be wise to test the design on a sample of users to understand how they might approach using it.

B. Social Risk
How can physical design provide people with the tools to calibrate their social risks?

Alternatives and Adjustments
How can props provide tools for, and prompt, the actors?

"Small moves [of chairs] say things to other people," William H. Whyte wrote about the social signals of chairs. "If a newcomer chooses a chair next to a couple or larger group, he may make some intricate moves. . . . Sorry about the closeness, but there's no room elsewhere, and I am going to respect your privacy, as you will mine" (1980: 35).

The spatial relationship between people is a strong signal about their actual or potential social relationship, and thus adjusting how we sit next to each other allows us to calibrate our intended interactions. The social relationship may be between individuals or small groups, but we also like to be able to adjust our relationship to the flow of people and activity. Sometimes front-row seats are desirable, and other times we like to be backbenchers. Thus designers should provide both adjustable seating and a choice of types of places to sit (see chapter 13).

Likewise, a comfortable civic place provides both a variety of microclimates (e.g., sunny spots, shade near a pool) and means to manipulate the microclimate. Table umbrellas are perhaps the leading example of a prop that allows adjustment of the microclimate. One could imagine a walled plaza with operable "windows" to allow adjustments of wind flow, misters, fountains whose flow could be adjusted by users, or devices that allow a site manager to direct the flow of waste heat from adjacent buildings under walkways. Adjusting one's microclimate certainly is an issue of physical comfort, but it may also be determined by social comfort. One is more on display in the sunlight than the shade. Being out in the wind may provide an excuse to share body warmth. Public fountains are often the symbol of sociability as well as physical comfort.

In addition to providing choices and adjustable props, the designer can create prompts to social interaction. Life-size and tabletop chessboards invite games. Jack Mackie's 1982 bronze dance steps cast into the sidewalks of Broadway in Seattle provide such a prompt for social interaction. A couple often comes across the steps; one cajoles the other into trying to dance, and passersby comment or applaud.

To support a rich social life in a civic place, designers should provide the tools for nuanced interactions between citizens. The dance of the commons is full of subtle gestures.

between audience and actor may be subtler. Simply walking down the sidewalk may make one part of the show for the people watchers. A couple having lunch may enjoy watching the people watchers.

A sense of stage and audience may provide tools for people to play the game of seeing and being seen. A formal stage or gazebo, of course, provides a clear set of territories. Children, in particular, delight in taking to these formal stages. On the other hand, lovers, whom one finds in some of the most prominent places in public, tend to shun the *formal* designation of being on stage. They may kiss at the photogenic center of an entranceway, but, at least when the square is inhabited, a kiss on the gazebo is a bit too much of a display.

The central field of a square (see "Frame" and "Field," chapter 10) is naturally a stage on which the edge zone focuses. Sight lines and lighting should support the creation of a stage. Entrances can also serve as stages, particularly if they are slightly raised above the field and are easily viewed. An entranceway fit for the belle arriving at the ball provides another social stage.

There may also be stages and houses within the edge zone. A group of chairs or benches may form an "L" or "U" whose focal point becomes a miniature stage. Seating that has a commanding view of the civic room can itself become a stage. Think of the king's pavilion at an arena, or box seats in a theater. Porches and balconies can serve this dual role of prime viewing spot and stage.

All of these stages depend on good sightlines and reasonable distances. Football-stadium skyboxes don't typically have the power of a theater box because they are too far away to clearly see or hear the occupants.

House vs. Stage
Does the design allow individuals to move fluidly on and off stage?

At a large meeting, good speakers stand to take the floor. Standing, they can be seen over the heads of their neighbors; their voice carries farther, and it clearly signals that they have moved from audience to actor. In civic rooms, the distinction

Social Conflict
How can designers and planners manage conflicts between groups?

When the bicycle became popular in the 1890s it was one of the fastest land vehicles, and pedestrians, particularly the elderly, complained about "scorchers" (bicyclists riding rapidly past pedestrians) (McShane 1994). Currently, some people complain about skateboarders and succeed in getting skating banned from public places. A whole spectrum of inter-group conflicts, from concerns about rowdy Hacky-Sac games to the dominance of drug gangs, play out in civic places.

Some of these conflicts are difficult social issues best handled by the police and courts. Other conflicts may be within the purview of designers and managers. There is a whole literature on diagnosing, negotiating, and mediating such conflicts (see Cosner 1956; Breslin and Rubin 1991; Susskind, McKuaran, and Thomas-Larmer 1999). Ric Richardson, an expert on public dispute resolution at the University of New Mexico, suggests that public disputes are a natural component of the public realm and that the objective of a planner or manager should not be to make them go away, but to help shape them into a creative rather than a destructive force. For example, teenagers may need to distinguish themselves from their elders with their clothing, grooming, and demeanor. Providing a venue for the display of such dress and ritual may be a critical role for civic places, despite its potential to shock. Creating events such as Fifties day at the market may help illuminate the vagaries and roles of dress.

Physical design approaches that may help mediate inter-group conflicts are to create (1) subspaces so that different groups may claim different zones, (2) multiple entrances and exits so that it is more difficult for a group to dominate the entrance, and (3) circulation routes that are adjacent to rather than in the subspaces so that groups may pass each other without entering the subspace.

Planning and management approaches include (1) hiring a plaza "mayor," (2) providing mediation training to those who tend a civic place (whether they are employees, volunteers, or board members), and (3) hiring a consultant to perform a conflict assessment or to act as a mediator.

William H. Whyte suggests that the success of many New York squares is due to the fact that they have a "mayor." The "mayor" may be a doorman, vendor, gardener, or taking a cue from Wal-Mart, may be someone hired simply to welcome people. A "mayor" can help defuse potential conflicts simply by being a potential witness, but a good "mayor" also sets a tone of civility and may diplomatically intervene before conflicts arise. In small towns the town elders sitting on the barbershop bench once filled the role of plaza mayor.

Additionally, just as it is prudent to develop an emergency management plan and train staff, it is wise to send the staff of a public commons to training seminars in mediation and consensus building. A strong seminar may help staff assess events, define and understand the process of consensus, clarify their potential roles, seek to understand stakeholders' fundamental interests, understand the need for joint fact-finding, and build relationships with outside resources. The manager of a street festival, for example, may have native people skills but certainly could find herself in need of a toolbox for consensus building. Finally, some conflicts will call for outside assessment or mediation.

C. Crime Prevention
In what ways may physical design aid in crime prevention?

There have been numerous studies that show a concentration of certain crimes at certain places (see Eck 1997). For example, most convenience stores have few robberies or none, but a small portion of them suffers many (Crow and Bull 1975). The existence of these hot spots suggests a relationship between place and crime.

However, the relationship between the design of places and crime is not clearly understood. There have been strong claims and theories promoted that are strongly rejected by others or for which no conclusive evidence has been gathered. For example, lighting is often believed to reduce crime because it increases the ability of the general public and police to see a crime, and many street-lighting projects were funded based on this belief. A 1979 nationwide study of lighting for the National Institute of Law Enforcement and Criminal Justice was unable to make a conclusive answer to the question of the effectiveness of lighting (Tien et al. 1979). A 1997 review of place-based crime prevention studies comes to the same (non)conclusion: "Almost 20 years later [than the above study], we know little more about the effectiveness of lighting" (Eck 1997: 7–31).

Nevertheless, there appear to be three approaches to reducing crime and disorder through physical design that are both promising and also apply to the design of civic places.

Broken Window Theory
What does the "deportment" of a place say about safety?

"Social psychologists and police officers tend to agree that if a window in a building is broken, *and if left unrepaired,* all the rest of the windows will soon be broken," James Q. Wilson and George L. Kelling wrote in their article "Broken Windows" (1982). "One unrepaired broken window is a signal that no one cares, and so breaking more windows costs nothing. (It has always been fun)." They use this observation as an example of a larger phenomenon—"serious crime flourishes in areas in which disorderly behavior goes unchecked. The unchecked panhandler is, in effect, the first broken window."

In his 1983 book *Design against Crime,* Barry Poyner encapsulates the results of various studies on crime in school buildings. His design pattern 7.1, *"A well-kept school,"* generally supports the broken-window theory. However, he points out that the research evidence is not conclusive. Rather than well-kept grounds preventing vandalism, "Well-kept grounds may be in that condition because they have been less vandalized" (91). A more predictive theory may be that of "occupancy proxy." This theory suggests that maintenance that shows someone cares about a place may be effective when it indicates that someone is on the grounds (in this case a school caretaker). It may not be the work so much as the worker who is the deterrent to crime.

Good maintenance of a civic place, nevertheless, helps reduce hazards and has other benefits in addition to its potential for reducing crime and thus may be part of a total management approach. Consideration should be given to scheduling maintenance at times when the presence of the workers may provide critical surveillance and to training them to work with the police.

Natural Scrutiny
Can design help us watch out for each other?

Jane Jacobs's *The Death and Life of Great American Cities* (1961) and Oscar Newman's *Defensible Space* (1972) promoted the concept of natural surveillance—the idea that places that are overseen by people on a regular basis are safer than those that are isolated from other activities. For example, building entryways or courtyards that can be seen from multiple apartment windows are safer than those that are visually remote. Poyner's 1983 study concluded that natural surveillance has been found to be an effective strategy in various conditions (13).

According to the theory of natural surveillance, the provision of sufficient and even lighting should reduce crime although the inconclusive nature of studies on lighting mentioned above is frustrating to many. A recent, apparently well-conducted study of homicides in retail workplaces concludes that providing bright exterior lights appears to reduce the rate of homicides (Loomis et al. 2002).

Surveillance can work both ways. In Poyner's description of the activities of pickpockets at bus queues in Birmingham, England, he points out that the pickpockets can easily watch people in the line to observe where the victims keep their wallets (Poyner 1983: 68). Correspondingly, an island of bright light around an ATM may simply serve to put cash-machine users on a bright stage where they can be examined but cannot see people in the surrounding dark.

Even with these unknowns about lighting, natural surveillance appears to be a reasonable approach to crime reduction. It is a cornerstone of the Crime Prevention Through Environmental Design (CPTED) movement (see Crowe 2000). Moreover, it is an approach that fits well with the nature of commons. Seeing and being seen is a critical component of the life of a civic place.

Lighting Dark Alleys
Are certain physical and social settings ripe for crime? If so, can they be restructured?

Poyner's proposed solution to bus-queue pickpockets was to provide a physical barrier between the queue and the sidewalk so that the pickpockets could not easily jostle their victims. In her study of bus-stop crime in Los Angeles, Anastasia Loukaitou-Sideris made a similar recommendation (1999: 47). This approach to crime prevention is known as situational crime prevention—design methods for blocking crime opportunities.

Target hardening—tamper-resistant parking meters, anti-graffiti paints—is one component of situational crime prevention. Care should be taken with this approach so that the plaza doesn't become an uninviting fortress. Many of the temporary measures conducted in response to 9-11, such as blockading streets with jersey barriers, evoked a sense of siege. Large landscape rocks, well-designed bollards, and other features may provide the same protection as a jersey barrier but also help create a pleasant environment.

The more difficult component of situational crime prevention is to provide a physical intervention in a pattern of behavior such as the bus-stop pickpocketing mentioned above. To design successful interventions requires careful observation of the condition. This is an approach ripe for well-conducted research.

part three

GENIUS LOCI

ON THE EARTH, UNDER THE SKY

Or speak to the Earth and it shall teach thee.

—Bible, Job 12:8, King James Version

It is a glorious fact that at the very heart of our towns and cities—the place where we gather for celebrations, to stage political rallies, and to honor our heroes—rain can fall, wind can blow, and the sun can shine on us. We are creatures of the earth and our civic places should remind us of that fact. Moreover, the land and the sky offer a phenomenological palette that can greatly enrich the design of a commons. "[The] simple phenomena of nature . . . in their silent greatness wield an immediate power over the human mind" (Grimm 1883: 582).

The philosopher of environmental studies David W. Orr wrote in *The Nature of Design,* "The [ecological design] problem is not how to produce ecologically benign products for the consumer economy, but how to make decent communities in which people grow to be responsible citizens and whole people" (2002: 12). To approach this problem, we must build civic places that are part and parcel of the landscape and our communities. We must make places that embody care for the land and that find essential meaning in the enclosure of a bay, the trickle of a stream, or the cut of a stone.

"The genius of the place, the *genius loci,* is a mythological person taken over from antiquity and given a new meaning. The *genius loci,* if we put it in modern terms, is the character of the site, and the character of the site is, in a town, not only the geographical but also historical, social and especially the aesthetic character" (Pevsner 1955). Searching for, building upon, and illuminating this character or spirit supports the sense of conviviality—it roots us in a landscape and a community.

There are two scales of design in which we address the *genius loci*. First, we place urban commons within the landscape and atmosphere. Does the town square directly overlook the bay, or is it nestled on the floor of a steep valley? What is the relationship between the settlement and the landscape? Secondly, we craft the products of the landscape to build the civic place. The grain and color of local granite, the cadence of the rain on tin roofs, the taste of water, or a particular way of building a doorway or sidewalk can all evoke the spirit of a place (see chapter 9).

Outdoor commons can allow us to be simultaneously

immersed in the life of the mind, the life of a community, and the life of the land. When it literally rains on our parades, the roots of the metaphor are nourished. Design can help illuminate our connections to the earth and sky.

"From the beginning of time man has recognized that nature consists of interrelated elements which express fundamental aspects of being," Christian Norberg-Schulz wrote in *Genius Loci*. "The landscape where he lives is not a mere flux of phenomena, it has structure and embodies meanings" (1979: 23). To design a place that helps root us in the landscape, to give us in Norberg-Schulz's terms an "existential foothold," a designer must make a built claim about the structure and meaning of the landscape.

The basin and range landscape of the intermountain west, the oceanlike expanses of the Midwest, and the cliffs and bays of the Oregon coast each provide an underlying structure of places. Interpreting this structure to build meaning is an essential aspect of design. A plaza that opens on one side and frames an expansive view of the horizon asserts that this view has substantial value. A courtyard that encloses an artesian spring claims it as a resource for the members of the court. Whirligigs make light of the wind, while a king's banners attempt to dramatize its force.

The Folds of the Land

What are the spatial characteristics of the landscape? How do the town and the urban commons sit within these forms?

Quebec City sits atop and around a hill that commands the Saint Lawrence River. The original lower town had, like many French-American settlements, a square at its dock. The heights, however, provided locations for an additional place d'armes and fortifications overlooking the river. Seen as a military landscape in an age of naval power, the hill of Quebec offered a command of a strategic location. At the beginning of the twenty-first century this same prospect offers a grand overview of the natural, industrial, suburban, and agricultural context of the city.

Clovis, New Mexico, like many railroad towns of the Great Plains, is a checkerboard grid on a flat expanse. Originally, the civic focus of the town was the railroad depot, park, and hotel. Main Street originated here and ran at right angles to the track. Unlike Quebec City, whose locus is created by features of the landscape, Clovis is a set of human lines drawn upon a seemingly endless field. It is a place of Cartesian geometry oriented to the landscape of the continent and planet—a crossroads of the east-west railroad and a north-south main street. The designers of a civic room along the heights of Quebec City have a very different palette to work with than the designers of a square in Clovis.

Evoking Mediterranean and Northern European mythologies, Norberg-Schulz describes three types of landscape—one in which the sky dominates, one in which the sky and earth are in balance, and one in which the land is the dominant feature. Clovis sits in a *cosmic landscape* dominated by the sky that "seems to make an absolute and eternal order manifest" (1979: 45). Quebec, in Norberg-Schulz's terms, is part of a balanced *classical landscape* in which we find "an intelligible composition of distinct elements: clearly defined hills and mountains . . . imageable natural spaces such as valleys and basins" (1979: 45). The Appalachian Mountains with their groves and deep woods, hollows, ridges, and folds fit Norberg-Schulz's third category, the *romantic landscape* with "an indefinite multitude of different places."

This typology illustrates how we might begin to think about the architectural character of the landscape. However, I believe there are a multitude of other types of landscape, different ways in which the sky and earth shape places. Puget Sound and the inland waterway of British Columbia and the Alaska panhandle, for example, combine features of Norberg-Schulz's romantic landscape, such as the multitude of places within the forest, with distinctly defined islands and bays that might be characterized as belonging to a classical landscape, and the flat expanse of the ocean that evokes the cosmic.

Moreover, there are other traditional systems of understanding and composing within a meaningful landscape. The Chinese practice of Feng Shui and the Celtic practices of geomancy offer two currently popular examples. Native American tribes also developed existential landscape systems (see Nabokov and Easton 1989).

Figure 7.1a.
San Esteban del Rey Church and its camposanto *at Acoma Pueblo, New Mexico. The camposanto, or churchyard, is a strongly defined space that sits on the edge of the mesa within the enclosure of the valley. No photograph can adequately capture the sense that one is both in a strongly defined churchyard and enclosed by the larger landscape. Photograph, c. 1882, by Ben Wittick, courtesy of the Museum of New Mexico, neg. no. 15586.*

Acts of construction, particularly those that are prime components of the structure of the settlement such as a town square or protected harbor, help structure our conception of the landscape. The designer of a civic place should understand its place in the landscape and shape the place to evoke this poetic sense of living on the earth. Are we, at this place, ridge-top dwellers or valley people, contemplators of the horizon or the vault of the sky, people who live close to the ground or inhabitants of the heights?

The Fourth Wall

Can the volume of a civic room elide into the space of the landscape?

Box seats in the theater are both a small room and a place within the volume of the theater. A convertible parked on lovers' lane is both a private enclosure and a small point in the vastness of space. Likewise, a civic room may enclose its activities and be a portion of the larger landscape. We may be simultaneously immersed in the square and the countryside. Perhaps this is nowhere more powerfully accomplished than at the *camposanto* of the mesa-top San Esteban del Rey church at Acoma Pueblo (fig. 7.1a and b). One rises on a ramp from the town into the yard; on the right sits the church façade; and to the left a railing-height adobe wall with a picket of mud spirit figures encloses the other three sides of the graveyard. Beyond the wall the cliff gives way to an expansive view of the valley in which the Acoma mesa sits. The wall and its spirits hold the graveyard and frame the landscape beyond.

These spaces are not simply open to the larger landscape. People within the space can choose to perceive themselves as in the smaller or the larger enclosure, and switch from one conception to the other. In theater, the concept of the "fourth wall" arose in the French independent theaters of the late nineteenth century. The fourth wall is the fiction that the actors are so completely immersed in the world depicted on stage—that they are surrounded by and live within four walls, one of which the invisible audience can see through. Actors can, to dramatic effect, play with alternating between seeing and not seeing the fourth wall.

Figure 7.1b.
The wall of the camposanto showing the spirit figures that inhabit the border between the church graveyard and the larger landscape. Photograph, c. 1935, by T. Harmon Parkhurst, courtesy of the Museum of New Mexico, neg. no. 1987.

People can and do create these conceptual enclosures without the support of physical form, but a well-composed space allows groups of people to easily share definitions of conceptual place. The pattern "Implication and Elision" (chapter 10) discusses some compositional means that allow a place to be a component of more than one form.

The Japanese gardening technique *ikedori*, "capturing alive," provides a means for a designer to bring the sense of the larger landscape into the foreground composition (Itoh 1980). Trees from the mountain may frame the view of the mountain from a garden, as if the garden is simply a glade at the foot of the mountain. A garden designer may place rocks in a garden so that a hill in the background balances and completes the composition. A theater designer may incorporate the audience into a courtroom scene by placing them in jury boxes. A civic place designer may place a mountain glade or farm plot in the field of a square, or enclose a paved field along a river in a frame of river-edge trees. These spatial elisions of town and country blurring into one another allow us to partake of both and to contemplate the relationships between the two.

The Waters of the Earth
Wells and waterworks yield water, metaphors, and places to play. How should we drink?

> It has been well said that something about us, some lingering touch perhaps of the race's primitive days, gives to the running water of the city fountain that relation to public life which the fire in the open hearth has to private life. (Robinson 1903: 178)

There is an ancient and deep association between water and civic place. The idea of the city itself may have originated in the governance needed to build and operate irrigation systems. Some of the longest continuously operating forms of governance are the local associations that manage the ditches of farming towns, and these ancient systems for managing common resources provide critical models for some of the most pressing environmental problems of our time (Ostrom 1990).

Just as the water cooler in an office is a natural place of conviviality and gossip, the well or fountain of a town was a

Figure 7.2. *Children touching the water. Passing adults also frequently dip their hands in the water. Place d'Armes, Quebec City, 2002.*

natural gathering place. Many of the piazzas of Rome are places where the aqueducts fed fountains. Access to drinking water is a basic need, but in slaking our thirst we have found ways to meet our needs for companionship and social information. Just because we can now generally obtain water from sources outside of the plaza does not mean that the plaza should give up this basic attractor. A town that will not provide public drinking fountains in its squares has, to my mind, fundamentally abandoned the public realm.

The design of places that provide and display water is a delicate art because water is saturated with metaphor. "The comparative study of hydrologically inspired folklore clearly reveals that the fundamental cares of humankind—concern for nurture, fertility, relief and regeneration—are continuously expressed through water imagery" (Gribben 1992: 29). Historically, many cultures have holy wells; wishing and cursing wells; purifying, curative, and life-extending waters; and

various creatures and spirits of water. For evidence that these ideas still motivate us, one need look no further than the bottled water and spa industries (see Gribben 1992).

Water also provides an attraction and excuse for another of our basic needs—play. The true test of a good fountain design is not whether children will play with it (for only if it is foul or inaccessible will children avoid a fountain), or whether tourists gather about it, but whether it exerts a force like gravity bending the paths of people conducting their daily business. Do businesspeople come to touch it? Does it become the place to have lunch, to read a book, or to think about a difficult problem simply because to be near it, to hear it, to watch it is a kind of play? (see "City Water," chapter 15).

The sound of water can be a strong component of our sense of place. The fountain in the courtyard of the Boston Public Library can be heard in the surrounding reading rooms and is an essential part of the civility of the library. The Wave Organ, designed by Peter Richards and George Gonzales on a promontory in San Francisco Bay, has listening tubes placed throughout the promontory that capture and transmit the sound of waves. The timbre, meter, and volume of the Wave Organ varies with the weather and tide, and invites us to listen to the ocean as we would a song.

We use and delight in water and then pass it on. Historically, the dominant themes of fountain design have been the celebration of gathering and using water. Perhaps we should also take care with how water leaves our towns. Could the towns of Lake Tahoe celebrate in physical form the means they use to protect the clarity of the lake? Should the massive public works we build to handle wastewater be celebrated in ways similar to Rome's celebration of its aqueducts? Can we honor the drain as well as the fountain?

Local Sky

What are the temperaments of the sky? How does the design frame these atmospheres?

"The unique relationship between the open area of the square, the surrounding buildings and the sky above creates a genuine emotional experience comparable to the impact

Figure 7.3. *Skyline of Tom Quad at Christ Church College, Oxford, England, 2002.*

of any other work of art" (Zucher 1959: 1). What is the palette for this art of the sky?

First, the character of the local sky must be studied. Of course, each local sky goes through a repertoire of characteristics throughout the day and year, but there may be dominant or typical traits that characterize the seasons. The northwest coast's sky is milky blue. The towns high in the Rockies have a vibrant blue sky so that bright Victorian house colors vibrate in contrast. Montana and Wyoming are known for the expansiveness of their sky vault. During Seattle's winter, the sky does not appear as a vault; rather the rim of the horizon is prominent and long horizontal views are important to provide a sense of openness. Frequently, the lingering patterns of jets' vapor trails establish the height of New Mexico's sky. San Francisco's fog brings the height of the sky down almost to the ground. Knowing the pattern of colors, heights, and other characteristics of the local sky is akin to studying the traits of a picture to select an appropriate frame.

Secondly, the enclosure must be designed to capture the sky. The ceiling, the walls, and the floor of a square or courtyard can all help frame the sky.

The ceiling, of course, is most intimately associated with the sky. The ceilings of many great indoor commons such as Grand Central Station and the fictional dining hall in the Harry Potter books have clearly re-presented the sky. The open ceilings of outdoor commons, however, also cast the sky in a certain light. The tight canopy of a grove, for example, makes the sky a realm beyond that is glimpsed through a filter. A grid of wires and light bulbs can give Cartesian measure to passing clouds, contrails, or the colors of sunset. Banners and other windthings highlight the motion of the atmosphere.

Walls, however, can also strongly affect our perceptions of the heavens. White walls that take on the color of the sky and metals or glass that reflect light can highlight the time of day. The pattern "Cornice and Silhouette" (in chapter 11) discusses the walls' role in framing the sky. An open *fourth wall* of a room, in addition to framing a view of a landscape, will also frame a view of the sky (unless the room is very close to the face of a cliff). A room open to the west, for example, will be a place to contemplate the sunset and should be designed to bask in red sunlight.

The floor may also capture the sky. A pool will draw the color and movement of the heavens into a room. Textured pavement will highlight the angle of the sun. Paving with embedded quartz, glass, or other reflective materials will strengthen the play between shade and sun. In places and seasons where clouds scuttle across the sky, the play and activity of the sky will be echoed by light-catching pavement.

Wild and Cultivated
What is the story of humankind's inhabitation of this landscape?

"On arriving at the place where the new settlement is to be founded . . . a plan for the site is to be made . . . beginning with the main square," reads no. 110 of the Law of the Indies

Figure 7.4. *Oaks forming a colonnade and canopy in one of Savannah, Georgia's squares, 2001.*

In addition to embodying a claim of cultivation, a central civic place can also preserve knowledge of the pre-settlement conditions. The wild river runs out from the dam. A native outcrop of stone may pave part of a square. Native trees may flourish in the town park. Lithia Park in Ashland, Oregon, runs from the heart of town to the top of Mount Ashland a mile away. It literally connects the compositional center of town to a focal point of the larger landscape. Ashland Creek runs wild on the mountain but is structured by constructed falls, and its banks are gardened as it comes into town.

The pattern of frame and field, which informs many civic rooms, echoes and may ultimately derive from the meadow in the forest. It may embody our species' early acts of settlement—gathering on the edge of the meadow.

(Crouch, Garr, and Mundigo 1982: 13). Explicitly in the Law of the Indies and implicitly in many other traditions, the first act of settlement is demarking the central civic place. It is the first act in cultivating a landscape.

Thus a central civic place can embody a claim about our way of dwelling in the landscape. In Mesa Verde the Anasazi built their settlements within the protection offered by the overhanging cliffs. The landscape was itself their collective shelter. The mill towns of New England were built around falls or rapids transformed into sources of industrial power by dams. Here the power of nature was *harnessed* to make a living, and the dam, its lake, and the outflowing river was the central town-making construction. Seattle was settled by ship, and Elliot Bay remains a critical component of the economy and serves as the focal point around which the city is composed. Heirloom apple orchards, historic fish markets, irrigation canals, millworks, and other built places can embody the origins of the town's cultivation.

The Fruits of the Land
How can the products of the landscape enrich the spirit of a town?

The harvest can be a major component of the syllabus for a civic place (see chapter 4). Where and how do we gather the fruits of the land, and prepare, sell, use, and celebrate them? What facilities are useful and delightful?

Members of a Slow-Foods chapter meet for long, leisurely meals, to eat local and traditional foods, to talk about food, wine, culture, and philosophy (see www.slowfood.com or www.slowfoodusa.org). These "convivia" gave birth to the Slow Cities movement. The charter of the Slow Cities Association includes the goals of:

▦ implementing environmental, infrastructural, and technological policies that "maintain and develop the characteristics of [the town's] surrounding area and urban fabric, and

Figure 7.5.
*Santa Fe Plaza, New Mexico,
c. 1881–1883, showing a crop
(corn?) being grown in the
field. During this period of
time the county, which ran
the plaza, was short of cash.
Farming the plaza was
one means to raise funds.
Photograph by William H.
Jackson, courtesy of the
Museum of New Mexico,
neg. no. 15277.*

⊞ "safeguard[ing] autochthonous production, rooted in culture and tradition, which contributes to the typification of an area, maintaining its modes and mores and promoting preferential occasions and spaces for direct contacts between consumers and quality producers and purveyors."

Farmers' markets provide one means to implement these goals, and provide a direct connection between a town and its countryside. However, in addition to food, the use and production of the full range of products of the land could help nurture the spirit of place. In northern New Mexico, roadside vendors sell piñon firewood whose smoke provides settlements with a distinctive and pleasant aroma. The firewood, the forests, and the vendors are powerful aspects of the region's *genius loci*. The pattern "Local Craft and Local Stones" (in chapter 9) discusses materials that are incorporated into the construction of a civic place such as building timber, stone, or adobe.

Local Habitats
Can the hearts of our towns be shared generously with other species?

Bird watchers are a significant political force. Could we design town parks as prime habitats for migratory birds with good viewing blinds? Gardening remains a national pastime. Can the residents of a retirement community plant and tend the gardens of the town square? We are obsessed with getting out into nature by hiking. Can we create urban hikes that compete with our overcrowded national parks?

As we shape our towns we shape habitats for other species. Sometimes we do this with forethought and grace—providing shelters for bats under river-crossing bridges. Often we are blind to our actions and do things like creating ledges for pigeons where their droppings will line a sidewalk and threaten those who dare to walk.

How might we live, in town, with other species?

Excursion

COMMUNITY GARDENS

Volunteer-Run Neighborhood Commons

Andrew Stone

The municipal provision of neighborhood parks often suffers from a very narrow vision. Government often views parks and playgrounds as settings for specific recreational activities. The design of these spaces may not accommodate people seeking experiences outside this narrow range. Particularly overlooked has been the potential for new neighborhood open spaces to serve as neighborhood commons.

One type of open space that has proven effective at promoting interaction and cooperation among neighbors is the community garden. Community gardens have a long history, going back to the Great Depression and the two world wars, and reemerged in inner-city neighborhoods in the 1970s, often on vacant land that resulted from building abandonment and demolition.

Community gardens evolve in a variety of ways. Some are provided as a service, by municipal agencies, to individuals seeking a large, sunny garden plot. But the majority of community gardens in America, and virtually all of those in my city—New York—are a result of grassroots initiative. New York City gardens are also entirely operated by volunteer groups, typically under lease or license with the city's Green Thumb program or a nonprofit land trust (such as The Trust for Public Land).

The creation and sustenance of a community garden is often seen as an ideal neighborhood-organizing project by multiservice community organizations. Neighbors join together, frequently to clean up a lot that has been a community eyesore. Relationships develop out of this sense of common purpose. In most cases, the availability of plots to individuals and families encourages membership. Many of the most successful New York gardens require "plot holders" to volunteer to help maintain common areas.

Community gardens around the country take many physical forms. Typically, gardens in New York are within easy walking distance of a large number of residents, and vary in size from less than one-tenth of an acre to about one-half acre. To accommodate a range of community needs, successful gardens provide a mix of individual plots (generally for vegetables), communal planting beds (often consisting of flowers), and one or more areas for sitting and gathering. Most gardens in New York are fenced, with public access when members are present.

At West Side Community Garden in Manhattan, members with plots volunteer four hours each month in maintaining either flower beds, the compost system, or an offsite greenhouse for seedlings. At West Side, the opportunity for residents in one of New York's densest neighborhoods to grow their own food, to learn perennial gardening, or to help plant over ten thousand bulbs each fall provides a core group of volunteers that maintains a higher level of maintenance and horticultural excellence than is found in any other small park in the neighborhood. These volunteers, many of them retirees, provide a constant presence at the site, essentially eliminating vandalism and enabling this entirely volunteer-run space to be open from dawn to dusk.

There are many examples in New York of community gardens functioning as one of the few places where neighbors regularly come together across barriers of age, class, and ethnicity. Gardens frequently have intergenerational programs, and are a focal point for block associations and neighborhood gatherings. Sixth Street and Avenue B Garden on Manhattan's Lower East Side, with its active membership of over one hundred, draws on the talents of neighborhood volunteers to present over one hundred free cultural events and workshops. At Sixth and B, the ability of members to create and constantly re-create elements of the garden results in an enormous commitment to the garden and a willingness to lend their talents—in a fashion that far surpasses volunteers' commitments to most traditional city parks.

At the same time, there can be a downside to municipal programs allowing community volunteers to control land in this fashion. There are numerous examples in New York of individuals or very small groups taking control of community gardens and operating them as private fiefdoms. Sometimes this is benign. For example, I have seen numerous cases of a community-garden founder who has such high standards of how the garden should look, and how individuals should behave there, that they inadvertently discourage participation. In other cases, there are sites that are "community gardens" in name only, where a few individuals or families gain control of land and intentionally keep out other residents.

One of the goals of The Trust for Public Land in New York City has been the fostering of leaders who welcome broad participation as well as widespread and diverse use of these community gardens. Starting in 1999, with our acquisition of sixty-three gardens (which would otherwise have been auctioned by the city), we have also had an opportunity to require that these sites maintain public hours and conduct outreach for new members. We have a full-time community organizer available to assist volunteer garden leaders in this effort.

Community gardens provide an unusual opportunity to directly involve residents in creating and caring for neighborhood common spaces. As in-fill development occurs in urban areas, securing some land for these small oases is a worthwhile goal. Gardens provide ample opportunity for government, private developers, and local volunteers to work together effectively toward a common goal.

Andrew Stone is The Trust for Public Land New York City Program Director. Before joining TPL in 1988, Andy held positions as a Capital Projects Planner for the New York City Department of Parks and Recreation and Coordinator of the Mayoral New York City Open Space Task Force. Andy coauthored *Public Spaces,* an award-winning study of open space use, design, and management, published in 1992. He holds an M.A. in environmental psychology (1982) from City University of New York Graduate Center and an individualized B.A. in urban studies (1977) from the University of California at Berkeley.

SINGING IN THE RAIN

One must have a mind of winter
To regard the frost and the boughs
Of the pine-trees crusted with snow;

And have been cold a long time
To behold the junipers shagged with ice,
The spruces rough in the distant glitter

Of the January sun; and not to think
Of any misery in the sound of the wind,
In the sound of a few leaves,

Which is the sound of the land
Full of the same wind
That is blowing in the same bare place

For the listener, who listens in the snow,
And, nothing himself, beholds
Nothing that is not there and the nothing that is.

—The Snow Man, *Wallace Stevens (1923)*

There is nothing so delightful as a summer morning breakfast on the square. Outdoor public places are generally most used when they provide pleasant moderate climates, and design can help create these tempered conditions. Yet people will sometimes gather despite poor microclimates. Crowds gather at ice-sculpture festivals and outdoor hockey games; people leave their air-conditioned homes to sit in the heat near pools and fountains; splashing in puddles is an age-old sport; and windy knolls are prized for flying kites. Sometimes design can help us celebrate and enjoy immoderate climates.

A. Moderating

There are three basic approaches to creating moderate climates in outdoor rooms, and thus creating more good weather than the site would otherwise have. First, we may create spaces that provide a variety of conditions and let people move to the conditions they like best. Second, we may build places that selectively admit sun and wind to improve the microclimate, and finally we may condition the environment with the addition of energy (often in the form of cool water).

In any case, the aim is not necessarily to create an ideal climate but to make a tolerable climate that is noticeably better than the intemperate outdoors. Tempering the climate of civic places may also reduce the climate-control demands on adjacent indoor spaces (e.g., a shaded and cool set of courtyards around a building will reduce the cooling load on the building) and reduce the thermal shock people experience in going from a regulated building to a severe day.

The Sunny Side
Can we provide a variety of subspaces with attractive microclimates?

The primal microclimate strategy is migration—moving to the sunny side of the courtyard in cool weather. Civic places can be designed to aid migration both by (1) zoning activities by matching peak use times with appropriate microclimates, and (2) providing a set of differing microclimates within an outdoor room.

Zoning activities is an attempt to fit social patterns with microclimate patterns. For example, in cool climates, restaurants that cater to dinner crowds may wish to have afternoon sun warming the diners. In warm climates, the shady side of the square may be preferable. Donut shops may desire the opposite and try to maximize early-morning sun exposure.

One advantage of zoning activities by microclimate is that this tends to create a set of uses that peak at different times of day and thus provide activity in the civic room throughout the day. It can also simplify the climate-responsive design of the subspaces. The morning microclimate of a dinner restaurant is not critical. Thus the design can focus on the afternoon and evening microclimate. A note of caution is necessary, as the restaurant may at some point in the future wish to open for breakfast or may be sold and converted to a donut shop.

Providing a variety of microclimates allows different activities to locate in their appropriate comfort zone. For example, people playing basketball may desire shade while people sitting on a bench watching them could benefit from direct sun. Even within a set of people engaged in the same activity there may be a distribution of microclimate prefer-

ences. Watch people sitting down for a picnic on a temperate day. Some will sit in the shade, others in the sun, and many at the line between.

Sailing
How can we tune and refine environmental shelter in an outdoor room?

The bioclimatic chart developed by Arens et al. (1980) shows the conditions that they believe 80 percent of people would find thermally acceptable given a set of assumptions. These assumptions include that: for conditions above the shading line shade is provided, for conditions below the wind line, the air is still, "clothing changes are not commonly made during a single day," the site is at 45 degrees latitude, and people are not exercising. The comfort zone described under these conditions works well for typical office, home, classroom, and retail conditions, and is a reasonable benchmark for other conditions if properly adjusted.

The microclimate of a space can be brought into the comfort zone by adding sunlight in cool conditions, wind in warm conditions, or humidity in warm and dry climates (fig. 8.1).

Civic places can be designed to maximize the comfort zone during particular conditions. Thus in a cold climate we may open a square toward the south to maximize solar gain. However, many climates have seasons that call for potentially conflicting strategies (we may want to admit sun in the winter and provide shade in the summer), or fluctuate so that while in general it may be desirable to admit as much sunlight or air movement as possible, there are times when we would like to provide shade or block wind.

Seasonal adjustments may take advantage of differences in the angle of the sun, the location of seasonal winds, or other factors. If, for example, winter and summer breezes come from separate directions, then the walls of the square can be designed to block winter storms but admit summer breezes. Similarly, pavilion roofs and tree canopies may be designed to block summer sun but admit the lower winter light. As a thesis project at the University of New Mexico, Joel Condon designed a campus for the University of Alaska sheltered from

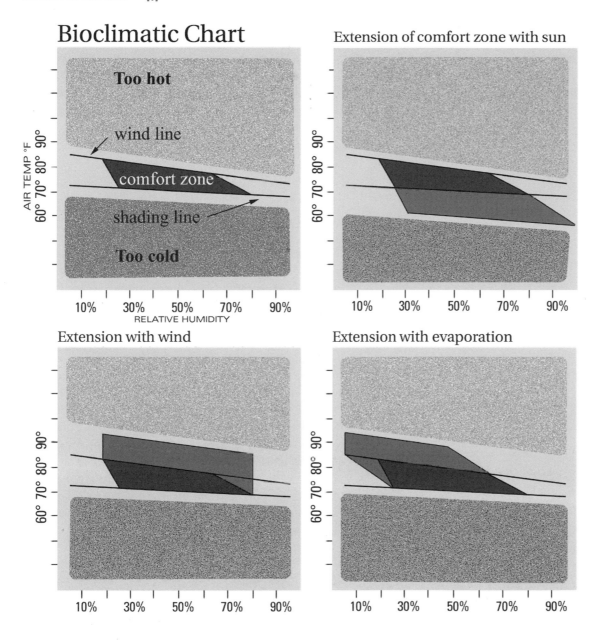

Figure 8.1. *Bioclimatic chart. Redrawn from E. Arens, P. McNall, R. Gonzalez, L. Berglund, and L. Zeren (1980), "A New Bioclimatic Chart for Passive Solar Design," in* Proceedings of the Fifth National Passive Solar Conference *(Newark, Del.: American Section of the International Solar Energy Society), 1202–6.*

Figure 8.2. *Proposal by Joel Condon for an ice wall for the University of Alaska campus. In the winter the ice wall shields the campus from winds and in the summer disappears to allow the flow of summer breezes. Inset: mock-up of ice wall. Courtesy of Joel Condon.*

Shaping the Shade
How can we shape and adjust solar gain to temper the room?

People treat a shadow line as a kind of wall or territorial edge, and thus in essence the sunny and shady spots are subspaces within a plaza. A number of computer modeling programs provide a means to track the sun and shadow patterns created by a design. For designers using pencil and paper, G. Z. Brown and Mark DeKay explain how to create and use sun path diagrams in their book *Sun, Wind and Light* (2001). In either case, the daily and yearly pattern of shade and shadow is a critical component of the design.

Above about 75 degrees F (~24 degrees C), shade is required for comfort. Nonetheless, except in the warmest climates, designers should consider orienting the civic room so that sunlight is admitted and then providing shading devices such as trees and awnings within the square to block the sun on appropriate days. There are two reasons for this recommendation. First, it is easier to provide shade in a sunny space when needed than to reflect sun into a shady space. Second, sunlight is attractive for reasons other than the temperature and climate. On a hot day people may hang out under trees on an arcade but are still attracted to a place that overlooks a sunny field. Adjustable shading devices within a courtyard allow fine-tuning of the microclimate. Awnings, table parasols, and velariums (large cloths used to shade a large portion of an outdoor room) can be deployed. Deciduous trees and vines can be placed so that their leaves provide seasonally appropriate shade.

Water Tempered
How can we maximize the climatic benefits of a fountain or other source of water?

During the late summers of the eighteenth and early nineteenth centuries, Romans would plug the drain of the fountain in Piazza Navona, and ride their carriages around the ensuing piazza-lake (Kostof 1992: 145). In less dramatic and more sanitary ways, fountains have historically provided a cool respite from a hot city.

Water can cool by conduction, evaporation, and to a

winter winds by an ice wall. During the summer the ice melts, admitting breezes (fig. 8.2). A square may also be designed to take advantage of strong daily patterns such as the location and angle of morning versus afternoon sun, diurnal beach or valley winds, or regular summer afternoon thunderstorms.

Adapting to more variable conditions requires the provision of adjustable devices such as awnings, fountains, and wind baffles (see the next three queries). Operating these devices is akin to trimming the sails of a boat. To obtain the maximum effect, people must understand the goals, pay attention to the conditions, anticipate changes, and make multiple small adjustments. If there are no people inhabiting the square who are willing to do this, then sailing devices will not be effective.

lesser extent by radiation and reflection. Anyone who has dipped her toes in a fountain has enjoyed conductive cooling. Water pulls heat away from us faster than air and thus feels cooler.

Evaporative cooling is one of the magic features of water. As it changes from liquid to vapor, water takes in heat. In hot and dry climates, evaporating water can provide very effective air conditioning, as people standing in the mist of a fountain will attest. Cafes in Phoenix provide misters above their outdoor tables to improve the microclimate. A pavement that wicks moisture up from the soil below can provide effective cooling in a hot, dry climate. In well-enclosed courtyards or squares, evaporative cooling towers can significantly lower the air temperature. At the University of Arizona, Moule and Polyzoides Architects provided the courtyard of a dorm with a tower that draws in air at the top. The air passes through wet pads and picks up moisture, raising its humidity and lowering its temperature. The cool air sinks down the tower, pulling more air in the top of the tower, and spilling cool, moist air out the bottom of the tower into the courtyard.

The thermal mass of a pond can help moderate the climate of a space by gathering "coolth" (the opposite of warmth) at night and releasing it during the day. For example, a pond can provide a cool place to dip one's toes, a fountain can spray cool mist into the air, or a cool pond can lower the radiant temperature of an arcade. Coolth may be gathered by allowing the water to radiate heat to the night sky. Because the rate of radiation is directly related to the surface area of the water exposed to the sky, designing methods to increase the surface area of a pond at night and decreasing it during the day (when it would gather heat from the sun) can be an important part of this approach. For example, a fountain may release its water to flood the field of a plaza with an inch or two of water at night. Then in the morning the cooled water may be recirculated into the bowl of the fountain.

It may be possible to effectively use water to transport heat to and from the deep ground. A few feet below the earth's surface, the ground is near the average temperature of a region. Water from a well is thus cool on a warm day, and warm on a cool fall morning.

Water from the ground can also warm a commons. In Glenwood Springs, Colorado, water from the Yampah hot

Figure 8.3. *The thermal pool at Glenwood Springs, Colorado, 1999. In a sense, the pool serves as the town plaza.*

springs fills a large outdoor pool. While the pool is privately owned and admission is charged, many of the townspeople have passes. The pool serves as a membership commons shared by a significant portion of the town. In the pool teenagers flirt, businessmen talk shop, kids play, and newcomers get acquainted. In effect, the pool is a plaza under a few feet of warm water (fig. 8.3).

Water, of course, provides much more than thermal comfort, and any design should treat water as more than an air-conditioning liquid. That water cools or warms us is just one of its joys.

Admit Breezes, Block Storms
How should we shape the wind in a civic room?

Wind above thirteen to nineteen miles per hour raises dust, disturbs hair, and can make sitting uncomfortable. Above

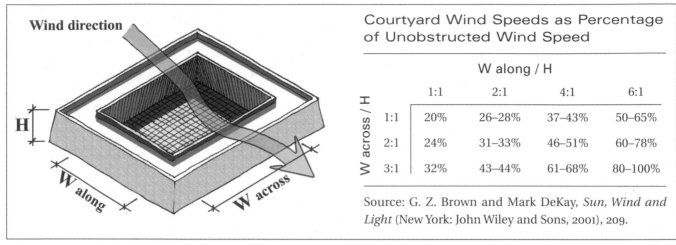

Wind direction

H

W along

W across

Courtyard Wind Speeds as Percentage of Unobstructed Wind Speed

		W along / H			
		1:1	2:1	4:1	6:1
W across / H	1:1	20%	26–28%	37–43%	50–65%
	2:1	24%	31–33%	46–51%	60–78%
	3:1	32%	43–44%	61–68%	80–100%

Source: G. Z. Brown and Mark DeKay, *Sun, Wind and Light* (New York: John Wiley and Sons, 2001), 209.

Figure 8.4. *Courtyard wind speeds as a percentage of unobstructed wind speed, drawing by Mark Childs.*

about thirty miles per hour, wind makes walking difficult. Nevertheless, a light breeze on a hot day can be invaluable, and in places like the knoll in Gas Works Park in Seattle, a stiff breeze brings people out to fly kites. Buildings and parts of buildings may be used to shape the wind. Buildings, plantings, and walls may act as windbreaks providing calm to their lee. A skyscraper or wind tower may reach up to catch stronger winds aloft, or a line of buildings may act together to funnel wind down a street. The value of these winds depends on the temperature and on the uses of the place.

The amount of calming produced by a windbreak is a function of distance from a wall or hedge and its solidity. To create a calm courtyard or square, the walls acting as windbreaks should be tall in proportion to the width of the courtyard, and there should be few openings into the courtyard (see fig. 8.4).

On the other hand, in warm conditions we often wish to admit wind. A breezy outdoor room should have short walls and have multiple openings. To create breezy streets and maximize the potential for cross-ventilation through abutting buildings, the streets should be straight and continuous, wide and oriented at about 20 to 30 degrees from the prevailing cooling breeze. This angle produces slight positive pressure on two sides of buildings and slight negative pressure on the other two sides and thus induces ventilation through the structures.

Wind speed tends to rise with distance above the ground. Wind-catching towers have been used to take advantage of this phenomenon and cool traditional Islamic buildings. These towers may be adapted to bring a breeze to a small courtyard (see Rudofsky 1964; Brown and DeKay 2001). However, skyscrapers adjacent to a forecourt or square often create the design problem of excessively turbulent wind. On the windward side of a skyscraper there can be a strong downward flow known as downwash. On the edges wind can be accelerated above the ambient speed, and on the lee side a skyscraper may create strong upward-flowing eddies. These turbulent flows can be reduced at the ground by rounding the corners of the building, creating a two- or three-story base wider than the tower, or building rigid awnings and other structures to block and break up the tower-associated wind before it reaches the ground.

Adjustable parts can allow users or managers to trim the wind admitted to a civic place. A windbreak wall, for example, could have shutters or hinged sections to admit breezes or block storms. The tops of wind towers could fold closed in the winter. Could we build inflatable wind foils, or gust-activated shutters?

Water Harvesting
Can we design our civic places to
capture rain and supply water?

Rain, like sunlight and manna, is a resource given from the heavens. Many places are experiencing significant water shortages and the careful use of rainwater can be an effective means to increase supply. Five components are needed to harvest this bounty—a collection surface, a conveyance system, a filtering and possibly a purifying system, a means of storage, and a distribution system.

The roofs of buildings encircling and in a civic place and the floor of a square or street can serve as collection surfaces. Different collection surfaces will add different impurities to the water. A parking lot, for example, will impart a larger range of pollutants than will an enameled metal roof. Careful design can help reduce the impurities. For example, roof catchments can be made less attractive to birds by putting spikes on the ridgeline and eliminating other places where they might perch. The height of the collection system will also affect the nature of the distribution system. Roof catchments may allow an entirely gravity-fed system. Floor systems will be limited to watering roots and downhill levels or will require pumps.

A conveyance system of gutters, downspouts, etc., can also serve to house part of the filtering system and in some cases as part of the storage or detention system. Initial screening, to keep large debris out of the system, and "first flush" separators are often part of the conveyance system. The first water off a catchment system is loaded with debris and other contaminants. Eliminating this first flush of water from the harvesting system can significantly increase water purity.

The need for additional filtering and purification naturally depends on the water quality and the uses to which the water is put. Water-purity requirements can be subtle, and an expert should be consulted. For example, copper nails added to a shake roof may beneficially inhibit the growth of moss on the roof but also harm plants in a garden fed by the roof runoff.

Storage systems allow rain to be distributed over time. Their capacity, height relative to grade, and visibility are critical components. To size a cistern, one must prepare a rain

Figure 8.5. *"Downspout Garden" by Buster Simpson on Vine Street in Seattle, Washington. Photo courtesy of Buster Simpson.*

budget that shows amounts and patterns of rain (e.g., size and frequency of storms by season, the drought cycle), the size of the collection field, and the demand for water. The height above grade for the outlet of the cistern determines what areas can be watered by gravity. Finally, the location and character of the tanks determines the legibility of the water harvesting. Tanks placed in a plaza can advertise the system. A gauge tied to a float in the tank to indicate water levels or a meter measuring the outflow of the tank could add interest and educational value.

Finally the distribution system must be carefully designed. If harvested water is used in conjunction with municipal water, for example to flush toilets, devices must be installed to prevent backflow and cross-contamination. If harvested water is returned directly to the watershed, rather than through the sewer system, then the temperature, speed, turbidity, contaminants, and other characteristics of the returned water should be considered to maintain the health of the watershed.

The infrastructure of water harvesting need not follow the path of late twentieth-century infrastructure and create monofunctional and frequently ugly structures. Rather, we should follow the example of the great public works such as the Roman aqueducts and fountain-plazas and design for function, pedagogic value, and beauty.

High Water
How can our civic places help moderate floods?

Cisterns and tanks used to harvest water can also retain water that otherwise would contribute to flooding. For small storms, cisterns may allow a site with impervious surfaces (e.g., buildings and paving) to mimic the runoff characteristics of an unbuilt site. The cisterns take up the rain that would soak into the soil of an open lot. A tree canopy can also assist by retaining light rains. Regulating the runoff from small storms is important to help stabilize streams and to maintain healthy stream habitats. The pulse of water created by even a one- or two-year storm on a highly urbanized and impermeable watershed can seriously erode streambeds and silt up fish-spawning grounds.

A water-harvesting system is unlikely to have the capacity to retain significant amounts of water from a large or long rain. However, flood-detention capacity can be built into courtyards, squares, basketball courts, parking lots, and other civic places. The fields of these places can be lower than their surrounding walkways and buildings and, by regulating the size of the drainpipe, can be designed to retain a few inches of storm water. Care should be taken when designing this flood zone to avoid water damage and other hazards (e.g., electrical outlets in the flood zone). In some conditions, additional capacity may be gained by designing the ground under an urban field as a gravel- and sand-filled french drain. Fountains or ponds may also be designed to have storm-water capacity.

Even downspouts can be designed to temper surges of water from a short downpour. A fat downspout has a bottom outlet sized to a maximum acceptable flow rate. If water enters the downspout at a flow rate greater than this outflow rate then it begins to fill the excess volume of the downspout. An emergency overflow near the top relieves the flow should the downpour exceed the fat downspout's capacity. Such systems simply spread a surge over time and may not be advisable in some conditions.

Sometimes, instead of civic places being designed to aid flood control, flood-control facilities are designed to provide civic places. In Albuquerque, New Mexico, and King County, Washington, basins designed for flood control also host playfields and parks. Like Boston's Fens, the urban flood plains of streams and rivers can serve as multifunction greenbelts.

B. Celebrating

Sometimes we shun comfortable microclimates to play in the snow, dance in the rain, and fly kites in the wind. How can we design places that help us enjoy "bad" weather?

In Jukkasjärvi, Sweden, there is a popular tourist hotel built of ice, including ice beds (see Chelminski 2001). Throughout the cold-weather areas of the United States and Canada, people flock to ski resorts and towns hold ice-festivals. Likewise, sailboarders have descended on the towns of the Columbia River Gorge in Oregon and Washington because of the gorge's winds. The town of Hobbs, New Mexico, has a "hot summer nights" festival that includes a sidewalk egg-frying contest. The design of a civic room and artworks within the place can certainly aid and abet this play (see chapter 15).

Observe and Measure
*Can we make a civic room **the** place to talk about the weather?*

There is truth in the old saying, "If the weather didn't change once in a while, most people couldn't start a conversation." The weather provides a common experience that allows strangers to talk. Providing places at which the effects of the weather are particularly noticeable can nourish this social grace.

A plaza with a view of the ski slopes or ocean surf would provide aficionados a place to hang out and monitor conditions. Maybe this overview could be augmented with posted weather reports. Even for people with only a general interest in the weather, a view of oncoming storms can be attractive.

We speak about the weather in the present, past, and future tense, and the design of a civic place can prompt all three types of discussions. For example, steps down into a stream help measure the current level of drought or high water. Monuments placed on those steps could mark historic floods, as could scientific (or otherwise) predictions of floods based on upstream urbanization.

Means to measure, record, and predict other aspects of a local climate could also nourish celebration and knowledge of the weather. When have migrating birds or butterflies returned to a site? When have the first and last frost been? How intense is the current ultraviolet light? Where are we in the solar storm cycle and how might this be manifest in a civic place?

Small Doses
Can we make places that allow people to calibrate their exposure to the weather?

Porches, arcades, gazebos, and pavilions provide partial shelter. We can inhabit these places and, for example, enjoy the turbulence and taste of a storm without bearing its full brunt. Just as people differ in their definition of the perfect microclimate, they will differ in their desired exposure to immoderate weather. The layers of an urban room may be designed to provide a variety of environmental exposures—for example, a swimming bay and beach are open to the full summer sun, a grove of trees and picnic tables frames the beach, and an encircling covered dock and boardwalk provide complete shade.

In severe weather, devices for sailing the microclimate, such as deployable windscreens and parasols, may not be able to produce a perfectly comfortable microclimate. Yet they may create havens in which people can enjoy the weather. The ability to choose and to modify one's degree of exposure may produce psychological comfort that compensates for the lack of complete physiological comfort.

We need to balance protecting people from severe weather to encourage use of civic places with allowing people to feel and live in the environment. The main walkways to and through a public place should be semiprotected spaces. Completely enclosed and climate-controlled walkways, even those with floor-to-ceiling windows, significantly distance us from the here and now by limiting our experience of the environment to the single sense of sight. We can watch a snowstorm on TV nearly anytime we wish. Overly damped reality is kin to virtual reality.

Play
How can we design to capitalize on the opportunities of each season?

Perhaps the very idea of the bioclimatic comfort zone is easily misunderstood when applied outdoors. The comfort zone describes conditions in which we are well sheltered and the climate is nearly unnoticeable. However, when outdoors we may desire to notice the weather: to dig our toes into warm sand, smell oncoming rain, chase snowflakes, fly kites, or otherwise play.

Rather than seeking passive comfort, another approach to the climate is to find delight in each season and in the change from one to another. Providing places and facilities to play in and with the weather can support this alternative attitude. For example, a summer wading pool that becomes a winter ice rink may serve as the central field for a playground that capitalizes on the seasons (see also "Sky Light," "Wind-things," and "City Water" in chapter 15).

Might we make town parks in which to hold solar-oven cook-offs, design fountains that create ice sculptures, or line the main street of a prairie town with whirligigs? Can we use the energy of water rushing through a downspout to create music, run a motor to heat a bus shelter, or animate a sculpture?

Sometimes very specific climatic conditions are valued. Albuquerque hosts the hot-air balloon fiesta because of its particular combination of cold fall mornings and layered winds. Pacifica, California, and Ji Lin, China, have fog festivals. What other places can we create to play with the rain, snow, sun, or wind?

Traditional festivals are a good source of knowledge about shaping humankind's relationship with the weather. Harvest, winter, and spring celebrations afford excuses not only for play but also for poetry. That many of these festivities are clichéd does not necessarily mean we should abandon them, but rather suggests that we need a new generation of poets of place that can revitalize and re-enchant.

Contrast
When and how should we heighten the sensations of the weather?

Sitting next to the fire is more delightful during a storm than otherwise. The creation of contrast can often make conditions more legible and more interesting. A prime example is the traditional roll in the snow during or after a sauna. Saunas, fireplaces, swimming holes, and other places that offer a contrasting microclimate are frequently the attractions around which groups gather. These places often are membership or neighborhood commons, but they may also

function in civic commons. Classically, the fountain serves like a hearth for a square.

Places that allow us to calibrate our exposure to the weather (see "Small Doses" above) can provide some contrast. For example, a shade canopy of leaves or a trellis can highlight the intensity of the sunlight, and being in the relative calm of an arcade in which we feel only the echoes of gusts may allow us to appreciate the gales in the courtyard.

We may also wish to create some places where the contrast is as great as possible. A downspout, for example, could let roof water cascade in front of a window. Likewise, a pavilion roof that transmits the sound of rainfall can emphasize the provision of shelter. Devices that measure the weather (see "Observe and Measure" above) can also help make the contrast legible. The dance of a whirligig or pace of a windmill allows us to see just how calm it is in our bus shelter.

This contrast may be made not only within a space but also at larger scales. We may enter though a gateway from a hot, dry street into a shaded and moist oasis, from the winds of the open road into the calm of town streets in a fold of a mountain, or from the open seas into a harbor.

Excursion

A WINTER CITY

Alf Simon

The city of Winnipeg, in the province of Manitoba, Canada, is located on the northern edge of the Great Plains at 49°57'N latitude. The city of approximately six hundred thousand was developed about the confluence of two large rivers, the Assiniboine flowing from the west and joining the Red, flowing from the south. While it has many fine qualities, Winnipeg also has the dubious distinction of being one of the coldest cities of its size in the world.

The average daily temperature from November to March is −12°C (10.4°F), with 119 days annually when the temperature does not rise above the freezing point. In January, the coldest month, the average daily minimum temperature is −23.6°C (−10.5°F), with extremes as low as −43°C (−45°F). Cold January winds flow down from the northwest, effectively dropping temperatures even lower with the wind-chill factor. Snows that start to fall in late October stay on the ground until well into March. Add to this, very short winter days with just under eight hours of daylight on the shortest day of the year.

Photographs on the Tourism Winnipeg Web site overwhelmingly depict the city in the green summer season. While denial is certainly one method for coping with such an inhospitable climate, many of the residents have genuinely incorporated harsh winters as a way of life. There is a compelling and poetic beauty in Winnipeg winters, when a fresh snowfall covers the city in a smooth blanket of white, in the crunch of dry packed snow underfoot, in the crisp, cold intensity of the air; in the bright, clear light and the sparkling texture of snow crystals, in the finely sculpted snow drifts, in the solitude, and in the suspended stillness and purity of land and life being cleansed. There is also a sense of stoic pride in the challenge of coping, surviving, even thriving, against the odds of winter.

During the cold winter months people spend less time outdoors in the public spaces of the city, and they engage those spaces differently than in the summer. Designers of urban public spaces in northern climates have traditionally held a summer perspective, developing places that are pleasant and comfortable in the warmer seasons but ill adapted for use during cold months. Since the early 1980s The Winter Cities Association of North America and other similar associations worldwide have actively promoted strategies for improving the livability of northern cities through intelligent planning and design. Northern urban spaces, like people, need to adapt and transform through the seasons. Although I would not characterize Winnipeg as a leader in urban design for winter conditions, there have been some interesting adaptations in public spaces and their use over the years to sustain the quality of life for the city residents during long cold winters.

The strategies for adapting to the cold can be broadly categorized as: providing shelter in situations and places

Figure E2. *A fence designed to capture and display snowfall. Design and photograph by Dr. Alf Simon.*

where it would not be necessary in warmer climates, providing venues for winter outdoor activities, celebrating winter as a fundamental aspect of Winnipeg's identity, and finding alternatives to "rolling" forms of transportation and movement over snow and ice-covered terrain. These strategies can be seen in all of the public spaces of the city. Most of the adaptations are ephemeral, appearing in the cold months and then disappearing, many literally melting away when spring and summer arrive. Most of those that provide shelter are permanent, embedded into the spatial and architectural character of the city.

Shelter

Pedestrian spaces are the most frequently used areas in the public domain. On popular promenade streets such as Corydon Avenue, the main shopping/business street in the Corydon urban-village area, summer use is very heavy.

Restaurants along the street spill out onto the sidewalks for outdoor dining, and many strolling pedestrians enjoy the dynamic social atmosphere. In winter people don't spend much time along the sidewalks, but scurry from cars to warm shops or restaurants, or into the protection of the substantial, sometimes heated, bus shelters. In below-freezing temperature with winds, being outside is at best uncomfortable, and more often almost unbearable. In the downtown these conditions can be exacerbated by accelerated winds blasting pedestrians on the unprotected sidewalks. The dwindling pedestrian traffic in downtown Winnipeg (due to a decline in the downtown area typical of North American cities) would be further diminished in the winter months, except for one factor: the city has developed an extensive system of "plus fifteen" walkways. (They are one story above grade.) The 1.2 miles of pedestrian skyways weave through buildings over the ten blocks that comprise the downtown's linear corridor, and are slowly moving into the adjacent heritage and cultural district to the north. The skyways pass through office and government buildings, a large urban shopping mall, and cultural venues, blurring the distinction between public and private space. Some of the newer sky bridges have incorporated small shops and kiosks. The bridges are really large trusses that form architectural spaces for pedestrians, and they differ in character and appeal. Almost all of them are glazed, letting in light and celebrating the idea of crossing over the downtown streets. The ones that incorporate shops tend to be more interesting spaces to move through, but some of the designs that reveal the structural system in the interior as the aesthetic of the space are also successful. While the street-level sidewalks and plazas are deserted in the depths of winter, a person working in one of the office towers at Portage and Main can spend their lunch hour walking through and over the downtown doing chores and shopping in climate-controlled comfort.

The University of Manitoba, a public university, is a 274-hectare, relatively isolated suburban campus located at the south end of the city in a low-density residential suburb. Exposure to the prairie winds at the agricultural fringe makes pedestrian movement around the campus in winter particularly uncomfortable. To mitigate these conditions, the university has built an extensive system of subterranean tunnels connecting many of the fifty buildings on campus. The tunnels, which also house infrastructure such as steam pipes and electrical conduits, provide a warm if somewhat drab pedestrian network for the considerable daytime population that gives the campus the status of being Manitoba's "third largest city" each weekday during the school year.

Outdoor Activities

Winnipeg has over 850 public parks within the city limits and several public golf courses that enjoy the benefit of river-water irrigation. Developed and managed by an active Parks and Recreation Department, the parks vary from small community sites the size of a residential lot to regional Olmsteadian-style parks of over 150 hectares (370 acres). The parks and golf courses are very popular and well used by residents of the city, particularly in the late spring, summer, and early fall.

In deep winter, when the lush green and multicolored spaces of summer and fall are blanketed in white, the parks are visually and functionally transformed. Many city residents wax up their cross-country skis and spend winter weekends gliding along miles of wind-buffered trails through the river-bottom forests in most of the larger parks and golf courses. Others like to put on snowshoes and trudge over the surfaces of deep snow-covered fields. Kids love the toboggan slides that are installed in many of the parks. The long iced slides send toboggan loads of people at tantalizing speeds down the slopes and racing over a flat snow-covered plain.

In other parks the banks of the Red and Assiniboine rivers become informal toboggan runs, propelling the sledders down the banks and across the thick river ice. On neighborhood community-center sites, soccer fields and baseball diamonds are dormant in winter, replaced by skating rinks as the popular hubs of community-center activity. The rinks accommodate both pleasure skating and hockey, and the board structures that surround the hockey ice surfaces emerge each fall as city crews transport modular units to sites all over the city and construct them in place.

Built on two rivers, Winnipeg has over one hundred kilometers (sixty-two miles) of navigable waterways. The rivers are public space, but in warmer seasons only those with access to boats, or who take one of the commercial river excursions, get to experience the unique and surprising perspective of the city from the river. In deep winter the ice-covered rivers are not navigable by boat, but the city clears a wide swath on the ice surface for miles to create a skating path. Driving over one of the city's many bridges on a nice winter weekend day it is quite common to look over the snow-covered river corridor and see strings of skaters, their breath condensing in white clouds as they skim along the tree-lined prairie river, well below the city street level in the muffled silence of winter. Many of the bridges that cross the two rivers also serve as river-access points, in the summer to get down to the river trail walkways, and in winter for the skating trail.

Celebration

Winter carnivals and festivals are common in northern cities. These events bring people out from the interior isolation that the cold promotes into the public spaces of the city. The social celebration of winter not only brings people together but also recognizes the profound impact that climate has in shaping who we are. Annually the community of St. Boniface, located across the Red River from downtown Winnipeg, hosts Festival du Voyageur, the largest winterfest in Canada. The festival, which attracts people from all over the city, the rural areas, and well beyond, celebrates French culture in western Canada, showcasing the era of the voyageurs and the fur trade. Events such as an international ice-sculpture competition, dog-sled races, fiddling and jigging contests, and voyageur cuisine bring people onto the streets and public spaces of St. Boniface.

At the Forks, a popular festival marketplace development on former railyards at the confluence of Winnipeg's two major rivers, winter is celebrated throughout the season. Each year a winter park for public use is constructed on the site featuring snow walls, ice sculpture, skating trails, a snowboard park, curling ice, cross-country ski trails, a dog-sled trail, and many other activities specifically suited to winter. Visitors can warm up in one of the kiosks provided in the winter park or in the market buildings at the hub of the Forks site.

Students in the Faculty of Architecture at the University of Manitoba developed the annual "Ditchball" event, which brings people out of the tunnels and outside for at least one day in the winter. The students arrange for snow cleared on campus to be dumped on the large lawn in front of the Architecture Building. In February, when the pile has grown into a mountain of snow, a front-end loader carves out a dog-leg trench some forty feet long, ten feet wide, and fifteen feet high. The trench is iced and teams of students, heavily padded in hockey equipment, compete against each other, scoring points by successfully passing a large, heavy cloth-covered ball to their "goalie" stationed up on bridges at either end of the "ditch." Crowds gather along the top of the ditch to watch the games amid a celebration of music, food, and other events including the Dean's snow-volleyball tournament.

Alternative Modes of Movement

A severe blizzard will shut the city down, closing schools, offices, and businesses. Deep snowdrifts can cover cars and even reach the eves of houses. In these conditions the streets are impassable to cars and can remain so for two or three days until basic snow clearing has been done. Emergency services are performed by the use of snowmobiles, and snowshoes or cross-country skis provide two of the few nonmotorized ways of getting around. During a Winnipeg winter, the city sidewalks need to be plowed after every snowfall for them to be fully usable pedestrian ways. As winter wears on it becomes very difficult to plow every sidewalk in the city, and the surfaces start to accumulate hard-packed snow and ice. Residential-area sidewalks are the last to be plowed and most of the residents have learned to navigate the tough conditions, outfitted in winter boots with good snow treads. For some, such as the elderly or handicapped, the conditions can be frustrating and dangerous. In the residential areas parents who use strollers on dry pavement trade them in for sleighs

of various kinds that glide more easily over the uneven, packed surfaces. In recent years snow cleared from the streets has been hauled away by trucks to large dumping areas. Prior to this practice, plows would push the snow onto the boulevards, and as the winter progressed streets would be transformed into urban winter canyons, with high walls of snow on both sides. One of the important site design criteria for private lands is providing areas that can be used for snow storage.

The fundamental low-technology solution for making outdoor spaces in winter cities useable is to create microclimates. Winnipeg, unlike like some other northern cities, has not been aggressive with this strategy. A space that is sheltered from the wind, has good sun exposure, and is designed to reflect and focus the sun's rays can be very comfortable even on a crisp winter day. If well designed, acknowledging the annual sun path, shadow patterns, and wind directions, this space can be made to be comfortable in every season. Urban spaces also have to be flexible with respect to use and adaptable to some degree of reconfiguration on a seasonal basis. Finally, urban designers in winter cities ought to recognize and promote the intriguing possibilities for the ephemeral landscapes that winter conditions offer.

Alf Simon holds a Master of Landscape Architecture degree from the University of Manitoba in Canada, and a Ph.D. in Geography from Arizona State University. He is currently the director of the graduate Landscape Architecture Program at the University of New Mexico. His interests are in landscape and infrastructure, cultural landscape studies, and urban design. Dr. Simon has been the principal of a Landscape Architecture and Architecture office and is a Fellow of the Canadian Society of Landscape Architects.

LOCAL 9 STONES

Yet stones have stood for a thousand years, and pained thoughts found
The honey peace in old poems.

—To the Stone-Cutters, *Robinson Jeffers (1924)*

The materials we use and the tectonics of how we use them to build the floors, walls, and furniture of our civic rooms can evoke a sense of place. The character of stone from a local quarry, for example, can help distinguish a town. A region's expertise in tile work, bicycle manufacturing, clock making, or building hot-air balloons can provide unique resources for the design of a civic place (fig. 9.1). Materials and designs that demonstrate a long-term investment in a place give assurance to others to invest their lives in the town and become attached to the place. Designs that provide this sense of durability and allow current and future generations to add to the collective work provide for a living tradition.

The Pedagogy of a Hand Pump

What natural forces and human wisdom can the civic place and its furnishings help illuminate?

On a hot day when a child hauls cool water up from a dark well, she learns about the thermal properties of the earth, the mechanics of pulleys, and the origins of multiple myths and sayings. A hand pump, particularly one whose various parts are clearly articulated, illustrates not only the work necessary to lift water but also shows the mechanism by which the task is accomplished. On the other hand, an electric water pump, particularly one whose only visible part is an electric switch, is a species of obscuring magic because it creates the illusion of effortless work.

"Buildings and landscape reflect a hidden curriculum that powerfully influences the learning process. The curriculum embedded in any building instructs as fully and as powerfully as any course taught in it," David W. Orr writes in *The Nature of Design* (2002: 128); and he continues, "Is it possible to design buildings and entire campuses in ways that promote ecological competence and mindfulness?" While the answer to this question does not require that we eliminate electric pumps, it does mean that we learn from the hand pump.

What natural forces and what human wisdom can be made evident in the design of a civic place? Much of the history of construction and design is an exploration of gravity. Can the walls of a civic room recapitulate and introduce our young to this history? Is it possible for a courtyard to illustrate the water cycle, algebraic axioms, the lunar cycle, or the procession of the planets? What grows here and why?

Figure 9.1. *Proposal for the redesign of Fourth Street Mall, Albuquerque, New Mexico, by Devin Cannady and Rick Martinez, inspired by Albuquerque's International Hot Air Balloon Fiesta.*

Shedding Skins and Durable Frames
Will different parts of a design wear or be outdated at different rates?
Can we create component systems that allow more rapidly changing parts to be repaired or replaced without altering longer-lasting parts?

We expect civic rooms to endure through generations, and in some ways they often do. The plazas of Santa Fe, Taos, and other New Mexico towns are still central features of those towns nearly four hundred years after they were created. Likewise Jackson Square (Place d'Armes) in New Orleans has persisted through three centuries of floods and wars, and the courthouse square of Oxford, Mississippi, is nearly two hundred years old. Often, however, the persist-

ence of a civic room is more like the continuity of a river than that of a museum piece—while the general scheme remains, every component has been replaced and often altered over time.

The location of a plaza within the topography of the landscape is not often subject to change, although in western towns we have literally moved mountains, and many cities have moved shorelines. A plaza's relationship to institutions such as churches and town halls and to other civic places such as streets is often remarkably durable. However, a square's location within the morphology of a town changes as the town changes. Los Angeles' old plaza was once the center of town, and is now the center of a district in the metropolis. A civic room's relationship to aspects of a site (i.e., landscape, urban morphology) is highly durable but not immutable. Thus the greatest care and consideration should be expended on this most durable decision.

The framework of a civic room—its size, shape, and lines of enclosure—is the most stable aspect of the room itself. Santa Fe's plaza was transformed from a rectangle to a square during the Pueblo Indian occupation of the town but has held its shape and framework since. The surfaces such as the paving and building façades that flesh out the framework, however, change with more frequency. The town square of Jackson, Wyoming, was a place to park horses until the 1920s, when it was transformed into a town park. The façades facing Santa Fe plaza in the early 1900s were Victorian and were recast in Santa Fe style after New Mexico was admitted as a state (see Wilson 1997). Thus the structural systems of enclosing buildings and the foundational earthwork and drainage paths of the field should be more durable than the façades and surface pavements. Moreover, it should be possible to make changes in these skins without revising the underlying structure.

Monuments, attendant buildings such as kiosks, and furniture have unpredictable lifespans. In 1877 the swan boats first took passengers on the short ride through the pond in Boston's Public Garden. They have outlasted numerous buildings surrounding the garden. On the other hand, one of the first memorials in the United States, an equestrian statue of George III in New York City, had a lifespan of six years before revolutionaries destroyed it (Gilmartin 1995: 3).

It seems reasonable to guess that political icons will have shorter lives than elements that speak to more general aspects of the human condition, but the evidence is fragmentary and unclear. Given this uncertainty, a reasonable design approach may be to design these elements as props for a play on a permanent stage. The play may have a long run, but the stage is built to admit new casts and new stories.

These different rates of change allow a civic room to provide a sense of historic continuity and allow current inhabitants to add to the tradition. To be a living place rather than a preserved specimen, people must be able to imagine that they too can make their designs and leave their imprint on a place. Both the initial designers and subsequent redesigners of civic places should balance historic continuity with current and future uses.

Artisan Made
How can we structure the process of construction to strengthen the design?

Figure 9.2. *Roof slater in Edinburgh, Scotland, 1985.*

During the twentieth century in the United States we seem to have divided construction into three modes—contract labor, artistic production, or design/build. In the majority of cases, construction is labor that follows precise contractual instructions and standards documented in blueprints and specifications. When something is missing or there are contradictions in these instructions, an elaborate process of change orders ensues. In special cases, artists are hired who are empowered to construct and design a portion of the work (e.g., a tile floor). Often artists are allowed to refine their design during the process of construction. Sometimes, particularly on smaller projects such as houses, teams of designers and builders work together throughout the process.

Developing means to allow construction workers to act as craftspeople or artists who have a degree of design autonomy can benefit the design of a civic place in a number of ways. First, this approach allows decisions to be refined as the totality of the place emerges. Despite 3-D computer modeling and other visualization techniques, even seasoned designers often discover new aspects of a site and a design as the place is constructed. Rigid contract documents make it difficult to respond to this new knowledge. Second, it creates a set of local people with a strong sense of authorship who may act as stewards for the place; and third, more design attention is frequently given to the details if the craftspeople are allowed to express their skills.

This evidence of craftsmanship, of consideration in the details, conveys that thinking humans rather than machines built and cared about the place. Of course, if the craftspeople don't care or have poor skills, this is also embodied in the construction. Older building traditions were of necessity craft-intensive, and thus we tend to think of highly crafted places as reminiscent of, or perhaps even nostalgic for, historic building styles. However, artists have explored means to craft nearly every modern material available, and recent computer manufacturing techniques allow inexpensive production of "crafted" work.

Creating the organizational means to support craftsmanship is a complex question of economics, legal structure, professional conventions, and risk-taking. In his book *The*

Culture of Building, Howard Davis explores many of these issues (1999). The nature of construction becomes part of the character of the commons.

Local Craft and Local Stones
How can local materials and local knowledge benefit the design?

Every design project adds not only to the physical town but also to the local language of building. A project could, for example, require that the architects and builders learn the details and quirks of a new type of recycled material. Perhaps a historic craft is required and the project becomes a workshop to train a new generation of craftspeople, or the quantity of stone required is sufficient to reopen a local quarry. If most of the skills and materials for a project come from outside of a community then an opportunity to enhance the local language of building has been lost.

Why should we care about a local language of building? There are social effects, physical design effects, and cultural opportunities.

Social effects include the economic impact of providing local jobs. Governments' willingness to fund public works often stems as much from this immediate economic stimulus as from the creation of the built form. We in the United States owe the existence of numerous town parks and other civic places to the New Deal agencies such as the WPA (Works Progress Administration) that were created to provide jobs during the Depression.

The use of local trades can create a body of people who have an ongoing interest in the vitality of an urban commons. It is well known that if the local community is involved in painting a mural, then graffiti taggers tend to respect the mural. A similar respect and pride in participation may be nurtured in the construction of a civic place. Frequently, public art projects such as a tile mosaic composed of tiles decorated by local schoolchildren serve this role. However, the potential exists for all the participants, including the gravel truck driver, the architect, the tree planter, and the banker, to be local stewards.

Social effects on the culture of building are important

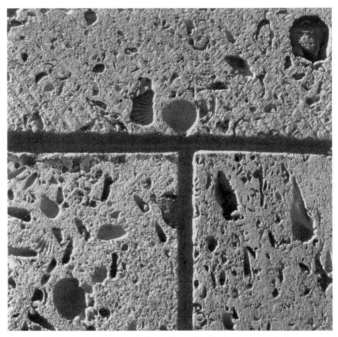

Figure 9.3. *Limestone with fossils, a building material native to Texas hill country.*

in their own right, but carefully considered they can also improve the physical design. If a civic place is built with local materials by local craftspeople, then future maintenance, replacement, and repairs may be easier than if the community needs to reimport the materials or skills.

If a material has been previously used locally, then there is a body of detailed knowledge about it. Knowledge of how a material weathers, if it leaches plant-killing substances, or how it shines in the fog can help refine a design.

Local languages of building are important because they provide a diversity of cultural approaches to building and creating our habitat. Just like ecological diversity or diversity in an investment portfolio, building-language diversity provides a more resilient system than would a uniform approach. For example, traditional building systems such as adobe, straw bale, and sod roofs have provided techniques and insight for the past few decades' work on environmentally responsible

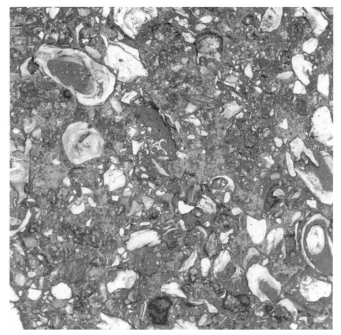

Figure 9.4. *Oyster-shell sidewalk in Savannah, Georgia. Similar sidewalks are found in many coastal communities.*

design. Perhaps as lumber becomes scarcer in the United States, masonry traditions will provide important information. Likewise, the fabrication skills held by Boeing aircraft workers in the Seattle region are an important economic and cultural asset that could be nurtured outside of the corporation.

Moreover, the use of local materials and skills embeds a design within a language of building. A regional-design character is rooted not only in architectural styles and building typologies but also in the local tradition of building materials and techniques. Like a regional dialect or language, a regional vocabulary of construction styles and skills can express identity and embody history.

Just as we think of a living language as one that adds new stories and even new words, a living language of building needs new projects and challenges. Modern adobe builders may build an ATM kiosk using twentieth-century machinery to form their bricks and twenty-first-century

chemistry to test their clay. Likewise, knowledge of the local environmental benefits and drawbacks of massive walls of adobe buildings may inform the design of concrete-block buildings, or inspire the development of new materials such as pumice-based concrete.

A design rooted in the local culture of building will, through its materials and craftwork, speak to the larger issues of regionalism, local identity, and ongoing tradition.

Storied Stones
Materials can have histories. How can these embodied stories inform a new design?

It takes a bit of work to quarry stones and bring them to a site. If a ruined stone building is nearby, these abandoned materials are frequently more efficient to use than new stone. As an added benefit, these old stones add an aura of antiquity and may link the new building to the history of the ruined building or its culture.

Reused building materials can be environmentally and economically efficient and culturally resonant. The forecourt of the Federal Building in Seattle, Washington, incorporates terra-cotta elements from the buildings that were torn down for the skyscraper. The floor of a square may incorporate the foundations or pavements of earlier structures. The archway of a building may be reused as a gateway to a courtyard.

The narrative associated with materials may be of something other than a previous building. As a symbol of their ties, Portland, Oregon, donated one of its Benson drinking fountains to its sister city Sapporo, Japan. Ballast stones from merchant ships have been used to pave the streets of many port cities. The vigas in San Esteban Church at Acoma Pueblo were cut on Mount Taylor, a sacred mountain to the north, and carried on shoulders the many miles to the mesa-top pueblo. The story makes vivid the effort and care expended to build this church.

Perhaps the main benefit of incorporating tiles imprinted with neighborhood children's hands or other culturally resonant material is the creation of stories that link people and the built place.

Scales of Context
What does "local" mean for design?

Normally we think of "local" as implying a small, immediate vicinity. A more nuanced view of the concept, however, may capture more territory. The first definition of "local" in the *Oxford English Dictionary* begins, "pertaining to or concerned with place." Based on this definition, if the designers are concerned with where material, labor, or ideas come from, then that aspect of the design is local. The opposite of "local" in this case is "generic" or "placeless."

But simply considering the sources of materials and traditions does not fulfill a concern with local design. The scale that "local" refers to depends on the issue at hand. Humankind is local to the solar system, and from this perspective local design can tap the material, historical, and intellectual resources of the planet (and occasionally beyond). The "local school," however, does not mean any school on the planet. How might we decide the scale of a design's context?

A number of social and environmental systems offer frameworks for considering the territory implied by a concern with place. The scales of governance, for example, provide one such framework. A federal courthouse is part of a nationwide set of buildings and should answer to this context. A city-police substation, however, does not have the same imperative. The catchment from which the majority of users come can provide another means to conceive of local. A neighborhood grade school thus will have a different context than an airport. The environmental footprint of a design can also provide a framework for thought. In what ways and to what extent does the design affect the various natural and human infrastructures? The watershed may be the local system for issues of potable water and wastewater, but the planet's atmosphere

is the local system for greenhouse gases. Likewise, the scales of economic systems provide a context. If the city is funding the project, then the use of city-based labor and materials will be of interest. The sloped tin roofs of northern New Mexico–style buildings reflect not only the superior weather protection of a sloped roof compared with a flat mud roof, but also mark the arrival of the railroad and the region's integration into a larger economy.

All of these frameworks provide a narrative that defines the context. For example, we can tell the story that the airport is a threshold between a town or region and a global web of airports, or that a parking lot is part of a watershed. Other stories such as those associated with history, nations, or cultures, of course, also provide a definition of local.

Scales and types of localness may be nested within and overlap each other. A city square, for example, may fluently perform roles as the center of a business district, a place built of the native granite, part of a watershed, and an outpost of the Mormon intermountain West.

Lying over these various narratives of place is the more difficult framework of reputation. Architects building a career, as well as clients and users, desire respect for a design. Typically, the larger the scope of recognition the better. The problem arises when this desire for a national or global reputation causes other scales of narrative engagement to be ignored, downplayed, or denigrated—one may be too busy trying to be hip to a New York audience to learn from and respond to the urban history of Pocatello. Tellingly, however, many great designers, like many poets and novelists, are known for the regional resonance of their work.

A concern with place is not a simple matter. Shaping the nature and extent of that concern is a critical part of the substance of architectural, landscape, and urban design.

part four

URBANITAS

CIVIC ROOMS

Half way between Pooh's house and Piglet's house was a Thoughtful Spot where they met sometimes when they had decided to go and see each other, and as it was warm and out of the wind they would sit down there for a little and wonder what they would do now that they had seen each other.

—*A. A. Milne,* The House at Pooh Corner, *128*

How do we create places between buildings that are strong figural chambers rather than leftover spaces? How can these rooms become the heart of the town, region, or nation? The grounds of Taos Pueblo are one conception of the center of the world; Times Square is another.

A. Gestalt

The early gestalt theorists of perception such as Wolfgang Köhler, Kurt Koffka, and Max Wertheimer observed that there are forms we perceive that are dependent on the whole structure of an image. The magic squares in fig. 10.1 provide a prime example. If you cover the enclosing forms you will not see the implied square.

This puzzling observation has lead to a long dialog of theories and experiments about the nature of human perception. Why do we see the magic square? Gestalt theory holds that we are looking for the best propositions about the whole set of things we see, and that we use principles of simplicity, regularity, and symmetry to define *best*. An alternate methodology, the inferential approach, suggests that we use prior experience to organize what we see.

For the purposes of this book, the more important point is that we do experience the implied form. "The essential thing of both room and square is the quality of enclosed space" (Sitte 1945 [1889]: 20). Our problem is: how do we create and give character to the magic square?

Magic Squares
What makes the space between buildings into a distinct figure?

In fig. 10.1, two-dimensional forms are implied by the agreement of the adjacent forms. They are shaped as if there were a central form. There are significant perceptual differences

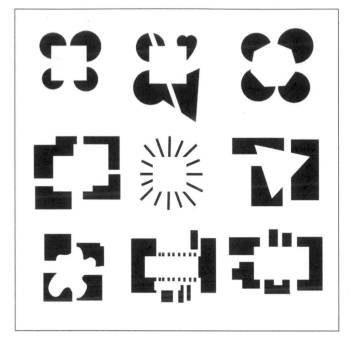

Figure 10.1. *"Magic Squares." Most observers see a bright figure of white that seems to sit above the background of white. The character of the surrounding black figures implies the existence of the white figure.*

Figure 10.2. *Most observers see white figures in the top two images, but not in the bottom two. Minor changes in the form of the corners are critical to the perception of the implied figure.*

between viewing a two-dimensional plan from above, and walking in and around a three-dimensional plaza. Yet the phenomenon of implied space seems to take place under both conditions. If the enclosing forms are shaped in the mutual agreement that a volume exists, then we sense the shape of the volume.

In *Visual Intelligence*, Donald D. Hoffman (1998) summarizes research on visual perception, and the reader is directed there for a discussion of the nuances of perception. The nature of corners is critical for the creation of figural civic rooms. The top objects in fig. 10.2 provide an example. On the top left the ends of the lines have sharp convex corners. When these corners are rounded as in the bottom left, the image of the central circle fades. The rounded corners focus on the line, while the sharp corners allow us to imag-

ine a larger circle with its focal point at the convergence point of the lines. Corners are places with large amounts of information about forms.

There is a long tradition of creating simple plans for courtyards and plazas. Many courtyards are purely a square of raked gravel or perhaps a stone path surrounding a lawn enclosed by four similar walls. The field of Boston's Post Office Square is an oval lawn. Portland, Oregon's park blocks are rectangles with a pathway down the center. This simplicity in the central field aids in the legibility of the implied figure of the chamber. The wall of building façades may depart from geometric regularity, the frame may have complex detail, a central fountain may erupt in sculptural exuberance, but the form holds. Even in dynamic and subtly complex places such as Michelangelo's Campidoglio an overall simplicity of geometric forms is at play. Perhaps the figural quality of a civic room is akin to rhyme and meter in poetry. The figure provides a coherent compositional infrastructure within and against which the play of nuance is visible.

Does the creation of perceptual figures matter in any way beyond visual composition (although this joy may be reward enough)? Oscar Newman, in his book *Defensible Space,* suggested that crime could be deterred by the creation of perceived territories: "There is a language of symbols which has come to be recognized as instrumental in defining boundaries or a claim to territory. . . . Some represent real barriers: U-shaped buildings, high walls and fences. . . . Others are symbolic barriers only: open gateways, light standards, a short run of steps, plantings, and changes in the texture of the walking surface. . . . These symbolic barriers are . . . found to be identified by residents as boundary lines in defining areas of comparative safety" (1972: 63). I suggest that we can extend the observation to say that people can associate a set of social practices with a perceived space as well as with a building. In other words, the territory of a front lawn or a town square may be as strongly a socially defined place as a church or a bar. However, if the place is not clearly perceived, then the social territory is not easily defined.

In addition to aiding the legibility of the implied figure and territory of a civic room, simplicity of character also aids in maintenance and in the adaptability of the space for multiple unanticipated uses. However, the place should not be dull. A Canadian study by Joardan and Neill (1978: 488) found a strong preference for "visual complexity" (including items such as fountains, trees, and flower beds; sculptures, nooks, and corners). Finding a balance between figural simplicity, supporting the syllabus, resonating with the landscape, and providing visual complexity is one of the overarching questions for the design of civic rooms.

Figure and Ground
How can we mediate between the figural qualities of a civic room and its surrounding buildings?

Like the Oscars' best-supporting-actor awards, perhaps the architectural community needs to create awards for "best supporting building." If it is paramount for a civic room to have a strong figural quality, then the enclosing buildings should not only face the room but work together to take a profile determined by the form of the room. In plan, the buildings will be the shape of the dough left between cookie cutters. These leftover shapes between forms are often referred to as *poché*. These fabric or background buildings frequently present significant and intriguing design problems, but they often do not get the press garnered by figural and monumental buildings. This potential lack of attention can be a problem for a client who desires an iconic building and for a designer building a career.

Historically, working with an irregular site determined by the shape of streets and squares was common. Even the self-important Parisian *hôtels* of the seventeenth century fulfilled their "duty" of making the street wall (Dennis, 1986). Buildings were often poché between the figures of courtyard and street or square. In late twentieth-century North America, we typically used parking lots and planting beds as the poché between figural buildings and figural roads. If we are to make well-enclosed squares, some of our buildings will again need to be the ground in which the figure of the plaza is set.

There are additional approaches to forming the figure of a square. A freestanding arcade or a screen wall of columns, trees, or kiosks and stands can form a coherent inner line of enclosure (see "Arcades" and "Onion Skins," chapter 11).

Implication and Elision
In order to create a strong sense of enclosure and to create the figure of a chamber, how much of the wall must exist?

Part of the dynamic tension of Michelangelo's Campidoglio in Rome is between opening to the view and holding the sense of enclosure. This room has no solid corners and is missing a wall (fig. 10.3). Yet it is coherent. The mirrored façades and inflection of the wings, the strong figural floor, the visual alignment of the arcades with the edge of the Palazzo del Senatore, the proportion of the height of the wings in relationship to the width of the open wall, and the balustrade with its skyline of statues are all critical to holding the sense of enclosure. If, as

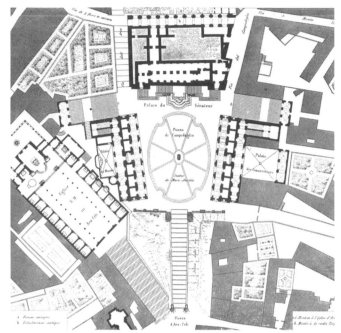

Figure 10.3. *Piazza di Campidoglio, Rome, Italy. Image from Werner Hegemann and Elbert Peets,* The American Vitruvius: An Architects' Handbook of Civic Art *(New York: The Architectural Book Publishing Company 1922), 26.*

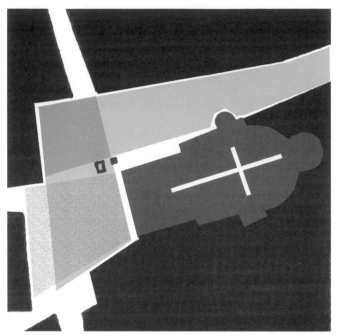

Padua

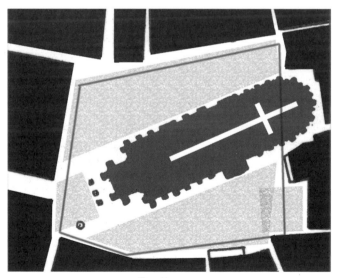

Freiburg

Figure 10.4. *Diagrams of two forms of spatial elision. In Padua the rooms overlap, in Freiburg an implied square is subdivided into smaller rooms. (Figures redrawn from Sitte 1945 [1889].)*

in this case, all the details work to make the enclosure, then a significant portion of the solid walls can be left out.

M.I.T. architecture professor Morris Smith propounded a rule of thumb about how much of a form was necessary to imply the rest: three-fifths. That is, if you build roughly 60 percent of a form, then the mind will recognize the complete figure. Corners have more figural power than other portions (Smith 1980–81). Thus four posts, particularly if they are detailed to make an inside corner, can imply a room.

Careful use of the three-fifths rule can allow us to design spaces that overlap and elide into each other (fig. 10.4). This allows us to suggest subspaces within a chamber that are both separate territories and part of the larger place. The *portales* around Santa Fe Plaza, for example, are both part of the plaza and distinct places. A subtler example is provided by the prototypical Elm Street. Each front lawn is separately owned and maintained, yet they elide into a single form. These overlapping forms allow people to redefine the appropriate uses of a place simply by seeing it differently. It is no wonder that children have a hard time staying out of a neighbor's front yard; sometimes it is just part of a larger playground.

Small, Medium, and Large
How big should a civic place be?

Jan Gehl has expressed the best rule of thumb for the appropriate size of a civic place, "Whenever in doubt, leave some space out" (Gehl 1996: 93). We are gregarious and, as William H. Whyte documented, we like to self-congest (Whyte 1980). "Everyone" at a party is in the kitchen not only because that is where the food is, but also because that is where other people are. On the other hand, civic rooms need to be large enough to allow civic interactions.

Edward Hall studied the distances at which people engage in various kinds of activities (Hall 1966). Based on his observations of the social meanings of proximity and how close together a space requires people to be, we can distinguish three sizes of civic places.

Coves
Neighbors or acquaintances place themselves between 4.5 to 12 feet apart for conversations. Thus very small front yards, narrow sidewalks, and small seating nooks (under about 4.5 feet) make it difficult for people who are not relatives to have comfortable conversations, and we can say that civic space (as opposed to private or intimate space) must allow people to be a minimum of about 5 feet apart. Two or more people in a space with dimensions that cause them to be within 12 feet of each other will be within each other's personal space and would have to work at ignoring each other. A drunk in a pedestrian tunnel narrower than about 18 feet can unintentionally dominate the passage because people cannot pass without entering the drunk's personal space. Civic coves thus need to be open, overviewed by passers-by, and easily exited.

Rooms
A "social" courtyard or square allows people to be far enough apart (about twenty-five to thirty feet) to easily practice civil inattention (see chapter 2), but is not so large that people cannot read facial expressions (a maximum of about one hundred feet). Kevin Lynch suggests that squares of this size have a "pleasant human scale" (1971: 194).

At distances of up to about 250 feet people can follow sports events or gestural performances. This gives the maximum distance from a dance stage or a playfield and suggests the limits of a civic room. Kevin Lynch observed that 450 feet is the maximum length of successful historic squares (1971: 194).

Grounds
Places that stretch significantly beyond a dimension of 450 feet are intended for large groups who are either a collection of independent parties or are mass audiences responding to the presence of the emperor, a rock star, or other central person. These large places are grounds. Moreover, the ability for a space to feel like a room dissipates with size. Depending on the height and coherence of the walls, the sense of volume disappears and the room becomes a park or other civic grounds.

These dimensions should be considered rough guidelines. The sense of enclosure is dependent on more than the minimum floor dimension. The height and character of the enclosing walls, the nature of the windows and doors overlooking the space, the manner in which the place opens into other spaces, the slope of the floor, the temperament of light in the space, and many other factors help shape the perceived size of a civic place.

A Place to Sit, A Place to Dance
Can we define compelling realms or territories of use within civic rooms?

The civic room can be thought of as the symbiosis of two milieus—the central field and the frame. Perhaps, this arises from deep in our history as forest-edge creatures (see Hildebrand 1999). Frame and field have different physical requirements and defining characteristics. The frame needs places to sit, lean, talk, and watch. Furniture, screen walls,

Room Size and Perceptual Distances

Room Type and Size	Notes	Reference
Intimate nook < 12 ft.	This scale covers Hall's "circle of involvement."	
Personal: < 2.5 ft.	People can easily touch each other.	Hall 1996: 119
Arm's length: 2.5–4 ft.	The viewer's 15° cone of clear vision covers the upper face of subject.	Hall 1966: 120
"Umbrella space": 4–7 ft.	Close social distance. Viewer's 1° cone of sharp vision covers one of the subject's eyes.	Hall 1966: 121
"Table distance": 7–12 ft.	Far social distance. The full figure of the subject is visible at a glance.	Hall 1996: 122
Neighborly courtyard: 12–40 ft.		
Public distance: 12–25 ft.	A person can take evasive action to move away from another. The viewer's 1° of sharp vision covers subject's entire face.	Hall 1966: 123
Town forum: 40–80 ft.		
40–80 ft.	"Pleasant human scale."	Lynch 1971: 194
65–80 ft.	Maximum distance to read facial expressions.	Lynch 1971: 194
Spectator square: 80–450 ft.		
230–330 ft.	Maximum distance to clearly follow events.	Gehl 1987
450 ft.	"Limit of successful historical enclosed squares."	Lynch 1971: 194
Civic Fields: > 450 ft.		
4000 ft.	Limit of detecting a person.	Lynch 1971: 194

Figure 10.5. *Room Size and Perceptual Distances.*

and the infrastructure of the place inhabit the frame. The field should be open and easily set and reset with props.

Frame

The frame is where we settle to watch the show, where we eat lunch, have a long conversation, read a book, or play chess. Alexander et al. suggest that the edge is the most critical component of a square: "The life of a public square forms naturally around its edge. If the edge fails, then the space never becomes lively" (1977: 600).

A study by Joardan and Neill of plazas in Vancouver, British Columbia, found that 99 percent of the six thousand people they observed carried out activities near physical artifacts and not in the open field (1978: 489). Jan Gehl also notes the edge effect: "the preferred stopping zones also are found along the borders of spaces or at the edges of spaces within the space" (1996: 151). Gehl notes the opportunities for refuge and prospect in edge places, and also reminds us to pay attention to the obvious. The edges of a plaza are the places closest to the indoor uses: "It is relatively easy to move a function out of the house to the zone along the façade. The most natural place to linger is the doorstep" (152). Likewise, outdoor restaurant seating will be most typically and easily near the door to the restaurant.

Good frames provide a variety of places to settle. People need places to sit alone or in groups. They need tables or ledges to eat lunch and play games. They need places to lean and hang out. They need a variety of microclimates—some places in sun, some in shade, and a number in between.

Creating a comfortable and attractive frame is critical to the success of the square, forecourt, or courtyard. First, the frame should be thick. There is no rule of proportion between frame and field, partially because in a good civic room the boundary is fluid and open to interpretation. The width of the two University of Virginia arcades together is about 10 percent of the width of the lawn. Alternatively, if we count the original buildings, gardens, and the second row of student dormitories as the frame, then the lawn is only 25 percent of the width of the entire composition. At times a square may be nearly all frame. For example, the field of café chairs may grow on a Saturday night from the edges all the way to a central fountain. The frame should have some permanent thickness that allows a variety of ways to hang about the place.

Within the frame there should be subspaces—civic coves with edges and fields. For example, two benches may face each other creating an alcove, a formal gateway may create an entrance hall, or food pavilions may enclose a field of lunch tables. One could conceive of this as a fractal pattern—each frame should contain frames and fields.

These alcoves allow people to temporarily claim a territory. Researchers have coined the term *refuge and prospect* to describe a place in which your back is protected and you have a view of what's coming. Studies suggest that subspaces that provide refuge and prospect are strongly preferred over open "unprotected" areas (see Hildebrand 1999; Kaplan et al. 1998).

Finding the appropriate balance between the isolating refuge qualities of these alcoves with the public open qualities of a square is a delicate act. One approach is to provide a variety of sizes of alcoves that also vary in their degree of removal from the central field and main paths. Creating a set of layers to the frame can help provide a variety of places and provide more territory for edge uses. A deeply layered edge provides opportunities for people to select their degree of exposure—sometimes we like front-row seats and sometimes the back of the theater is preferable. These layers may also provide various degrees of exposure to sunlight, allowing people to find their preferred microclimate. The ability to be hidden in shade while overlooking the sunlit field may also provide psychological comfort.

The elements that define the inner layers of a civic room should be subtle, perhaps suggested by paving patterns, to allow people to easily redefine the extent of the central field. The next layers may be a few steps or bollards that grow out of the pavement, then perhaps a screen wall, followed by a walkway or street, then an arcade, then the walls of the initial ring of buildings. Beyond the walls of the room, the streets that lead into a square may introduce the square's paving patterns or street furniture, a district sharing architectural character may cluster about a plaza, or a ring of parking garages could serve the district and suggest a village wall (see "Onion Skins," chapter 11).

Fields

Lively central fields are also critical for civic rooms. They may be game fields, as illustrated by ice skaters at Rockefeller Center and Frisbee players in a town park. The fields are also places for public dancing, parades, festivals, and holiday displays. Lovers' meetings and partings, toddlers' toddling, and conversations between the mayor and banker—the theater of the everyday—taking place in full public display embeds these actions in the life of the community. Political rallies and weddings take place on these fields because here is the heart of the public realm.

A well-designed field is supportive of its role as public stage. The edges should overlook the field as a theater's seats view its stage. Daylight and artificial light should give the field prominence, and perhaps actual stage lighting should be provided. Even if the field is dedicated to a particular use,

Figure 10.6. *Rollerblade rink in Battery Park City, New York City, 1999. The rink is the central field and is lined by concentric frames of benches, boats, and skyscrapers.*

and thus drain life from the edges. Approaches to designing for the uninhabited life of a plaza's field include (1) absorbing the field into the edge, (2) designing an imminent field that suggests that something is about to happen, and (3) adding elements such as fountains or whirligigs that have an active presence.

Movable chairs and tables provide one of the most common ways to transform a field into an edge. In the same way, pushcarts, display panels, or mobile artworks may be deployed. Approaches that are not dependent on people moving objects into the field include water fountains (with nozzles flush to the pavement) and nighttime laser shows.

Confetti littering the pavement evokes yesterday's parade even if a square is nearly deserted. An imminent field has physical features that call to mind its lively uses. The Mardi Gras gates in downtown Galveston, Texas, for example, speak to Mardi Gras year-round. Similarly, a stage suggests the possibility of and evokes the memories of plays and concerts. In addition to being imprinted with its uses, an imminent field may evoke a pregnant sense of time, season, or era. Stonehenge is alive with shadows and speculations.

such as an ice rink or swimming pool, it should be adaptable so that props and sets can recast its character.

The central field may not be intended for human occupation. For example, a duck pond, flower garden, or archaeological ruin may provide a compositional focus, a center of attention, and a sense of openness to a civic place.

It should be noted that the field of a civic room might predate the frame. Edges may be added to lively fields such as a rock-climbing cliff or a pond. Often civic rooms with their own frame and field can open out onto preexisting active landscapes such as a harbor, urban river, or ski run (see "The Fourth Wall," chapter 7). For example, the walkway along New York's Battery Park City overlooks the Hudson River.

Fields intended for human inhabitation must also be designed to be delightful when lightly used. When not fully occupied, overlarge or dull fields can feel bare and empty

Hard or Soft?

Is the civic room intended as an oasis from the city, a living room and community hall for the town, or a balance of both?

Urban oases such as a town park or rose garden tend to (1) have significant amounts of plantings, (2) be, at least in part, composed of organic forms, and (3) have subspaces scaled to small groups that are out of the flow of traffic. The center field is typically paved by a garden or lawn, and entrance points are heavily planted. To set the place apart from the street, walkway pavement may contrast in material and level from adjacent sidewalks. Crusher fines and other soil-like pavements may help evoke the sense of a garden, and materials and flora taken from the local countryside can help the oasis evoke a hike on the mountain or a day by the lake. These oasislike rooms are sometimes referred to as soft plazas.

Civic rooms that are more of a community gathering spot or community hall are typically signified and supported by paved, hard central fields, clearly defined geometric forms, and spaces that allow both small and large groups to interact. Surrounding sidewalks should lead seamlessly into the community hall so that people simply find themselves in the square in the course of their daily business. Both primary and secondary seating should be provided near to and facing pathways.

Hard rooms tend to support our gregariousness, and soft rooms our biophilia. These two types may exist in nearly pure forms, or they can be combined. A hard center may have an oasislike frame. Likewise, a garden may be framed by active walkways. An ensemble of chambers may provide both community halls and oases, or a single room may have both a hard and a soft center. The field of many of Savannah's squares, particularly in the residential wards, are occupied by garden beds, but framed by a net of streets and sidewalks.

With finesse, the typical characteristics of one type may be used to create the other type. New England greens are community halls with the pavements and flora of an oasis. The courtyard of the Boston Public Library is a hard-surfaced, geometrically composed refuge. It is the total composition in context that suggests whether the place is hard or soft.

B. Where?

A courtyard and its enveloping building can easily be seen as a single composition. Likewise, a square and a district are interdependent. Both types of urban rooms are symbiotic with the surrounding buildings.

The square is a living and vital place because of the institutions, stores, parking garages, subway stops, and houses that cluster around it. In response to a prospering urban commons, the surrounding district prospers. Thus designers of a square or courtyard should be aware that they are operating on one component, perhaps the keystone component, in a web of relationships. Just as heart disease can be caused by failures in other systems and can cause other organs to have problems, weaknesses in an urban commons may have complex causes and effects. What then should we consider about the relationships of these parts?

Catchments
Who are the potential inhabitants of a civic room? How do they arrive? Where are they coming from and where are they going?

A catchment is the area from which most users of the civic place arrive. With the proper modifiers this area can be measured. For example, one could define the 80-percent walking catchment as the area from which 80 percent of the people who visit a particular square walk to the square or the 95-percent residential catchment as the area that houses 95 percent of all people who visit a plaza more than once a week. Fig. 10.7 lists some rules of thumb for catchment radii.

Knowledge of the characteristics of a civic place's catchment can suggest (1) desired facilities in or near the place (e.g., places to buy and eat lunch; see chapter 4), and (2) formal characteristics. For example, college students may arrive by bus or subway on one side of a square and then diverge onto two or three routes. This morning divergence and afternoon convergence could give physical shape to the entrances, paths, fields, and frames of the square.

District
What is the structure and form of the district that a civic room serves? Where is the heart of the district?

If a catchment is an area of social influence, the district is the area of formal and compositional influence. District and walking catchments typically overlap but are not necessarily coincident (see fig. 3.3).

Civic rooms—courtyards, forecourts, and squares—should be central to the area they compose. For a square the area composed is a district. For a courtyard the area is the courtyard building, and forecourts compose the relationship between building and street. Thus the surround of a room depends on its type and raison d'être. Playgrounds should be the nucleus of neighborhood play, and the town square should be the heart of the life of the town. The arithmetical center of a district, however, is not necessarily the compositional hub.

In their pattern "Eccentric Nucleus," Alexander et al. (1977: 150–55) argue that the centers for neighborhoods should

Guideline Catchment Radii		
Catchment Type	Maximum Radius	Reference
Walking		
Daily errands (70% of Americans will walk)	500 ft.	Untermann 1984
Average length people will walk to a plaza	900 ft.	Lieberman 1984
"Comfortable walking distance"	2000 ft.	Calthorpe 1993: 56
75% of office-related trips in Manhattan	2000 ft.	Pushkarev and Zupan 1975
80% of all walking trips	3000 ft.	Pushkarev and Zupan 1975
Bicycle		
5-minute bike ride (2 minutes parking)	.75 miles	Federal Highway Administration 1978
10-minute bike ride (2 minutes parking)	2 miles	Federal Highway Administration 1978
Automobile		
5-minute suburban trip (3 minutes parking)	.5 miles	Federal Highway Administration 1978
10-minute urban trip (6 minutes parking)	~1.5 miles	Federal Highway Administration 1978

Figure 10.7. *Guideline Catchment Radii.*

be near the boundary of the neighborhood so that they may serve as meeting places between subcultures. The French colonial settlements in America embodied a similar pattern for the town center. The *place* was typically on the edge of the settlement at the waterfront. This was the natural meeting place and place of exchange between the town and the world.

Centrality for a square or a building's courtyard should thus be measured by the raison d'être of the civic room—as a place of gathering, of meeting. Where will people in the course of daily life naturally meet? For example, Louis Kahn created mini-meeting areas with blackboards in the halls of research centers to aid spontaneous discussions among scientists from different labs.

The pattern of previous design decisions and uses will suggest where an existing community believes its centers are. What is the hierarchy of streets? Where does the shopping district begin and end? Where is there an "anchor" building

that is a regular destination in and of itself, such as the county courthouse, the church, the high school, or the movie theater? Better yet, where is there a cluster of such anchors? Where do the informal trails lead? Where do teenagers hang out? Where do you see people having lunch despite the lack of pleasant facilities?

Sometimes it is not a matter of creating a center but of reinforcing it. Changes and additions to the infrastructure of a district should support the center. Bus stops should immediately serve the square, and traffic lanes should not overwhelm the pedestrian nature of a square. New parking garages for a symphony square district, for example, should be within a short walk (about nine hundred feet) of the square. The pedestrian entrances to the garage should be from the sidewalk, not from an internal link to the symphony hall. This requires people to walk through the district, past shops and restaurants. It also requires that there are good drop-off points near the symphony for those who have trouble walking and that the sidewalk between the symphony and the parking garage is pleasant. It may also be appropriate to make formal links between places. A commuter train station and plaza may echo formal characteristics of the central city plaza from which the train comes.

To reinforce a courtyard as a place of meeting within a building complex the supply of food should be in or accessed from the courtyard. The courtyard should also be part of the natural path from the entry but may be just off the flow. Its presence should be allowed to permeate the complex of buildings. For example, on a pleasant day the sound of a fountain in the courtyard might be heard in adjacent offices if they have operable windows. The ends of hallways could face the courtyard to provide both visual access and a sense of orientation.

To gather people, a square or courtyard should also gather the infrastructure and buildings, the streets and hallways, the public institutions and restaurants.

Streets in the Square
When and how should automobile streets be allowed in a square?

Vehicular traffic has historically been part of the life of squares and plazas. Wagon trains arriving from the United States on the Santa Fe Trail would, following custom, unload in Santa Fe plaza. The central square in Portsmouth, New Hampshire, is, like many New England squares, a crossroads. Portland, Oregon's new square, Pioneer Courthouse Square, is ringed by streets and serves as a terminal for light rail. Trolley stops and parking spaces bring people to an urban commons and in many cases may be essential for businesses. Trafficked streets provide passive and police surveillance. The parade of vehicles through a place can provide entertainment akin to watching people walk by. Yet modern traffic can easily overrun a pedestrian space, and places such as Quincy Market in Boston and campus quadrangles attest to the delight of (nearly) vehicular-free civic places.

Because the automobile has so severely eroded our cities, it is advisable to extend existing motor-vehicle-free city spaces wherever this is feasible. Places adjacent to institutions and residences may be separated more readily from auto traffic and parking than commercial spaces. A time-share schedule that gives the street to pedestrians during the summer, on weekends, on afternoons, or for regular events can help enlarge the pedestrian realm. Likewise, temporary and experimental street closures may provide a means to determine where and how a particular space may be permanently "liberated."

Nevertheless, the automobile cannot and should not be eliminated from all civic places. When a design calls for balancing traffic needs with the pedestrian nature of a civic place, streets should be designed to limit the car's intrusion and maximize their supporting characteristics. Limiting the number of edges occupied by auto streets, and their width and speed, can confine intrusions. Generous crosswalks should be provided and gracious sidewalks should line both sides of the streets. Stoplights and traffic-calming measures should be used to slow down traffic, provide a safer environment, and allow fleeting interactions between the parade of cars and people in the square. Pedestrians arrive from bus stops, trolley lines, taxi stands, and short-term parking spaces, and these places are the stages for the drama of arrivals and partings. Vehicles bring people who would not walk long distances to a square. Chapter 15 discusses various other means of sharing a space with automobiles.

Ensembles
What are the reasons to create a suite or ensemble of civic places?

The Pike Place Market District in Seattle is a suite of shared streets, pedestrian alleys, arcades, a grand stair, and a few courtyards. The Riverwalk in San Antonio, Texas, may be thought of as a pedestrian street strung through a set of overlapping rooms. These sets of rooms and paths create a larger civic place than a single socially scaled room could provide, and they provide a variety of different social settings such as promenades, oases, community living rooms, and quiet alcoves.

Camillo Sitte suggests that one of the principal delights offered by clusters of civic rooms is that they provide a variety

Figure 10.8.
"Neighborhood unit subdivision, looking from Market Square toward the commons and school" illustrates a composed ensemble of urban commons. From The American City, *March 1927, p. 291.*

of artistically different views, and that they allow a single monumental building to enliven multiple squares (1945 [1889]: 35–38). For example, Piazza di San Marco in Venice, Italy, is composed of two overlapping rooms providing a frontal and a side view of the Doges' palace (see fig. 3.2). The larger *piazza* provides an enclosed interior space where the cafés spill out onto the pavement, and the smaller *piazzetta* is a place of arrival open to the Grand Canal.

As in Piazza de San Marco, these rooms often overlap and flow into each other. Careful use of the three-fifths rule (see above) allows the rooms to retain their sense of identity while they blend into each other. This allows people to move from one space to the other without crossing a distinct territorial boundary and thus feeling that entry might be restricted. It also allows the collections of rooms to be perceived as a whole. At Pike Place the pieces are more distinct and one speaks of the hillclimb, Post Alley, or the park, yet we also refer to them as a single place.

Town Patterns
Can we shape districts and towns through the development of patterns of civic places?

The original town plan of Savannah, Georgia, featured a repeating pattern of wards centered on squares. In the first phases of the town's growth, this pattern was simply extended (see fig. 3.9). The existing set of squares knit together the historic town. From each square one can see to the next. The squares have taken on the character of their wards so that those in the more commercial areas have larger expanses of pavement and those in the residential wards are gardens or playgrounds. This variety in detail within the overall regularity of pattern gives both legibility and coherence to the town plan.

The history of town design, of course, offers many more examples of composing streets, squares, greenbelts, and other city spaces to provide a coherent framework that those designing new towns or subdivisions should study (for examples, see Arendt 1999; Hegemann and Peets 1988 [1922]; Kostof 1992; Reps 1965). Washington, D.C.'s French baroque *rond points* and boulevards, Olmstead's networks of greenbelts and parkways such as Boston's "Emerald Necklace," and the American campus-planning tradition all provide models. Subdivision and town designers need to compose the framework of civic spaces to give focus and coherence to a development and allow for future change and growth.

The problem of redesign, however, is frequently more one of *civitas* than *urbanitas*. It takes political will and organization to rebuild urban commons. In *New City Spaces,* Jan Gehl and Lars Gemzøe present case studies of mostly European cities that have systematic citywide public space plans (Gehl and Gemzøe 2001). Strasbourg, Germany, has used the introduction of a trolley line to redesign existing squares and streets and to add a string of new public places. Lyon, France,

balanced a program of renovating its historic squares in the city center with providing new civic places in the periphery. They developed a kit of parts of furniture and pavements for use throughout the city. This kit both eases maintenance and provides a sense of coherence. Gehl and Gemzøe note that underlying most of these extensive plans is a dedicated, visionary individual or group that developed a public space plan to address a set of interrelated issues such as traffic management, environmental responsibility, urban pride, and quality of life.

The set of squares, streets, urban frameworks, and other civic places are a significant component of the character and functioning of our towns. Moreover, these places are generally under the control of our collective will as expressed through our municipal government. A comprehensive city spaces and public works plan ought to be a vital component of municipal comprehensive plans.

WALLS, FLOORS, AND CEILINGS

The essential thing of both room and square is the quality of the enclosed space.

—*Camillo Sitte*, The Art of Building Cities, 20

O utdoor rooms, just like indoor rooms, have walls, floors, and ceilings. However, the architects of adjacent buildings often make the walls, traffic engineers and the forces of parking attempt to control the floor, and utility companies claim the sky. Square designers must recast these separate agendas as a congruent whole, to make well-enclosed space.

A. Walls

Walls provide enclosure. This sense of enclosure is critical to the character of the space and could be said to make the chamber. Take the enclosing buildings away from the lawn at the University of Virginia and one is left with an expanse of grass. It is the framework that gives this picture its power.

Active Walls

How can the walls of a civic room provide more than architectural enclosure? How do they support the active use of the commons?

As much as possible, and in a variety of ways, walls should be used and inhabited, and these uses should front on the square. This rule may be tempered a bit when a room or a subspace of a room is intended as an oasis or a membership commons. But even an oasis should not become an isolated back alley.

Window-shopping storefronts and sidewalk cafés, of course, are a prime means of activating the critically important ground floor. Providing a zone in which the stores may freely spill out into a square or plaza aids this symbiosis of the civic room and the commercial establishments. Double-loading this zone so that the sidewalk passes between the

Figure 11.1. *The traditional quilt pattern "Robbing Peter to Pay Paul" illustrates how two figural forms can interlock forming a complex edge zone.*

Figure 11.2. *Times Square, New York City, 1999. The full force of the advertising industry creates engaging billboards that help activate the walls of the square.*

storefront and the outdoor sales area increases the exposure of the business and the potential delight of the stroller. The traditional narrow and deep shop maximizes the number of shops that can face a square.

On a residential square, front porches large enough for a chair or three, small front gardens, and a sidewalk with places to sit and places to play are classic and effective means of enriching the ground floor. The residential streets of Charleston, South Carolina, provide a wonderful model of how individual residences may border a public street. The short sides of the houses and garden walls hold the edge of the sidewalk. The garden gates, front doors opening onto side porches, the upper levels of double- and triple-decked porches, and the side windows of the houses all provide glimpses into the private realms and give a sense that the sidewalk is overseen and cared for by the community.

Not all civic rooms can be continuously bordered by

cafés, shops, or homes. Some are walled by banks, movie theaters, supermarkets, private offices, and other uses that frequently have large sections of closed façades. Blank walls, parking lots, and other "unfriendly" or "empty" uses can break the relationship between active wall and civic room. Some buildings, such as movie theaters, may be dark boxes, which inherently have large parts of their perimeter that must be impermeable. The sidewalk edges of these buildings should be wrapped with open-edge uses. The wrapping may be independent stores, parts of the dark box that can be opened, or where these are not possible a thin wall of ATMs, display windows, drinking fountains, telephone booths, interactive public art, and other street furniture. The empty

Figure 11.3. *The portal along the plaza in Albuquerque, New Mexico (2000), is a traditional place for native artisans to sell their wares.*

boxes of parking lots or undeveloped lots may also be lined with a thin wall in a similar manner.

Many dark boxes have portions that can come to light, and designers should make an effort to unearth these possibilities. The lobby of a movie theater obviously can be opened to the street, and an interesting extension of this is to design the snack bar so that it both serves the lobby and has a window serving the sidewalk. Some grocery stores have given independent storefronts to their flower, coffee, and deli sections. Live theater houses can have their costume shops both serve the theater and provide rentals to the public through an independent storefront.

The upper floors can also support the life of a civic room. Windows provide the possibility of eyes on the commons. Picture windows of upper-floor fitness clubs and restaurants not only provide views of the commons, but views from the commons of the diners and bodybuilders.

Balconies and bay windows allow people to come out into the space of the commons and possibly interact with those below. In Spain, I have walked through small squares and streets filled with song from caged birds hung in the balconies of the surrounding homes. Even billboards on the upper walls can add life to the square (see fig. 11.2).

Arcades
Can the walkway that naturally lines an active wall become an architectural feature that helps unify the civic place?

The Law of the Indies required that the plaza mayor be lined with portales to provide a place for the "considerable convenience to the merchants who generally gather there" (Crouch, Garr, and Mundigo 1982: 14). The buildings behind the portales might vary in size, purpose, ownership, and detail, but these walkways gave the plaza a unity of composition and provided for the functions of the plaza. The covered boardwalks around Jackson, Wyoming's square also illustrate this principle. The buildings can even be absent. At Saint Peter's Square in Rome, Bernini used freestanding arcades to enclose the grand forecourt of the church (fig. 11.4). The Hopkins Oval at Johns Hopkins University also employs wings of arcades. The firm of McKim, Mead and White were masters of using the arcade, as can be seen in their Court of the Universe in San Francisco or their Burke Foundation Hospital in White Plains, New York.

The space within the arcades may feel to varying degrees like subspaces within the open room or as spaces that surround but are beyond the square. This sense of being "in" or "adjacent to" is created by the size and proportion of the openings, the depth of the arcade, whether the floor of the square continues into the arcade or is broken by steps or material changes, and to what degree the arcade protrudes from the line of façades.

The space of the arcade may functionally be related to the adjacent indoor rooms, to the square, or contain a set of its own activities. This may correspond to the architectural expression or it may not. For example, an arcade that seems to be part of a square may be owned and used by the storefront business to hold sidewalk sales. Likewise, plaza pushcarts

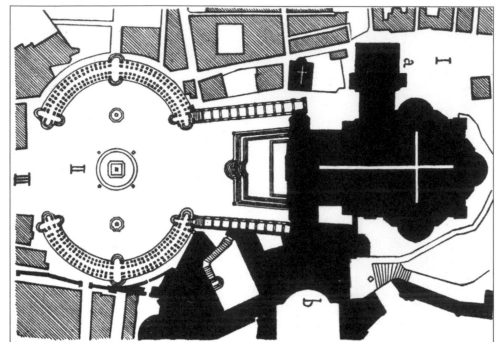

Figure 11.4.
The two arms of arcades compose Piazza San Pietro, Rome, Italy. From Werner Hegemann and Elbert Peets, The American Vitruvius: An Architects' Handbook of Civic Art *(New York: The Architectural Book Publishing Company 1922), 20.*

may have tables and chairs within an arcade that feels like an adjacent space. This mixing and blurring of indoors and outdoors is part of the role of the arcade.

There may also be vendors, vending machines, or other activities that live solely within the arcade. Vendors sell their wares under the shelter of the portales in Santa Fe and Albuquerque. Providing for the use of the arcade as more than a passageway, whether used by the storefront or independent vendors, requires adequate depth to the arcade, and suggests the provision of amenities such as seating places and electrical outlets. It also requires clarity of ownership, rights, and responsibilities. Otherwise storefront merchants may be in conflict with separate arcade merchants or street performers.

The enclosing walkway may take forms other than the arcade and help provide definition to an outdoor room. A line of bollards separates the implied street from the field of the campo in Sienna, Italy, and provides a subtle sense of unifying enclosure. The following pattern discusses other means to create a screen wall.

Onion Skins
Can multiple layers of enclosing walls be used to refine the sense of enclosure?

A line of columns wraps three sides of Pioneer Courthouse Square in Portland, Oregon (fig. 11.5). This screen wall establishes a more intimate proportion to the space than would be created just by the surrounding buildings. In addition, it allows the designers to compose an ordered wall for the space when they did not control the surrounding buildings, and makes the streets into layers bordering the core of the square. A line of trees, a picket of lampposts, a hedge of civic furniture, or other elements could create a similar screen wall (see "Furniture Habitats," chapter 13).

Building façades, arcades, or both can form the next layer of onionskin. Behind this initial layer of façades another layer may be established. Perhaps a square exists well enclosed by a set of historic buildings, and there is a desire to add skyscrapers to the district. Adding them to the façade line could

Figure 11.5. *Pioneer Courthouse Square, Portland, Oregon, c. 1997, designed by Will Martin. Note the free-standing line of columns that define an inner edge to the square.*

easily destroy the proportions of the room. However, it may be possible to create a new larger volume in which the civic room and its wall of buildings sit (fig. 11.6).

The degree of conformity of a layer speaks to the nature of the agreement that formed the commons. Perfectly matched sets of walls indicate that a single designer was at work. A variety of buildings that nevertheless are a coherent group suggest a coherent social dialog.

Thus we may conceive of an urban chamber's enclosure as a set of onionskins or perhaps Russian dolls sitting within each other. Each layer can provide different types and senses of enclosure. A uniform screen wall, for example, may be built to add order when chaos threatens. A line of independent vendors' booths may add variety and the possibility of growth when rigid conformity sets in.

Historic-preservation regulations have often led to the protection of portions of buildings. These remnant façades can be used as screen walls to preserve enclosure of the street and the space where the body of the building was. For example, in downtown Portland, Oregon, a building façade was left in place helping to enclose a parking lot that on weekends becomes an outdoor market square (fig. 11.7). Thus this

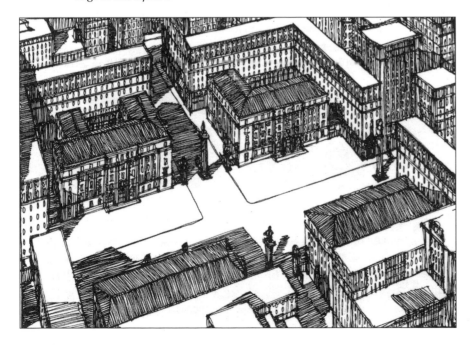

Figure 11.6.
This drawing by Franz Herding illustrates a civic center grouping with an inner ring of buildings nested within a second and third ring of structures. From Werner Hegemann and Elbert Peets, The American Vitruvius: An Architects' Handbook of Civic Art *(New York: The Architectural Book Publishing Company 1922), 149.*

Figure 11.7. *Skidmore Fountain square in Portland, Oregon, c. 1997. The arcade is the remnant of a former building, but now serves to provide an edge to the square and to contain the parking lot/market space on the building site.*

Urban Design: Ornament and Decoration (1995), proposed a typology of corners (see fig. 11.8). The "street corners" require careful attention to sightlines down the streets. What does one see? Does it tend to reinforce closure? Otherwise, we may perceive ourselves on a street rather than in a room. Tower and gated corners tend to emphasize the coherence of the room over the continuity of the street. Curved corners tend to require that the buildings shape themselves to create the form of the civic room: the square or courtyard is the figure cut from the ground of buildings. This figural quality emphasizes the primacy of the chamber. Angular corners strongly define an enclosure. There are, however, even in these most straightforward of corners, a multitude of possible relationships that may be expressed. Is the corner formed by a single building bending, two buildings intersecting, a building sitting within the embrace of another . . . ? An additional type of corner is the corner post (an object at a corner where the adjoining segments of wall are absent). Corner posts can be particularly useful for defining an inner center that elides into a space beyond the corner.

When a plaza or forecourt has multiple layers of enclosing walls, combinations of corner types provide for more nuanced corners. For example, a corner post can hold an inner line of enclosure that otherwise opens to a "non-corner." Likewise, an inner freestanding arcade can create a unified geometric field within a more fragmented set of building façades.

With a careful articulation of corners, an ensemble of squares, streets, and coves can overlap and elide (see fig. 10.4). In effect, people can be in two or more places at once and thus can redefine the place according to which room they choose to see as primary.

façade not only is a token of architectural history, but also is a beautiful screen that helps define two adjacent outdoor places. Despite our ample dedication of urban land to a poché of parking, we may be able to use arcades and screen walls to knit a new set of civic places.

Corners
How do the corners of a civic room affect the sense of enclosure?

If edges are critical to how we perceive a chamber, then corners are doubly so. Weak corners will diffuse and strong corners will reinforce the sense of enclosure.

Professors Moughtin, Oc, and Tiesdell, the authors of

B. Floors

"The floor plane, long neglected by designers, or sometimes timidly exploited, is an unexplored subject awaiting the artist to express the highest values of 20th century urban life" (Moughtin, Oc, and Tiesdell 1995: 97). The floor—its pattern, texture, and color; its pavements and plants; its seating ledges and game court; its steps, curbs, and slopes—can be

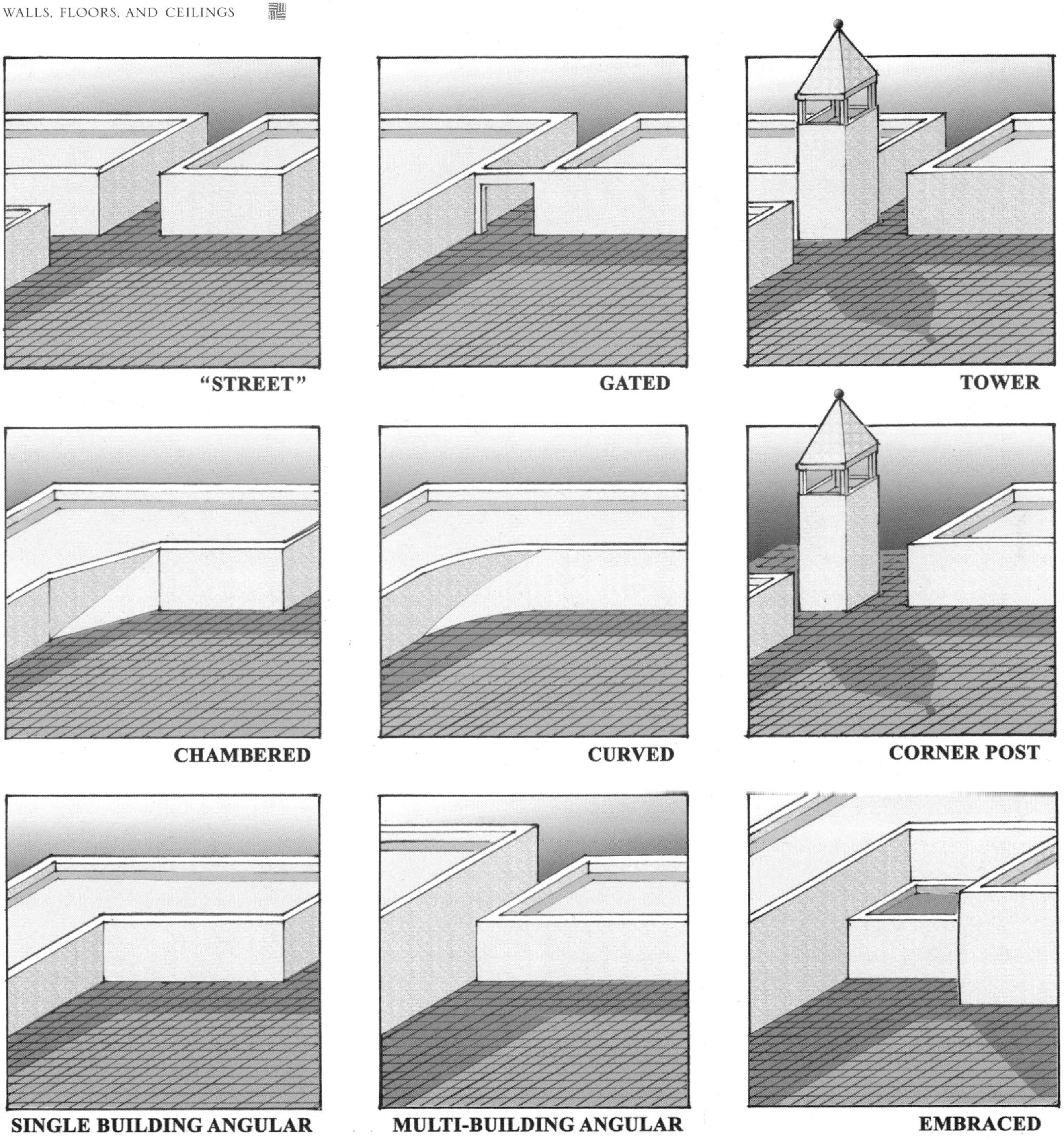

"STREET"   **GATED**   **TOWER**

CHAMBERED   **CURVED**   **CORNER POST**

SINGLE BUILDING ANGULAR   **MULTI-BUILDING ANGULAR**   **EMBRACED**

Figure 11.8. *Types of corners. Partially based on Cliff Moughtin, Taner Oc, and Steven Tiesdell,* Urban Design: Ornament and Decoration *(Oxford: Butterworth Architecture, 1995).*

Figure 11.9. *Patterned stone pavement in Penzance,*
United Kingdom.

Figure 11.10. *A labyrinth mowed into the lawn in*
Canterbury, United Kingdom, 2000.

the major component of a designer's palette. Walls may be essential to frame a chamber, but the floor is the place thus framed. If we replaced the lawn at the University of Virginia with a monolithic concrete pavement set with bronze statues, the place would have an entirely different meaning.

City Carpets
Can the floor itself be a work of art? What do our floors say?
What can they sing? What might they whisper?

The monotony of smooth black asphalt with white lines that dominates parking lots across the United States and much of the world could be seen as testifying to a hegemony of engineers serving a species of wheeled citizens. Michelangelo's pavement design at the Campidoglio in Rome speaks of another kind of power. The maze mown into a lawn in Canterbury whispers of the past and invites play. The simple carpet of lawn

and leaves framed by the brick-paved colonnades of the University of Virginia also provides an elegant floor. Pavements, both hard and soft, can provide basic utility such as a good walking surface and can be beautiful, comfortable, inspiring compositions. Pavements are expressions of our construction of the earth. We prepare the ground and pave the way for activities, draw lines in the sand to mark territory, and inhabit stomping grounds.

A basic utility of pavement is to provide good traffic surfaces. The best surface depends on the type of traffic. Thus, the pavement of the sidewalk often differs from that for the automobile lanes. Pavement may also function to separate a main path from a side route, indicate ownership, provide drainage, and aid navigation. Used well, it can be a critical component in the legibility of a place.

As the examination of a modern highway will show, the pattern of pavement is often critical as a traffic control and wayfinding device. Beyond the highway, pavement may show the pathway across an expanse, textured pavement may be used to warn the blind about hazards, patterns and materials may indicate parking stalls, places for vendors, or the stage area for a street performer or other territories.

Pavements can also aid in the more abstract wayfinding often called a sense of place. The oyster-shell sidewalks of southern seaports, the granite curbs of New England, and even the WPA stamp in concrete sidewalks throughout the West evoke a sense of place. Pavements can incorporate traces of earlier inhabitation such as building footprints or old roadways. Likewise, landscapes can echo native vegetation or a historic palette. These design gestures refer to and help define the uniqueness of the place.

Pavement is not simply two-dimensional. The floor of our towns is created of curved and bent planes. Crowns, valleys, and slopes direct water, catch sunlight, create pathways, direct our view. Our pavements can also be terraced. These layers can separate territories as the sidewalk separates pedestrians from vehicles. Pavement terraces may mimic geological or archaeological strata and suggest depths of time. Moreover, cracks, joints, gratings, holes, and translucent pavement may speak of tunnels, caverns, cisterns, basements, and other places of the underworld.

Some pavements can be used as a canvas for temporary works. Throughout Europe street artists create chalk drawings on the streets and plazas. Every summer in Santa Barbara, California, the *I Madonnari* Italian Street Painting Festival transforms a parking lot into a large canvas for teams of artists. Pike Place Market in Seattle has held similar events.

Finally, pavement can provide architectural delight. As city carpets, patterns in the pavement can help the eye read width and depth, suggest edges and subspaces, and, as every child knows, evoke games. Pavement texture can assist in defining paths and creating patterns of light and shadow. Perhaps the art and craft of quilting could inform the craft of laying asphalt and concrete. Pavement can unify and shape space and give scale, proportion, and measure. Part of the ugliness of the typical parking lot is its inarticulate expanse of asphalt. Like a mandala, the pattern of a pavement can engage the mind in pattern and play and evoke symbolic analogies. A floor can provide a memorable image and identity, serving as the icon for the place.

City Level
Outdoor floors are not flat. What potential for meaning and utility is there in a floor's slopes and levels?

Separated only by a six-inch level change and a few feet from where they could easily be killed, people will comfortably stand and chat. Sidewalk curbs may be one of the most powerful definers of territory and behavior in the modern city. They generally keep automobiles from invading pedestrian realms, provide clarity to vehicular routes, increase the relative height and hence the visibility of pedestrians, and can ease access to buses. In addition to the sidewalk curb, other layers, ramps, valleys, rises, berms, and knolls may help define and enrich the floor.

Above the street and sidewalk strata, we typically define a seating level (twelve to eighteen inches above grade), a table level (about twenty-nine to thirty inches above grade), and a leaning level (around forty inches above grade with a footrest at six inches). Forecourts can be successfully raised a few steps above sidewalk level. These few steps can give the chamber importance (it is literally set on a pedestal) and allow people sitting in a forecourt to be near eye level with those walking by. Depending on local conditions, a designer may wish to establish other levels. Perhaps the floor of a church or other institution could be extended to create a porch level overlooking a street level. Maybe actual geological or archaeological strata of the site or vicinity could help define levels. Perhaps the brick floor of a previous building could define the main level of the field, and a level of new pavement could sit two steps up and create the frame. These various floor layers can be composed and nested within each other in a manner similar to that described above for walls in "Onion Skins."

Slopes, knolls, berms, crowns, and other folds of a floor plane can allow for drainage and give character to a chamber. The central lawn in Boston's Post Office Square is not only raised up a step from the level of the walk, but rises slightly to the middle. These details allow for good drainage and ease of lawn trimming but, more importantly, separate the encircling path from the central lawn. People walk on the lawn when they go to sit, but typically do not casually cut across it. The enclosure of the International Fountain at

Seattle's old World's Fair Grounds is entirely created by the bowl in which the fountain sits.

Steps between levels create the condition where people like to hang out—the edge. Thus steps can provide good seating and a prime place for people to meet. Civic places can be created almost entirely out of steps, as Rome's Spanish Steps and many similar places attest.

For all level changes, design for universal access must be considered. Stairs should be designed with the frail in mind, and alternate routes for wheelchairs should be seamless parts of the design. Access to play in water fountains should not be overlooked. A one-in-twenty slope into a pool or fountain can allow wheelchair users and toddlers gentle entrée.

Texture
How can the texture of the floor enrich the design of a civic place?

God (or, depending on your attitude, the devil) is in the details. The texture of the floor can be critically important. Pavement must be firm, even, and sufficiently slip- and skid-resistant. Polished marble can be a hazard when wet. Textured pavements can help with both traction and drainage. A carefully designed system of textures can be an aid to navigation for the blind and the sighted. Warning strips, like rumble strips along a highway, can line a path and be placed before crosswalks or other hazards. The keys to success, as with any signage system, are legibility and consistency.

Subtle differences in material, pattern, and texture of the pavement will not divert, but may bend, most people's walking paths. People will generally go in the most direct route possible, but they may be induced to take a very gentle arc rather than a direct beeline. On the other hand, many people will avoid areas with very rough surfaces such as cobbles and large, loose gravel. As these surfaces are not handicapped-accessible and can be tripping hazards, they should only be used to designate areas people are not supposed to inhabit.

Textured pavement can also be used to capture and pattern light. By giving the same care to pattern and texture as a good swimsuit designer uses, a square designer can subtly shape space by this patterning of light. Paths can be given

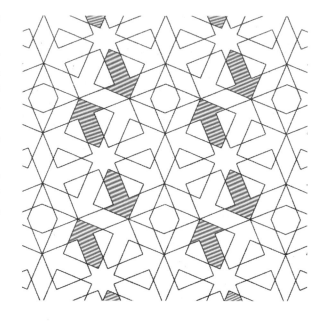

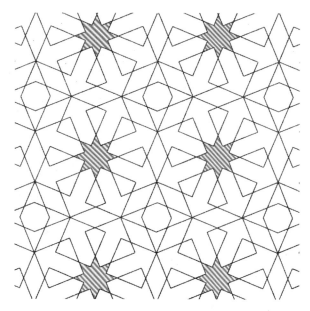

Figure 11.11. *Light casting shadows on ridged tiles can alter the perception of the pavement pattern. Both images have the same tiling pattern. The top image has light coming from the bottom right and the bottom image has light cast from the bottom left (90-degree separation).*

linearity and rooms a centralizing texture. Light-catching textured pavement will make curves in a path more legible than if the pavement is smooth. The angle of the sun, and thus the time of day, will be highlighted by a textured floor. A geometric paving pattern that allows multiple readings can be given different highlights at different times of day by the appropriate use of texture (fig. 11.11). The play of texture and light can be elaborated if the pavement has light-reflecting elements. Recycled glass, mica, or quartz could be added, for example, to the field of a plaza to make it sparkle in contrast to the surrounding frame. This play, in all likelihood, should remain subtle, and glare should be avoided.

Gameboard
Games often require specific boards.
What games will the field support?

One of the delights of an urban commons is playing in or watching the games. Sometimes this is the raison d'être for the place. During the summer, Portland, Oregon's Lovejoy Fountain is a place of water play. During the winter, the ice rink *is* Rockefeller Center and, of course, stadiums and sport courts of all kinds are dedicated to games. Historically, central squares have housed important community games. During the seventeenth century, Spanish bullfights were frequently held in the plaza mayor. Jousting tournaments, whose participants often included a king, were held in Italian piazzas and French *places* (Kostof 1992: 157–59). The swept area of Creek towns featured a manicured ground and a central goalpost used for at least two types of games.

Even in civic places that are not functionally or symbolically dedicated to a game, the public game can be a critical component. The everlasting chess games played just off Harvard Square, the card games played in New York's Washington Square, and pick-up games of Hacky-Sac across the country add life and character to the commons.

The *Oxford American Dictionary* defines "game" as "a form of play or sport, especially one with rules." These rules may be explicit and essential, such as those for Rollerblade hockey or bocce. They may be minimal, such as "keep the Hacky-Sac off the ground without using your hands." The rules may be implicit and subject to negotiation and imagination, such as those at a dance or in a sandbox.

There are specific requirements for the court or game board for each game. Life-size and tabletop chessboards, tennis courts, and the like have well-defined requirements. Games such as Frisbee and Hacky-Sac simply require an open, relatively smooth-surfaced space, preferably in a place where people can admire the players. Even the more negotiable games have specific needs. Sandboxes require sand in a contained area, space for the number of children expected, a surround of seating for parents, preferably loose parts for digging and fort building, and a supply of water.

The requirements for dances and other social games can vary from almost nothing but a floor to very complex affairs. Designers should divide the task of supporting these events into two realms—the infrastructure and the props. The props will depend on the current form of the game and should be developed by the current players. The designer of the civic room should provide the infrastructure such as the dance floor, the grand entrance, backdoors, places for quiet walks, refreshment areas, places that can serve as a stage, and sitting areas.

Deciding what games to support will be an interaction of the community syllabus (see chapter 4), the budget, and the available space. An artist or other designer may suggest a design that supports a game the community is not familiar with. This may require developing events along with the physical design to introduce the game. For example, a community may not have a critical mass of Go players to support the active use of a life-size Go board. However, if the construction of the board also includes a sustained effort to develop Go clubs in the local schools or senior centers, it may take root.

After the initial design is built, users may very well develop or bring their own new games. The designers and managers of civic places should not only anticipate this by leaving spaces open to interpretation but should consider encouraging play. Pavement patterns, movable props (e.g., a set of traffic cones labeled "PLAY!"), and complex but ambiguous artworks and structures can invite games. I'm waiting for an opportunity to fill a plaza with a variety of traditional and novel life-size game pieces, and watch as people move them about and invent games.

C. Ceilings

Civic rooms are open to the sky, yet they have ceilings. There is a sense of enclosure, a height that defines the space. "The subjective impression of a definite height of the sky is caused by the interplay of the height of the surrounding buildings and of the expansion (width and length) of the floor. It is strongly influenced by the contours of eaves and gables, chimneys and towers" (Zucker 1959: 7). Lighting, tree canopies, overhead wires, and trellises can also help define this enclosure. Like a physical ceiling in an indoor room, the height of the ceiling in relationship to the width and length of the chamber is critical. If it is too high people can feel dwarfed and oppressed. If the ceiling is too low in a chamber the space can feel undefined or too large. The shape, height, and character of the ceiling can help define the sky. Is the sun oppressive, requiring a filter of leaves to make life comfortable? Should the sky be clearly framed so that we see it as an artwork? Should the walls be painted sky blue to merge with the sky? Should we cast light boldly into the atmosphere, claiming space, or minimize lights so that the stars shine in?

Cornice and Silhouette
How can the walls imply the ceiling?

The implied sense of a ceiling can be created by the coherence of the enclosing walls; this is similar to the way the framing lines create the "magic square" of fig. 10.1. The implied form must consistently shape and be shaped by the surrounding forms.

A coherent cornice line is the single most important element in creating a strong implied ceiling. The cornice for these purposes is the place where viewers from the square or courtyard see the building end and the sky or remote buildings begin. There may be floors above this level as long as they are not visible from the ground. The cornice lines of various buildings need not be exactly aligned, but they must be in general agreement. A rule of thumb is that from the ground they should not be more than 1 degree apart (the angle of sharp vision). The traditional cornice has two

features that aid the framing of the sky: (1) a strong horizontal band that stops the flow of one's gaze into the sky, and (2) a projecting ledge that turns the eye from the rise of the building to the implied plane of the ceiling.

Just as a forest may have upper- and under-story canopies, a square or courtyard may have multiple levels of ceiling. A coherent line marking the height of the ground floor can reinforce the unity of the chamber and imply an "under ceiling" near the buildings. Likewise, a set of lampposts, flagpoles, trees, or other objects may suggest a secondary ceiling.

Spires, TV dishes, statues, and other forms that rise from the cornice line frame the field of the ceiling. A picket of white parapet posts could highlight blue skies but fade away against clouds. Celestial events, such as sunrise on the architect's birthday, can be marked both by silhouettes at the cornice line and by their shadows on the floor. A set of satellite dishes or telephone towers rising from a façade could cast a certain light on our relationship with the sky. An array of photocells would suggest a different conception of the sky.

Canopy
Without sealing off the sky, how can we filter and frame it?

In Seattle it rains. Snow and slush can dampen outdoor life in the North, and unmerciful sun can make unshaded skies unpleasant in the Southwest. At times we wish to filter the sky—for example, letting in the breezes but providing shade, or sheltering us from getting wet while we listen to and smell the rain.

Arcades, awnings, and balconies can provide shelter and a variety of microclimates along the frame of a square or courtyard. Instead of abandoning a chamber because of a brief shower, people may shelter in these edge spaces and then return to the larger space. During off-seasons, arcades, dining balconies, and such may harbor a critical mass of people and activity to keep the civic place an integral part of the town's life. Thus they should be sized for these seasons and designed with fields and edges to accommodate events.

We may also wish to filter the sky above the central field and the inner layers of the frame. Trees provide the most

Figure 11.12.
*The canopy
of trees gives
a ceiling to
this London
square, 2000.*

typical canopy. In southern Spain, vast sheets of linen held aloft on poles provide shade. In the central squares of the Dordogne region of France, open-air pavilions shelter markets and other activities. Trellises, ramadas, and small forests of umbrellas can also serve.

In poor weather, central gazebos and small pavilions offer a profound experience. One can sit relatively protected but surrounded by a snowstorm. One can feel both isolated in the midst of an unoccupied field and in the center of things framed by busy sidewalks and shops. Canopies can provide both physical and psychological shelter.

If we design a moon base, the ceiling of the commons will be an interesting challenge. The technical challenges of providing shielding would be just one component. Should the heavens be visible, giving a sense of openness, of living in the cosmos? How can a sense of scale, a way of relating the size of a single human to the size of the heav-

ens be established? How can a sense of enclosure be balanced with openness?

Under our bubble of atmosphere we face similar questions. How should we frame the heavens?

Light
Can we shape light to create a ceiling?

At night, strings of bulbs could weave a ceiling over a dance floor or café. Stadium lights create a volume of light. Columns of searchlights can stake a claim to an infinite sky. Floodlit façades can emphasize the edge and wrap of a chamber. Lines of lights can reinforce cornice lines. The color, intensity, and height of lamps in a square could contrast with those of adjacent streets, marking it as a special zone. A dance of lasers could sketch a ceiling, or minimal

Figure 11.13. *Tom Quad at Christ Church College, United*
Kingdom, 2002, showing afternoon light
illuminating the upper floors and spires.
Compare to fig. 7.3.

light could be used, and the field of stars framed by the cornice line could be the ceiling.

During the morning and evenings, horizontal sunlight
can be let in by streets and other openings to reflect off façades
and fill a courtyard or plaza. Patterns of shade and shadow or
reflective and absorptive materials on the floor and façades
can shape how this light is captured. For example, a white and
smooth cornice line above a darker façade may capture first
light in a way that holds it floating above a square.

Open Doors

Unscrew the locks from the doors!
Unscrew the doors themselves from their jambs!

—*Walt Whitman,* Song of Myself

Good squares are visually, socially, psychologically, and physically accessible. To be attractive, they must also provide a public resource. The resource may be access to other people (a place to meet your friends and perhaps someone new), a commanding view of the town and countryside, a place to play a particular game, a public market, the touchstones of history, a train station, or some conceptual doorway to another place or perspective. In a membership commons, the members share the resource; in a square, it is accessible to all citizens.

A. Physical Doorways

One of the physical distinctions we frequently make between a square and more exclusive chambers is in the elaboration of the doorway from street to room. Membership commons are frequently entered through lockable gates or doors; the doorways of public commons are typically only implied by passage through the plane of the enclosing wall. Forecourts and other privately provided spaces open to the general public fall somewhere in between.

Boston's Louisburg Square illustrates the use of different doorways to differentiate the membership nature of the inner green from the public nature of the framing streets. To enter the square, one must merely walk along a public sidewalk and pass into the space. To enter the green, one must have a key to open the chest-high gate.

Fuzzy Threshold
Is it possible to dissolve the sense of threshold to allow people to discover that they have already entered a room?

"The area where the street and plaza or open space meet is a key to success or failure. Ideally, the transition should be such that it's hard to tell where one ends and the other begins" (Whyte 1980: 57). A seamless edge eliminates the need to decide to cross the threshold and it reduces any sense of exclusion. Thus more people enter the civic place. How is such a transition created?

Public streets may overlap and elide into a square. As in many classic English market towns, the street may simply turn a corner and widen to blend into the market square so that path seamlessly becomes room. The key is that the street does not end at the edge of the square but legibly continues into and perhaps across the square.

Details are critical in creating this elision and interpenetration of spaces. Stairs break our stride and form boundaries and thresholds. Thus they should generally not be placed at the initial interface between two overlapping forms. Pavement patterns, on the other hand, can be subtle. The pavement pattern of a street and a square can be mixed as they overlap, allowing people to see either. A picket of bollards or other implied wall can both make an edge for one form and allow another form to be read through it. The Campo in Sienna, Italy, has such a detail. Walking along the implied street the bollards are seen as a curving line forming an edge to the street. From the field of the Campo, the bollards are seen against the enclosing façades and create only a minor edge.

The town square of Portsmouth, New Hampshire, presents another means of minimizing the sense of threshold. It is a knot of intersecting streets. The form of the square is created by the complex intersecting geometries, but entering from the major streets one reads the form of the street continuing through. These non-doors eliminate the need to decide to enter and thus are generally more open to the public. They also eliminate the setting for the grand entrance, and make it more difficult to read the room as an oasis or world apart. Overlapping spaces requires that the figural quality of each is partially eroded and implied. Carried too far, a civic room may lose its form and become a confusing wide spot in the road.

Porta Triumphalis
When should we create the full sense of a door into a civic room?

As discussed in the pattern above, we often wish to eliminate the sense of threshold into a square. We don't want to have people stop and decide to enter; we want them simply to

Figure 12.1. *Mardi Gras gate in Galveston, Texas, by Cesar Pelli, 1992.*

enter. We also want to eliminate any sense of exclusion. However, we may wish to have one doorway into a plaza or other civic room for celebrations. Moreover, we may wish to create a threshold and sense of exclusion for a forecourt or courtyard.

The *Porta Triumphalis* that marked the entry of a triumphal parade into the city of Rome and the *fornix* (triumphal arch) erected along the parade route to honor a victorious general provide one historic precedent for the celebratory gateway (see Favro 1994). This tradition was elaborated throughout Europe with the creation of both permanent arches such as the *Arc de Triomphe* in Paris and temporary arches such as the one Napoleon commissioned in celebration of his marriage to Josephine.

This tradition continues in North America. There is a ceremonial arch in New York's Washington Square. The borders of San Francisco's Chinatown are marked with elaborate gateways, and in Galveston, Texas, a set of decorative arches were commissioned to celebrate Mardi Gras (fig. 12.1). New Mexicans promoted statehood with parades and temporary archways, and downtown Reno has long had a welcoming arch.

We may also wish to create a gateway to aid the sense of enclosure when a street or passageway enters at a compositionally difficult point on the wall. This may be particularly true for a street that leads to a quiet residential neighborhood, a service alley, or other less public area. The gate may help keep the public in the square from wandering onto a quiet residential street.

To create an appropriate doorway, we should consider all the elements of a door—the threshold, jambs, head, and door—and use those that are needed. Actual doors are necessary to secure a doorway but are rarely used in celebratory gateways. It is also not always necessary to have an arch or lintel for a doorway. Freestanding columns, such as those facing the water at San Marco, may form an entrance. Conversely, a sky bridge or strings of lights may span from building to building forming a doorway beneath without articulated jambs. The articulation of the threshold to an urban chamber should depend on how thoroughly the doorway should be a place of its own. If the gateway also serves as a proscenium arch for a stage, then the threshold must extend out and create the floor of the stage.

Mystery
How may a doorway entice one to go through and beyond it?

Just at the edge of sight around the bend of the street, a great shaft of light floods out of a place barely seen but marked by a tower. The researchers Rachel and Martin Kaplan call the character of a scene like this "mystery." Through their research on visual preferences they have found that "[t]he desire to explore a place is greatly enhanced if there is some promise that one can find out more as one keeps going" (Kaplan et al. 1998: 16).

Differences in light between two sides of a gateway can produce an enticing sense of mystery. A gateway at the end of a narrow street that opens to a well-lit plaza will frame a view of the plaza that glows in contrast to the street. From the plaza, the gateway will offer a dim, cool, and enclosed alternative.

The material and character of the gateway can also suggest an enticing world beyond its threshold. At the end of a street of plain concrete buildings, a Chinese-red gate festooned with dragons promises entry into a different world. Of course, if the world on the other side is mundane, the gate will lose power.

Restricting the view into a square can also aid in the sense of mystery and drama. Thus a doorway that narrows the view from a street, or a curved street that gradually reveals what is around the bend, can pull people into a square.

Whether composing the curve of a street, a physical gateway, or a landmark, hinting at the value of the place thus marked is a critical part of the design brief.

Threshold
When called for, how can we design a strong sense of threshold?

A great gate can have characteristics of a civic room, a street, or both. Like a square, it has a floor, walls, ceiling, a field and frame, and often furniture.

The articulation of the floor can be critical in suggesting whether the gate is intended as more a marker of a border or as a porch along the square. Pavement that runs uninterrupted through the gate suggests that travelers should keep moving. Steps, a carpet of pavement associated with the doorway, or a screen of bollards suggests that the gate is a stopping place.

The walls and ceiling also participate in the articulation of the gateway. A thick wall can hold a cove within it and thus allow people to dwell between the two sides. A thin wall does not invite one to linger between places. In either case, the portions of the gate that frame the actual opening provide at least a small area out of the flow of the pathway. This zone may be enlarged and elaborated by pavement and furniture.

In addition to a cove within the thickness of a wall, a gateway can create coves on both sides. The walls of the gate can reach out and enclose coves. A carpet of pavement can spill out into the square and create a stage for both the drama of everyday arrivals and formal theater. Likewise the pavement may suggest a cove on the street side of a gate. This cove may serve as an antechamber. It may be a rendezvous point for people coming or leaving the square, a green room for theatrical performances, or a place for vendors when there is a large event in the square. Gateways can be elaborated into an entire plaza. For example, *Cincinnati Gateway,* by Andrew Leicester, serves as an entrance to a waterfront park called Bicentennial Commons. This gateway marked by pigs with wings on one-hundred-foot-tall columns is elaborated with wading pools, earth mounds, a bridge, walls, and multiple allusions to various aspects of Cincinnati's history. The gateway covers nearly 1.5 acres and creates an ensemble of civic places.

The relationship between the field of the square and the gateway also influences its role. To serve as a stage for the civic room, a gateway must enter directly onto the field, not into the back of the frame.

Building Entrances
How should the doors between enclosing buildings and a civic place frame their relationship?

The main doors of surrounding buildings should open onto a square. The pedestrian entrances of freestanding parking garages should also enter onto squares and separate tunnels or sky bridges should not be created to bypass a square. The surrounding buildings create the square formally, but they also supply people and activity. If people are directed away from the square, it loses vitality.

Different types of buildings along a plaza have different types of doorways. Most shops should attempt to minimize the sense of threshold. Ideally, shoppers don't have to make a decision to visit the store but, rather, find it easy to wander in. When a closed door is necessary, it should help people transition from the pace of the plaza to the slower pace of a store. Paco Underhill, the anthropologist of shopping, has spent years observing how people enter and use shops. He suggests that retailers either (1) accept that there is a necessary transition zone for people coming into a store and put appropriate items in this zone (he provides the example of a flower stall that people will see on their way in and shop at on their way

out), (2) increase the sense of threshold (with, for example, a squeaky door or a bell) so that people transition in a smaller space, or (3) try pushing the transition zone out from the front doors—get people engaged in the store long before they have actually entered the building (Underhill 1999: 49). The traditional café tables and sidewalk display racks do just this. Mr. Underhill also suggests that designers carefully watch how people walk: when do they slow down and look at merchandise and where do they look? Display windows and window-shopping signage should face the direction people are walking. Often this means placing signs perpendicular or angled to the façade. On the other hand, canopy-level signs are meant to be seen across a plaza and should be scaled to be legible and compelling from that distance. Likewise, the store façade may be composed of an entrance scaled to the plaza in which sit a set of display windows and human-sized doorways meant to be seen and used by pedestrians on the adjacent walkway.

Movie theaters, symphonies, and other large halls should have doors that allow large pulses of people, accommodate queues, and are of interest when not in active use. Placing these doors near the field of the square allows the field to serve as lobby. The marquee, ticket booth, and posters of the classic movie theater help animate the façade during off hours. The theater's refreshment stand could have a window to sell to the plaza crowd as well as the lobby, or the lobby could be opened so people can shop at the refreshment stand, the ticket booth, and the video arcade. This can help activate the façade and provide secondary income.

Upper-floor offices are often best served by a ground-floor lobby. The finest of these lobbies are often public forecourts or atriums rather than simply a guard's desk and a bank of elevators. These lobbies can be thought of both as thresholds to the square and as coves with their own entries, field and frame, and supporting walls.

Doorways to residences may be more discreet and hidden than those to more public functions. They must articulate the transition from the public to the private realm. There are two major alternatives—foyers and porches. Residential foyers may be more private versions of office lobbies. The art of porch-making is a critical and, I believe, currently understudied practice. The porch must prompt social transitions with physical transitions such as series of changes in level, direction, lighting, or degree of enclosure. Then again, the porch is not simply a path through layers. It is a place to be at home and in public. Children, particularly, are creatures of the porch (playing games, waiting for friends, watching the life of the square). Porches offer protection and selected interaction with the public.

Doorways are critical to making engaged walls (see chapter 11) and tying the life of the buildings to the civic room. Establishing an architectural language that allows people to read the different types of doors provides both legibility and visual richness.

Universal Design
How can we open doors and provide access with dignity to people with varying abilities?

The Americans with Disability Act (ADA) is a civil rights law that prohibits discrimination against people with disabilities. This discrimination includes designing public places that are inaccessible. Thus the Justice Department and various other agencies have developed guidelines for maximum slopes, the height of controls, the location and sizes of parking spaces, etc. (see, for example, Americans with Disabilities Act Accessibilities Guidelines for Buildings and Facilities, 36 CFR Part 1191, July 26, 1991). Universal design aims to go beyond the requirements of the law and provide places that are accessible with dignity. The Center for Universal Design at North Carolina State University defined universal design as "the design of all products and environments to be usable by people of all ages and abilities to the greatest extent possible." Many proponents of universal design also propose to eliminate where possible separate but equal facilities (Preiser and Ostroff 2001: 1.5). Where the ADA would allow an ugly ramp in a back corner that provides access for those who cannot climb a grand stair, proponents of universal design would suggest that the two facilities be integrated into one strong design.

Fountains are a delight; their play with sunlight, their musical drips and torrents, their cooling mists and fresh smells, and even the taste of the air can be glorious. Fountains engage all our senses and thus provide a model for universal design. Designs that rely on a single sense (often vision) are not easily accessible to people who are handicapped in that sense. Multisensory design can include more people. For example, careful texturing of pavement can help the blind read pathways and edges. This same texturing will also increase legibility for the sighted.

Another component of the public whose requirements are often overlooked in physical design are children. In addition to providing activities attractive to children, designers should consider their physical safety (particularly in places where cars and children mix), children's eye heights, and access to controls. Young children are often brought to a civic place by their parents. Ramps and curbcuts allow easy access for strollers and toddlers.

B. Electronic Doorways

One of the functions of civic rooms is as a place to see and be seen. Electronic media have extended and amended this role and will continue to do so. People regularly gather in Times Square to appear in the weather report of a national news show. One can be seen by many. Conversely, the other side of the public-appearance equation is fundamentally altered. Those who are viewing are not themselves on view and cannot directly interact with the life of the square.

The doorway of the TV camera has profoundly affected the social character of the public realm, and it has increased the importance of the photogenic and iconic qualities of architectural design. While everything from ancient coins and maps to coffee-table books have also attested to this off-site iconic role of design, each new medium has its specific point of view and audience that shapes the definition of success (fig. 12.2).

How should the design of a physical civic place extend into and interact with its media image and environment? Is being on TV an end in itself or do the conditions and context matter? How might a web page interact with the physical site? Should we provide public squares with wireless networks? Could we, and under what conditions should we, entice film producers to build film sets that then become public plazas? What other electronic doorways should we open?

Figure 12.2. *Scudo of Clement XI with Piazza della Rotonda from 1713. Clement XI had funded the redesign of the Piazza shortly before this coin was issued. Note the market stalls and people in the windows. Courtesy of the Ashmolean Museum, Oxford.*

Virtual Presence

How can new technologies promote conviviality?

Could someone sitting at home open a web page, choreograph fountains in a square, and watch as kids played in her composition? Could plazas in sister cities have video screens of each other so that passers-by could wave and perhaps talk to each other? Could a mannequin sitting on a bench be operated in real time through the net? Could a housebound child race a miniature sailboat across the duck pond?

Can the electronic viewers be connected back to the urban commons? How can the sense of belonging to a community and to a place be reinforced? Much of our electronic communication appears to be placeless. Where are the servers that run Google? Where is a chat room? Where, for that matter,

are radio stations? I suggest we play with mixing civic places with their ghostly echoes. How would we use a reader board in Berkeley's BART station that displayed e-mail messages? Would people come to play a game in a square that had a few remote players? How do you play cell-phone or digital photo tag, and where's the base? Could a symbiotic relationship be created between a plaza and a radio station?

Cell phones have liberated a significant portion of office work from the office. The presence of business people in squares and town parks talking on their phones has added a new life to these places. At a minimum, these people talking to the air provide a kind of spectacle and offer a glimpse into the operations of business. Out in public they may bump into colleagues or friends and engage in more traditional forms of public socialness between calls. They can see and be seen and are exposed to the world in a way they are not within their offices. Cell phones have also liberated people from waiting at home for a call.

What doorways into an urban commons will people use? Can these doorways offer the housebound a delightful and meaningful way to participate in the public realm?

Data Feed

Can electronic and other media be used to extend our perception of the landscape and our place in the world?

In addition to doorways *into* an urban commons, what doorways *out* into the universe should we open? We place television screens, stock ticker reader boards, and coin-operated telescopes in our plazas. Should Houston have a square where one can see live reports from all the current space missions? Should the square in Jackson, Wyoming, have a map that displays the migrations of elk herds? Perhaps Aspen should have digital displays of where skiers are on the mountain and in line.

Features of a plaza may also enhance our sense of time. When timepieces were new and expensive, the town clock provided a new order to the day. Stonehenge may be an astronomical clock. Stewart Brand and colleagues have proposed creating a clock that would run for ten thousand years (Brand 1999). Perhaps it should run longer and be built in a plaza near the Waste Isolation Pilot Plant (Carlsbad, New

Mexico) or near Yucca Mountain, Nevada, to indicate the time left until the radioactive materials have decayed.

These tools for looking beyond the immediate context of a square need not be electronic nor from the halls of a science museum. The Place de Célestins in Lyon, France, has a periscope that looks into the underground parking garage beneath it and displays its cavernous beauty. A sundial could mark the anniversary of the founding of the town or Dr. Seuss's birthday (March 2). The history of building on the site could be embodied in pavements and preserved building parts. Bus stops, depot parks, and other terminals could be designed to echo the character of their destinations. Farmers' markets bring the experience of the countryside in a very tangible way into the city. Perhaps they could benefit from expanding the sense of their goods from simply vegetables to a doorway into the landscape. For example, the Santa Fe Farmers' Market offers tours of farms and information about what is necessary to keep the small-farm landscape in business.

Access to the world beyond can be one resource a civic place has to offer. In a square, such a resource becomes public, part of the commonwealth.

Responsive Environments
What civic games, festivities, and media for dialog can a wired civic place offer?

Could a fountain have valves, levers, and gates to allow people to adjust its flow? What would happen if we placed a set of chalkboards or typewriters in a courthouse square? How would people interact with a digital camera that presented an ongoing exhibit of the customers of a hot-dog stand?

Researchers at MIT's Media Lab have developed various tools for responsive environments, such as gesture-based musical instruments and collaborative control interfaces. For example, *sensor-frames* is a set of two empty picture frames. Each frame tracks a person's arm movements and translates them into music. The frames may be played separately. "However, the *frames* are programmed to look out for similarity of movement between the two players; the more the two players follow each other, the more a special, easily

recognizable, chordal sound is produced by the dual instrument" (www.media.mit.edu, July 29, 2002).

What kind of games could be developed if the field of a square was equipped with position and gesture sensors? Could the same field also serve as a performance space for linking dance to music or light sculpture? Given electronic wizardry, what should the triumphal arch do when the parade master enters it? Most importantly, how can these devices and games serve as excuses for strangers to talk or perhaps play together?

C. Conceptual Doorways

Entering a territory may also imply entering new social relationships and concepts of the world as is illustrated by the medieval European saying, "City air makes free men." A similar sense of conceptual threshold may be evoked walking onto campus as a freshman, and I maintain that to some degree entering any vital urban commons is gaining access to a way of life.

Membership commons, such as the country-club swimming pool, must have conceptual and physical doorways that filter members from nonmembers. Public commons should not, but may invite all to move from one "world" into another.

Existential Thresholds
What ways of life or worldviews are being introduced? How can the physical doorway and threshold speak of the conceptual doorway?

The door may be a précis of the room. If the room represents a way of life then the door may provide an introduction, invitation, declaration, or defense of the social values held within. The entrance to the United States Supreme Court is a prime example of this didactic role.

To the extent that a square represents a community and its place in the landscape, its doors can represent the settlement. Memorials and town clocks have often claimed this role, and were placed as the jewel in the plaza setting. Gates reverse this relationship and serve as frames for plazas. Rather than implying that current life is centered around the monument, the gate suggests that history leads to the present.

Gateways may also frame a view out of a civic room into the city or countryside. As a *fourth wall* (see chapter 7) or a smaller window, they may lay claim to the surrounding lands or suggest the beginning of a path into other places. Pueblo Indian plazas appear to imply a bit of both in that the views of the mountains both center the plaza in the landscape and indicate the routes to other worlds.

Gateways may suggest an existential reframing through text and symbol, as a prop in community stories and legends, and as a place of orientation. Doorways embroidered with or made out of text and symbol are both an ancient tradition and a current art. Frequently, the account described by the doorway is part of a widely known story. Church doorways are a prime example of an existential threshold, and there is a long tradition of embellishing them with words and symbols to elaborate this role. An archway opening onto a campus, the grounds of a carnival, an outdoor theater, or the courtyard of a spa may also serve to mark the boundary between lifeworlds.

To introduce a civic place, gateways may become places of orientation. They may be coves where one may pause, get information, consider one's course of action, and perhaps even adjust one's image (take off a sweater, straighten a tie) before entering. Perhaps they offer an overview of activity in the square so that newcomers may survey the scene before plunging in.

There is a strain in American culture that resists the creation of gateways because of the walls and restrictions they often imply:

> *Before I built a wall I'd ask to know*
> *What I was walling in or walling out,*
> *And to whom I was like to give offense.*
> *Something there is that doesn't love a wall . . .*
> *—Robert Frost,* Mending Wall, *1914*

On the other hand, open gates can also imply opportunity. We can create gates that offer entry into new "worlds" and possibilities. *The Gateway to the West,* the Saint Louis Arch, was intended as such a gesture. Gateways into a town's civic places should strive to invite people into the commons.

PROPS

I have three chairs in my house: one for solitude, two for friendship, three for society.

—Henry David Thoreau, Walden, *section 6*

We come to the square to skate, to shop at the flea market, to eat lunch, or simply to sit and watch the world go by. All of these activities require props—a small building, furniture, equipment, or all three. Deciding which props to provide, where to place them, and what their character should be, is a critical component of the design.

A. Appointments

To "appoint" means to "provide with furnishings and accessories in a tasteful manner" (*American Heritage Dictionary* 1992: 736). To appoint a place with chairs, seating ledges, bollards, railings, drinking fountains, lampposts, street lights, and falafel vendors, designers must understand the roles and requirements of each.

Moreover, we must recognize that furniture, like clothing, is highly evocative of human activity and expression. We can see a group of chairs in conversation. A picnic table calls to mind picnickers. Tools suggest the worker and the work. In his essay "Meaning and Building," Joseph Rykwert wrote, "But the chair is only one of the many parts which compose our environment; and each one of them carries a proportionate charge of group memories and associations. The designer's responsibility then . . . is to create order not only in terms of a sensible arrangement of physical function, but also out of the all-but-living objects which we use and inhabit" (1982: 14).

Furniture Habitats
How can the furniture, equipment, and other props of a civic place be organized to avoid clutter and support the life of the place?

Over time, both streets and squares can become cluttered with the ad-hoc placement of utility equipment, vending machines, vendors, and other props. Sidewalks can become

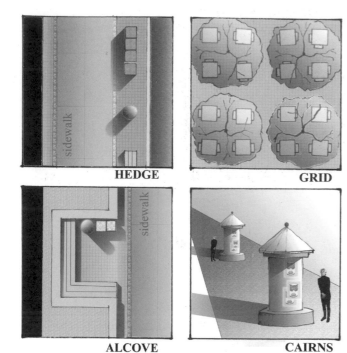

Figure 13.1. *Compositional patterns for street furniture. The upper left image shows a hedge of furniture along a sidewalk. The upper right illustrates a grid of café tables and trees. An alcove with seating and newspaper boxes is diagrammed in the lower left, and a pair of kiosks arranged as cairns along a path is shown in the lower right.*

people sit during a summer farmers' market, and where will they sit on a quiet Tuesday morning in the early spring?

Compositional patterns such as alcoves, hedges, grids and cairns, or axes of monuments can help create coherent social settings (fig. 13.1). An alcove of props creates a subspace for the activities suggested by the props. Benches flanked by newspaper racks near a bus stop suggest that this is the place to read the paper while waiting. A hedge of street furniture may help separate the sidewalk from driving lanes, or the aisle from the field of a plaza. Market stalls, chairs for an audience, and café tables are often organized into grids. There are, of course, a large variety of grid types, and a designer laying out a market or circus can benefit from studying the history of town plats. A market grid may recapitulate the pattern of the town. For example, the market in a square at the end of Main Street may itself have a "main street" terminated by a square. Finally, kiosks, fountains, telephone booths, or even telephone switching boxes can compose an axis of monuments that mark a path.

Seats
What makes a great outdoor seat?

"Ideally, sitting should be physically comfortable. . . . It's more important, however, that it be *socially* comfortable," William H. Whyte observed in his classic study *The Social Life of Small Urban Spaces* (1980: 28). A major design factor in providing for social comfort is the movability of the chair. People adjust chairs to form conversation groups, signal civil inattention (see chapter 2), watch passers-by, and express an infinity of other body language. In this sense, chairs, like clothes, can be an extension of our bodies.

The provision of chairs in a civic place is a social gesture that invites people to sit and stay awhile. The trustees of some civic places provide chairs and even lawn cushions, but because chairs need to be taken in at night, they are often under the management of a vendor or store. Cafés are the prototypical supplier. At some urban beaches, vendors rent beach chairs and umbrellas. The Fremont Outdoor Cinema in Seattle was b.y.o.c. (bring your own chair) and held competitions for the strangest seat.

As such a competition illustrates, chairs come in a

so full of props that it becomes difficult to walk. There is an understandable tendency in the redesign of these places to sweep the ground clean, eliminating most, if not all, of the props. Yet the mailbox, the telephone kiosk, the newspaper rack, the hot-dog vendor, and the gumball machine are part of the reason people come to a civic place.

Finding ways to arrange furnishings to make social settings, organizing them into zones and subspaces, is part of the job of making a civic place. Do the lampposts and the backgammon tables make a set? Can bollards, benches, a clock, and a newspaper rack complement the bus stop? Where will

Figure 13.2.
Moveable seating in the Refectory of Humboldt Park, Chicago. Image from The American City, *September 1915, p. 188.*

variety of forms. Designers should consider the opportunity. Lounge chairs, the typical café chair, lawn cushions, and stools all suggest different social milieus. Different subspaces within a square could have different furnishings. Perhaps two sets of chairs could be used to play life-size checkers.

The invitation made by chairs can be extended and elaborated by tables. Tables with umbrellas, misters, or lights not only provide a surface for activities but also a means to alter the microclimate. Child-sized tables and chairs attract children. Tables with built-in game boards can support a local players' club.

In many jurisdictions, seating has been reduced because "undesirables" use it. Following this logic, we should ban driving because drunks drive. The underlying problem is either one of social welfare and policing or one of social class and fear of strangers. The answer is not removing chairs from civic places. Adding more seating may dilute the problem presented by an "undesirable" or two who otherwise regularly take up the only places to sit.

Places to Sit
Where else will people sit?
How should these places be designed?

"Venice is noteworthy because all city furnishing—street lamps, flagpoles, statues, and so forth, as well as many of the buildings—are designed so that it is also possible to sit on them. The entire city is sittable" (Gehl 1996: 164). If we wish people to use civic places we should aim to follow Venice's lead.

The secondary seating provided by building walls, planter-bed edges, and street-lamp bases provides seating capacity for big events without making a place look empty when there isn't a crowd. These seats are also informal; one can sit without "taking a seat." Thus they suggest a different set of social possibilities than do chairs and tables.

The Project for Public Spaces suggests that secondary seating should provide about half of the seats in a plaza (PPS 2000). Based on extensive studies of New York City plazas, William H. Whyte recommends that (1) there be at least one linear foot of secondary seating per thirty square feet of plaza, (2) the seats be between one and three feet above grade with most of them about eighteen inches high, and (3) they are at least eighteen inches deep for single-loaded seats and three feet wide for double-sided seating.

Materials and finishes need to fit the environmental conditions. Properly finished wood provides a soft, thermally appropriate, and smooth seat. Metal is often uncomfortable in extreme climates. The thermal lag of a masonry sitting wall, properly sited, can provide a warm seat on a cool evening or a cool seat on a warm morning. In any case, not only should seating material be comfortable, but it should also look comfortable. A campaign focused simply on designing all city furnishings so that one can sit on them would create small social settings throughout the city, and show a concrete commitment to the quality of the city.

Places to Lean
What makes a great place to lean?

People lean in a number of different ways. Bollards and table-height ledges invite the half-sit and sometimes the one-arm lean. Railings with a surface that supports forearms and a bar on which to place a foot invite forward leans. Counter-height ledges tend to favor the one-arm lean in adults, but taller people will also use them to half-sit. Poles and walls are used for the shoulder lean or the back lean. Each of these positions sets up different body language. The forward lean, for example, is typically used either to overview an expanse or at a bar. In both cases, one's back is uncovered and one is usually looking away from the center of the space. Leaning against the wall is nearly the opposite condition.

In addition to the various types of leans, there are other assisted standing positions for which we should consider providing supports. A step or bar six to eighteen inches above the floor is useful for tying shoes. Lampposts could incorporate an appropriate ledge. Counter-height surfaces allow people to rest a package while they stand, or sit a toddler while they talk face to face. I have observed, in civic

Figure 13.3. *Taxi drivers' conversation centered on a bollard. During a nearly hour-long conversation, one or more of the taxi drivers was nearly always touching the bollard.*

places across North America and in Europe, long conversations taking place around a bollard. The bollard doesn't serve so much as a support for leaning as an anchor for the dance of body language during the conversation. Often, it is as if there is a rule that one or another of the group must be touching the bollard at all times. This "bollard effect" can be very strong. They serve as catalysts for conversations. In his observations of Siena, Italy's Campo, Jan Gehl noted, "nearly all standing activities are centered around the bollards" (Gehl 1996: 153).

Parking meters should be better designed to lean on, and indeed all of the equipment that occupies our sidewalks and squares should be redesigned to support pedestrian life. In addition to making civic places sittable, we should make them leanable.

Civic Fixtures
What other props should we provide?

The mechanical horse in the grocery store's covered sidewalk was the after-school rallying point for my friends. Occasionally, one of us would put in a quarter and ride. More often, we bought something from the vending machines or store and then hung out by the benches until the clock in the parking lot told us it was time to go home. This set of equipment, under shelter of an arcade wrapping a parking lot, was the attraction and excuse for my grade-school cohort to be in public.

Similarly, mailboxes and newspaper racks can attract people to a plaza. The designers and planners of a civic place may also want to search for unique or place-specific attractors. Features such as duck-food dispensers near duck ponds, a vending machine that will take your picture and displays it on a reader board, or other interactive artworks may serve as attractors.

Other fixtures such as trash cans and lampposts are not necessarily attractors in and of themselves. Rather, they support other activities. If these other amenities and seating are associated with an attractor, then people may be induced to stay a while. Designers should create subspaces around attractors. These subspaces not only help organize what can easily become a clutter of furniture and fixtures, but more importantly, they create social settings. They are prompts for conviviality. The mailbox becomes a place to talk to neighbors, and the duck feeder becomes a place where children make friends.

Civic Equipment
What roles can/should the equipment of our cities— manhole covers, meters, traffic lights— play in addition to their direct utility?

The systems of infrastructure that serve our towns run through our streets, parks, and squares. The accoutrements of these systems (e.g., telephone switching boxes) serve engineering roles and are not typically located or designed to directly support the civic vitality of the place they inhabit. Can the designers of the infrastructure and of urban commons work together to fulfill both sets of values?

Figure 13.4. *Manhole cover, Seattle, Washington, by Garth Edwards.*

Many U.S. cities have adopted a "1 percent for the arts" program, which budgets a portion of their capital improvements for artwork somehow associated with a building project. These programs have produced memorials and other traditional public artworks (appropriately and inappropriately), but they have also produced a new generation of civic equipment. For example, Seattle, Washington, has installed artwork and street maps on manhole covers, developed tree grates that educate passers-by about the tree, and transformed power substations into art parks. Could the poles for traffic lights also serve as poster kiosks for pedestrians? Could lampposts have seats at their bases or a bar-height shelf at which people could eat lunch? Could telephone switching boxes teach us anything about how the network functions?

Civic equipment can aid in place-making, wayfinding, and promoting dialog. In addition, civic equipment should properly fulfill its engineering roles. Additional functions must not diminish the efficiency of the equipment. For example, a map on a manhole cover doesn't affect the utility of the cover, but specifying special light bulbs for a plaza requires the city maintenance department to stock multiple bulb types and is often resisted by the street-light utility. The question for designers is how to intertwine the expressive possibilities and the engineering roles of the work.

Pushcarts and Booths

Who should design the temporary buildings of festivals, markets, and daily vendors? Where should they take up residence and what infrastructure should be provided?

Booths at the *Dickens on the Strand Festival* in Galveston, Texas, must conform to a set of design regulations issued by the festival organizers (fig. 13.5). The professional vendors I surveyed at this event, over the course of a few seasons, overwhelmingly preferred to have a themed fair that required these design regulations because themed festivals (1) draw larger crowds than those without overt themes, and (2) provide the best environment for teaching about the vendors' crafts. In addition to the image of the booth, ease of setup was a critical design factor. Cost and shelter from the weather were important to about half the vendors, and security was only of minor importance.

Design guidelines are often a happy medium between requiring a uniform set of predesigned booths and a completely ad-hoc assortment of booths. The creator of design guidelines must articulate what is necessary to make the overall design cohere without prescribing so much that the booth builders have no opportunity for creativity. Design guidelines should result in pleasant surprises. This is a problem akin to that of the urban designer of a square who must frame requirements for the architects of the enclosing buildings (see chapter 5). On the other hand, it may not be reasonable to enforce design guidelines other than health and safety regulations on pushcart vendors who move from venue to venue. The challenge for the designer of a plaza is to make good "campsites" or stalls for pushcarts and for festival booths.

The characteristics of vendor stalls vary according to the nature of the vendor. The majority of stalls at a local farmers' market or flea market may be tables at the back of

Figure 13.5. *Portion of the design guidelines for temporary vendors' booths at the* Dickens on the Strand Festival *in Galveston, Texas. Guidelines for dress are also issued to vendors. Image courtesy of the Galveston Historical Foundation.*

cars or small trucks, but some items such as corn and watermelons are best brought to market in a trailer. Not only do trailers take more space, but also customer access is best from the side rather than from the rear. Festivals typically require that the vendor's car is not parked at his booth, but vehicular access is helpful to deliver the booth and the goods.

In addition to space, a market or festival requires infrastructure. Access to electricity, water, restrooms, trash receptacles, and seating areas is critical. A square that regularly houses a market may also provide a shade system (e.g., places to clip on shade tarps or places for poles); a permanent kiosk, stand, or storefront dedicated to the market; and storage areas for equipment. Because market and festival use of a civic room differs significantly from daily use, the designer would be well advised to develop plans illustrating both conditions.

B. Attendant Buildings

We have inherited a tradition of small buildings that live within the frame and field of a square, forecourt, or courtyard. Each of these buildings has its traditional habitat, and gains meaning from its location within the civic room. The exact role of these buildings has evolved over time and will continue to evolve, and perhaps we may add a new member or two to this family of building types.

Care should be taken when adding permanent buildings to a civic room so that they don't unduly divide or fill the place. Yet a few small, well-placed structures may house activities and help form the chamber.

Figure 13.6. *Wedding in and about the gazebo in the Las Vegas, New Mexico, plaza, 2001.*

Gazebo
What roles can a gazebo play?

A gazebo is a small open-sided structure centered in the field, with a floor typically raised about a meter (2.5 to 3 feet) above grade. The classic octagonal gazebo form reflects the gazebo's role as a central marker.

It is unclear where the term *gazebo* comes from, but the *Oxford English Dictionary* suggests that it may be a humorous construction of "gaze" and the Latin verb ending "bo," thus meaning "I shall see." In any case, gazebos are places from which to look out upon the world. Hence their elevation above grade, open sides, placement in the middle of the field, and circular or many-sided plans.

Gazebos also serve as bandstands, wedding canopies, and other ceremonial shelters. They are structures at the central place of honor. They are not only places to look out from, but also to look in toward. Thus they may serve as icons.

The need to provide wheelchair access to gazebos challenges the tradition of raising the floor up a few steps from the field. It is often infeasible to provide either twenty or thirty feet of ramp or an all-weather mechanical lift. Yet the raised floor is critical to the gazebo's role. On a sloped site the gazebo may be placed along a joint line between two levels (fig. 13.7). On flat sites, multilevel gazebos or hand-powered lifts may help solve this design problem.

The emphasized centrality of a gazebo can lend an air

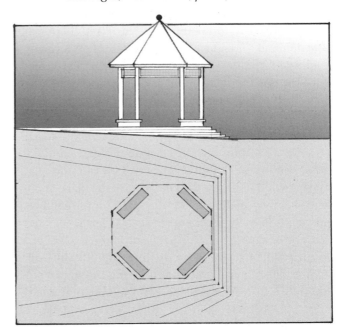

Figure 13.7. *Diagram of a gazebo at grade change allowing access for people with limited mobility.*

of importance to nearly any activity taking place within it. This setting is a B-movie cliché. Moreover, the design of gazebos seems to have frozen into a narrow set of nostalgic styles. A challenge for designers is to breathe new life into this old and powerful building type.

Stage
How formal a stage should be provided?

At least informally, a civic room, particularly its field, serves as a stage. It is a place to see and be seen. Stages facilitate plays without dictating their content. Can the field be not only a stage but also a place for festivals; a place to begin or end parades or to sell books; a place for buskers, politicians, and other street theater; and a place for as many other means to facilitate dialog as the community can imagine?

We may wish to designate a portion of the field as a formal stage for theater, music, politics, or lectures. An empty formal stage invites impromptu acting, but it also indicates a commitment to producing formal presentations.

The syllabus for the civic place should, of course, inform the degree of formality of the stage (see chapter 4). Is there demand for and a capacity to present performances? In addition, the designers should consider the degree to which the stage should dominate the place. Is a permanently raised stage necessary or can a temporary platform serve? Should only the framework for stage lighting be permanent or should the lights themselves be permanently installed?

A proscenium arch or stage roof creates a building within the urban chamber that must be carefully placed and shaped to reinforce the character of the place. A raised stage or sloped seating claims the space for formal theater, and begins to exclude other uses such as farmers' markets. It may be desirable to create a full amphitheater. For example, the Hearst Greek Theater on the campus of the University of California at Berkeley is a strong urban place. The dominance of a formal stage is a fundamental decision about the character and use of the place that typically requires trade-offs.

However, formal theater, music, politics, or education is not dependent on a formal stage. The art of street theater

is ancient. Designers can craft good places for street theater. These street stages need a flat stage area (often open to three-quarters or full theater in the round), an area for a standing audience two to three layers deep, good lighting, and, to the degree possible, good acoustics. The stage and audience should be near a main circulation route. The design of the pavement may provide marks that the performer can use to establish the area of the stage.

The stage is an integral part of a civic room. The shape or shapes it takes should be carefully considered.

Kiosks
How should we house support services, such as the exchange of information?

The word *kiosk* has been borrowed from language to language, acquiring new connotations. The Turkish word *kösk* referred to a pavilion used as part of a summerhouse. The French borrowed the term and some of the structural form, and the word *kiosque* referred to a small pavilion used to sell newspapers, and later to a cylinder on which notices are posted. In the mid-1800s, the English borrowed the term to refer to small structures used to distribute or post notices in public places. During the twentieth century, kiosks have expanded their role, and the term now includes places to exchange information in a number of media, or to obtain small goods. Thus telephone booths, ATMs, and structures housing ticket-vending machines and the like are now referred to as kiosks.

For the purposes of this book, "kiosk" will refer to a small structure in a civic place that provides support services, particularly the exchange of information. Kiosks may house a vendor or provide an awning, but are not typically entered by the public. Thus they are more objectlike than roomlike.

Kiosks should be placed along routes of circulation. They may serve well as part of gateways or screen walls. Particularly if a kiosk is designed as a distinctive figural object, it may also function as a meeting point and wayfinding device. A distinctive kiosk used throughout a district, city, or nation may become emblematic of the place or of a function or both. The English red telephone booth and the Parisian cylindrical kiosk are prime examples. There are a number of opportunities to create new iconic kiosks. A newspaper company could create a new type of newspaper box. A state farmers' market association could design a market kiosk, or a university could distribute a distinctive outdoor notice board throughout its campus.

Ceremonial Storehouses
Can we give architectural dignity or delight to the building in which we keep props for the field (game pieces, tents, etc.)?

The Zamboni ice resurfacer is typically either parked unceremoniously to the side of the ice rink or hidden away in a utilitarian shed. Could the minor ceremony of cleaning the ice be made more fun or otherwise enriched if the warning lights went on, skaters left the ice, and the machine and its rider emerged from the Zamboni temple?

If, instead of putting the props for the field away in a back closet or shed, we created buildings adjacent to the field that evoked or commented on a game or activity, then the game would have a presence even when it is not being played. The building can serve not only to house the equipment and as an advertisement, but also as a place to collect donations or fees; to post rules, notices of tournaments, records, and clubs; to distribute information about the history of the game and the plaza; and to sell paraphernalia and to meet fellow players.

How might we design a shed housing life-size chessmen? Should there be a single shed for both colors, or opposing barracks? Perhaps, next to a bocce court there is often no need to store bocce balls, but would a notice board and a covered bench for spectators and those waiting a turn increase the delight of the game? If the tai chi club had a support building, what would it be? Could more than one game be stored in a prominent storehouse, so that the players and aficionados of different games intermixed?

What are the metaphors that could inform the design of these storehouses? Should they be toy boxes, temples, wardrobes, game pieces, elborate gizmos, or smooth monoliths?

Who will hold the key to opening the storehouse? Should it be associated with other vending operations?

Stands
How should we house permanent vendors within a civic room?

An old diner converted into a police substation forms the short edge of Triangle Park near the University of New Mexico in Albuquerque. A pair of greenhouse-like structures frames the eastern entrance to Post Office Square in Boston. One greenhouse covers the stairs to the underground parking garage and the other a sandwich shop and deli. These small buildings illustrate both good form and placement of a stand within a square. They are small structures that allow people within them to feel connected to the outside. They are a part of the frame of the square and form the first layer of enclosure. Ingólfstorg, a new square in Reykjavik, Iceland, uses a similar compositional device—a pair of colonnaded buildings separates the composition into two rooms.

As a rule of thumb, stands should be (1) shorter than the enclosing walls, (2) as open as possible, (3) as small as possible, (4) near the major routes of circulation but with an outdoor area into which their activity spills (e.g., seating for a lunch shop), and (5) help form a screen wall. As screen walls, stalls may help fill a gap in the enclosing wall of surrounding buildings, help subdivide an area into multiple places, or create alcoves. Permanent stands may also serve as the "anchor" or starting point for a row of stalls for temporary vendors.

Stands in an active square can be highly valued real estate. With care, a symbiotic relationship between stand vendors and the trustees of a civic room may be formed. Attracting people to the square or forecourt and maintenance of the place is in the interest of both parties. There is a danger of becoming too focused or dependent on the commercial interests of the stands and slighting the rights of access and use of the general public. Stands, I suggest, should be leased, not sold, to vendors so that the stewards of the civic place retain control.

Pavilions
When and how should we add a roof to the field?

A pavilion is an independent, open-air structure in or at the edge of the field of a civic place. They may be permanent or temporary, such as tents erected for dances or concerts in the square.

In addition to promising shelter from the sun or a bit of rain, pavilions reiterate the roomlike qualities of a civic room. Temporary tents for a community dance emphasize the place—this is *where it's at*. Thus these pavilions often are, and should be, highly ornamental and figurative. They are signs of the festivity. Their celebration-marking function may even entirely replace the provision of environmental shelter. Strings of lights may be shaped like a tent and strung over the field to demarcate the dance floor. Possible configurations of these temporary structures and their infrastructure (e.g., outlets, tent-pole sockets, storage places) should be part of the design of a square.

Permanent pavilions are most frequently found in civic grounds, such as parks, where they provide picnic shelters and overlooks. The strongest tradition of permanent pavilions is that of public markets. In the early parts of the twentieth century, a number of public markets with permanent pavilions were built in the United States (Childs 2000).

Markets benefit from environmental shelter. Shade reduces heat and spoilage, and a roof can attract people to a market during a light summer rain. A market shed or pavilion also advertises the market even when it is not in session, and indicates a commitment to the continuation of the market. It provides a kind of political shelter.

If the market is seasonal or periodic, the pavilion must function both as a place reserved for a particular set of uses (e.g., vendors during the market) and as a flexibly used public place (e.g., hangout and playground during the week). A syllabus of uses and design documents showing both (or all) occupancies should be developed to verify that the space works well under all conditions.

No matter what the use, the larger the portion of civic place covered by a pavilion the larger is the separation from the landscape, and the greater the possibility that the space will be claimed for some private uses. Roofs tend to imply ownership. To ensure that a pavilion does not overly dominate, I would suggest that (1) the roof covers noticeably less than half of the field, (2) no spot under the roof is more than twenty feet from the edge, (3) the walls are as open as possible so that the space flows easily from under the pavilion into the field, and (4) the pavilion is placed to one side of the field and allows as many long sightlines across the square as possible.

CARS

To George F. Babbitt, as to most prosperous citizens of Zenith, his motor car was poetry and tragedy, love and heroism.

—*Sinclair Lewis,* Babbitt

The life of the city, and particularly its civic rooms, is mostly a life of people outside of their cars. In most cases, the rights of pedestrians must be championed. Automobiles have usurped a large portion of our city spaces but squares are at heart living rooms, not garages.

Yet cruisers, wedding caravans that circle the town square, and the everyday activity of hanging your head out the window to talk to someone on the sidewalk suggest that we can, sometimes, integrate drivers into the civic life. Moreover, the automobile brings people from the suburbs and countryside and can concentrate them in vibrant urban places.

Nearly every driver and passenger becomes a pedestrian in a parking lot. Furthermore, parking lots are used for the high-school car wash, hot-rod rallies, farmer's markets, skateboarding, and other nonparking activities. Therefore, the places of parking ought to be well designed for automobiles *and* pedestrians.

In my book *Parking Spaces,* I suggest a number of approaches to provide for both the car and the pedestrian (Childs 1999). Fundamentally, parking should be distributed and designed to support the pedestrian life of the town. To put it mildly, this has not been the guiding principle of the majority of our parking-lot design.

Moreover, parking places can and should begin to make civic places. This chapter changes perspective, recasts the patterns of *Parking Spaces,* and adds new patterns addressed to the designer of civic places who may need or desire to accommodate a few cars.

A. Parking Commons

When, where, and how can automobile parking share space with a civic square or courtyard? Automobile users have a strong tendency to overtake open spaces. How can pedestrian use of a shared space be defended?

The following patterns offer approaches to integrating some parking into squares and other commons. From diagram to detail, the designer of a successful shared realm must accommodate the requirements of both drivers and pedestrians but place the emphasis on the pedestrian.

Figure 14.1.
Motorcycles on the square at Portsmouth, New Hampshire, 2002. Groups of motorcyclists stop at the square to get a coffee and pastry and to hang out.

Parking Bread and Butter
Parking lots are critical components of commerce. Can this economic engine be tapped to support the creation and maintenance of civic places?

Ferry terminals and railroad stations gather people from large catchments and create lively gathering spots. Large parking structures could have similar effects, if we designed them as terminals.

For example, Post Office Square in Boston is a 1.7-acre park atop a fourteen-hundred-stall underground parking structure. The parking provides access to the district, and the park provides an attractive focus. Friends of Post Office Square, a group of local property owners and tenants, developed and paid for the project, because it was in their self-interest to provide parking *and* a park open to the public.

Care should be taken in the placement of pedestrian exits from the parking. Ideally the flow of people from the parking structure should pass through a portion of the square or park, providing life to the space. Vendor's booths, restrooms, and other support services thus can provide for both the square and the daily flow of parkers.

Likewise, automobile entrances should be placed to minimize conflicts with the pedestrian use of the square. Pedestrians should not have to cross the flow of commuters, and the entrance structures should not create inappropriate walls between the square and the surrounding buildings.

Squares may also serve as terminals for buses, taxis, and car-pool drop-offs. A pleasant square with good seating, shelter, a newsstand or coffee vendor, and other amenities can make waiting for the bus a delight rather than a necessary evil, and thus increase the desirability of public transit.

Parking-Lot Catchments
Each parking lot has a catchment from which drivers come to use the lot. How can knowledge about these catchments inform the design of a car commons?

A grocery store attracts about 80 percent of its customers from a 1.5-mile radius (Urban Land Institute 1999: 46 and 53). A regional mall, however, has a primary catchment of about 12 miles. A public library will have a driving catchment based on the distribution of libraries in the area, the specialization of the

Figure 14.2. *Car show at Heritage Days on the courthouse square in Portales, New Mexico, 2000.*

library, and access routes. Thus the catchment for a parking lot varies according to the use of its building. It may also vary by time of day, week, or year. Specialty groceries, for example, have a smaller catchment during the week than during the weekend.

The designer of a shared parking area should understand the demographics and habits of users of associated buildings. The designer can then attempt to complement the activities of these users (e.g., make places to read for library users), or supplement these activities (e.g., create a place for a weekend farmers' market in and around the empty parking lot of an office building).

A detailed understanding of the trade area or catchment can give an indication of the homogeneity of the customers (for example, grocery store customers are from a more tightly defined neighborhood than the customers of a regional mall); the times of day, week, and year when users typically come to the building (e.g., office lots may be empty on weekends); the socioeconomic characteristics of the users

(e.g., young high-income families); and their trip patterns (e.g., people making weekday evening grocery-store trips are on their way home and thus may not be willing to long engage in a secondary activity).

This catchment information can be gleaned from observing existing buildings, surveying users of these buildings about their trips to and from the location, and investigating census and other place-based information for the catchment. However, the designer must remember that with changed conditions at the site (the new design) the characteristics of the catchment will change. For example, more people may come to the grocery because of the demonstration garden next to the parking lot.

Dedicated Pedestrian Space
How can pedestrians maintain a primary claim to a place shared with automobiles?

Pedestrians make numerous claims to the use of our parking lots. We walk to and from our cars in the driving aisles; we stop and chat over grocery carts; occasionally, car washes take over a portion of a lot or the circus transforms the lot for a weekend. However, these are secondary claims with parking as the primary use. If we wish to make a place in which automobiles are guests, we must strongly stake the pedestrians' claim to dominance.

Cars must never run people out. There must be a significant and important portion of the place that is permanently dedicated to pedestrians. Thus people who are considering coming to the square don't have to remember or guess if the cars have taken over or if the pedestrian realm is open for business. Vendors, street musicians, outdoor chess players, and other core users can have permanent facilities.

The prime pedestrian spaces will be determined by the total context of the design, but two diagrammatic relationships should be considered: (1) entrances to the civic room should look into dedicated pedestrian spaces rather than parking areas; (2) pedestrian spaces should be immediately adjacent to the entrances to shops, halls, and other destinations rather than in a remote island, so that these adjacent uses may spill out into the square, forecourt, or courtyard.

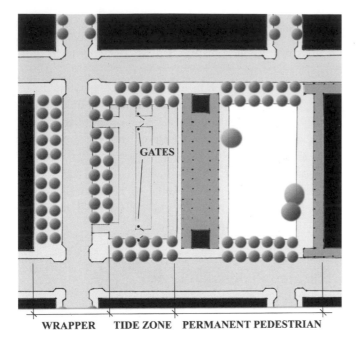

WRAPPER   TIDE ZONE   PERMANENT PEDESTRIAN

Figure 14.3. *Diagram showing permanent pedestrian zone, a tidal zone that allows parking at certain times, and a wrapper of active pedestrian space that surrounds the tidal zone.*

Intertidal Zone
Since parking lots are often partially or completely empty, can this excess capacity be put to good use?

If a shopping-center lot is designed to provide sufficient stalls for the twentieth busiest hour of the year (a typical standard), then at least half of the spaces are vacant 40 percent of the time (Urban Land Institute 1982: 12). Additionally, many lots are empty on weekends or evenings. Fig. 14.3 shows a strategy to capture the excess space due to the flux of cars. An "intertidal zone" may be created for parking at automobile high tide and pedestrians at low tide.

Critical to making the diagram work are either (1) gates to control the distribution of parking, or (2) inducements to make the stalls farthest from the pedestrian realm fill first. Inducements might include being closest to the automobile

entrance and exit; being closest to the building that the parking lot serves; larger parking stalls; cheaper parking rates; and simply prior use and occupation of the further stalls by basketball players, street musicians, or other users.

The pedestrian uses of the intertidal zone must depend in part on the frequency, duration, and time of parking use. For example, the overflow lots for a stadium, a church parking lot, and an office's employee lot are available for pedestrian uses at different times of the day and week.

The intertidal zone should be bordered by a wrapper of edge uses. Uses of the intertidal field to consider include: hard surface sports such as basketball, tennis, or roller skating; street vendors and markets; outdoor movie theaters, live theaters, and public dances; and fountains whose nozzles are flush with the pavement or protected in islands. Bordering the intertidal field should be an edge zone with uses such as an encircling path, places to sit and watch, permanent vendors, ATMs, soda dispensers, and other service machines. A frame of trees, gardens, walls, arcades, or other elements can enclose the field and edge zones to help make this place into a room.

The Language of the Street
How can the graphic language of the street be overwritten or opened up to allow for pedestrian life in a car commons?

Traffic engineers have done a remarkable and useful job of creating a strongly legible visual language for the spaces of the automobile—the freeway, road, and parking lot. White lines on black asphalt create a parking lot and strongly suggest the character of the space and its set of uses. Wheel stops, parking meters, and curbed islands are additional strong definers of the parking-lot language. If automobiles are allowed onto a portion of a civic room, their signs and symbols should be muted and transformed.

Rather than creating lines solely for parking spaces, pavement patterns that compose the floor of the entire place may also delineate where to park. Embedded reflectors, lines of bollards, or a grid of trees can replace the white lines to indicate the spacing of parking stalls.

The typical smooth black finish of asphalt can be

Figure 14.4. *Parking meter with graphic art in Albuquerque, New Mexico. Part of the Rhyme and Meter Project sponsored by the Downtown Action Team and the Design and Planning Assistance Center at the University of New Mexico.*

transformed. Brick or stone pavers, colored concrete, and engineered soils and gravels provide the opportunity for creating patterns and weaves. The typical topcoat asphalt can be replaced with "architectural asphalt," in which selected gravels are rolled into the finish coat to provide color and texture. Asphalt can also become a canvas for an artist using tumbled glass, metal inserts, tile fragments, or other materi-

als. Care should be taken to provide handicapped-accessible surfaces and to avoid tripping hazards.

Wheel stops and curbs can often be eliminated or replaced by bollards, landscape rocks with curblike profiles, and changes in pavement. Eliminating wheel stops and curbs not only reduces the parking-lot image, but also eliminates a significant source of tripping hazards, and allows for the smooth flow of pedestrians into the parking areas.

To help establish a sense of enclosure, parking zones should be broken into bays that are proportioned to the surrounding buildings. Secondary buildings, such as bus shelters, attendant booths, and ATM kiosks, can help provide enclosure and define visual and pedestrian connections. Artwork, plantings, and lighting should also be used to define the place.

Messy Beasts

Cars are messy beasts that leave oil stains and create air pollution. How can car commons be designed to be attractive and more environmentally sound?

One objection often made to the shared use of parking lots is the mess made by cars and their owners. The oil spilled by cars is unattractive, can create slipping hazards, and is an environmental hazard. In addition to oil spills, an early-morning inspection of a busy parking lot reveals that parking lots are often used as dumping grounds for all kinds of trash. A clean parking lot free of slipping hazards should be important for any owner, but when pedestrians other than those coming from and going to their cars use portions of the lot these issues become more important. The following approaches to the problem of messy parking lots follow a modified version of the environmental schema, "reduce, reuse, recycle."

Reduce: The best long-term solutions are to reduce the use of automobiles and to lobby for cleaner cars. If cars did not drip oil and deposit metals from brakes onto parking lots, a significant environmental and aesthetic problem would be eliminated. Civic places that provide support facilities for pedestrians, bicyclists, and mass-transit users can encourage people to use their cars less.

Littering may be reduced by providing trash cans in easy-to-use locations, containing overflow and blowout from dumpsters inside fences, and by having employees set an example by cleaning the lot when customers are present.

Resist: Various commercial sealers are available that increase pavements' resistance to oil staining. Additionally, the color and pattern of pavements should be selected to reduce the appearance of stains. Parking stall areas that receive the highest concentration of oil stains may require darker and more resistant materials than driving and walking aisles.

Gravel and crusher fine pavements may not show oil stains as easily as impermeable pavements. However, they are passing the oil and other pollutants into the soil and potentially creating a more indelible environmental problem.

Maintain: A regular maintenance plan for a parking-lot plaza is critical. The broken-window theory suggests that well-maintained places receive less abuse (see chapter 6). If trash is regularly removed from the lot, fewer people will litter in it. Additionally, the sooner oil spills are addressed, the easier they are to remove. A number of commercial products and types of cleaning equipment are available to clean oil stains. Some of these products and processes simply pass the problem onto the storm drain unless they are disposed of properly. Problem areas such as the front of parking stalls should be designed for frequent cleaning, and so that the pavement may be removed or repaired without requiring that the entire lot be replaced or recoated.

Remediate: Parking-lot runoff should be captured and treated. Trash and oil separators are required in many jurisdictions. Biological remediation by seeding the subsoil or pavement with oil-eating bacteria and treatment of parking-lot runoff (both above and below grade) may provide new approaches to the aesthetic and environmental problem of oil deposits.

Other environmental problems are caused by the typical parking lot. Their large impervious surfaces change storm flows in neighboring streams, and the typical expanse of black asphalt can significantly increase local air temperatures causing higher cooling costs and greater smog generation. Additionally, parking lots are often placed on sites in a manner that discourages other modes of transportation (e.g., making people walk across the lot to get to the front door from the sidewalk).

B. Shared Streets
How can the full width of a street become a pedestrian realm shared with automobiles?

The following two patterns illustrate conditions in which pedestrians have access to the drive lanes of streets. Before the advent of the automobile, streets were typically shared by pedestrians and multiple types of vehicles (horses, carts, trolleys, and bicycles). Conflicts certainly arose, but the city street was closer to a multiuse plaza or square than a monofunctional utility for vehicles. It provided space for the life of the town.

Cul-de-sacs
Why are cul-de-sacs and loop roads so strongly desired?

At the beginning of the twentieth century, Raymond Unwin convinced the British Parliament to reverse its ban on cul-de-sacs. Unwin argued: "[The ban on cul-de-sacs] had, no doubt, been taken to avoid unwholesome yards; but for residential purposes, particularly since the development of the motor-car, the cul-de-sac roads, far from being undesirable, are especially to be desired for those who like quiet for their dwellings" (quoted in Southworth and Ben-Joseph 1997: 42).

Cul-de-sacs also offer an informal neighborhood commons that is immediately accessible and requires minimal maintenance. Block parties, gossiping, and children's games claim this space. Various studies indicate that cul-de-sacs are more frequently and safely used by children than are through streets (Sanoff and Dickerson 1971; Cooper 1974; Je 1986; Eran 1995). Moreover, cul-de-sacs offer a defensible space. Residences' front doors and windows oversee the street, and strangers are clearly not just passing through. Some studies indicate that patterns of cul-de-sacs reduce traffic accidents and crime in the cul-de-sac neighborhoods (Mayo 1979; Newman 1995). It is unclear whether or not the traffic accidents are exported to the arterials.

However, cul-de-sacs present three potential problems. First, they are rarely designed to support their use as neighborhood commons. The techniques of streetyard design (see below) could be fruitfully applied to the typical

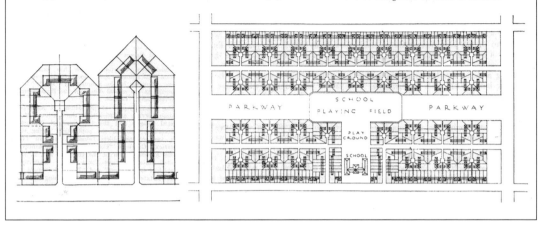

Figure 14.5.
*Portion of a 1928
article promoting the
cul-de-sac. From*
The American City,
November 1928, p. 104.

cul-de-sac. For example, manhole covers can be placed to serve as home plate for baseball games. An island of trees may provide a miniature neighborhood park. Short walls may serve as informal seating, and the cul-de-sac may be lighted for pedestrian use.

Secondly, the local commons created by cul-de-sacs may be excessively closed and defensive. A neighborhood of six houses does not provide hope for a great variety of neighbors, and the defensive nature of the form may separate this tiny group socially and physically from the larger neighborhood and town. Often the larger subdivision pattern of multiple cul-de-sacs and loop roads also serves to disconnect the residences from the town. "The [cul-de-sac subdivision] pattern as it has evolved is usually difficult to conceptualize because there is so little apparent structure, no unifying element, or clear describable pattern. . . . One lacks the sense of being part of the whole, of being in a neighborhood or town that is truly one's own, with a sense of civic identity and spirit" (Southworth and Ben-Joseph 1997: 122).

Finally, cul-de-sacs and their subdivisions tend to make circulation difficult. Due to their limited number of access points and through routes, they concentrate automobiles onto arterials. They often make automobile and pedestrian trips longer because of their circuitous routes. This excess distance may reduce or eliminate pedestrian trips. I have measured route lengths between cul-de-sacs and neighborhood schools that are more than ten times the length of a direct route.

"Live-end streets" offer an approach that could open up cul-de-sacs and provide more direct pedestrian connections (see Childs 1996a). The live-end street is one on which automobile traffic ends while the pathway for pedestrians continues. On my own street, which joins a pathway, I've measured nearly twenty times more nonmotorized traffic than on a comparable neighboring true dead end. A number of neighborhood children take the path to the park, and I've met numerous neighbors from other streets walking my street. The plan of Radburn, New Jersey, offers a set of live-end streets, and neighborhood street grids in Seattle, Berkeley, and elsewhere have been transformed into networks of live-ends through the addition of street diverters and closures.

Cul-de-sacs and live-end streets are attempts to balance the social and automobile use of the street.

Streetyards and Streetcourts
**_Where and how can pedestrian-based commons
share space with an automobile route?_**

The Dutch planner Niek De Boer developed the concept and
designs for _woonerfs,_ or streetyards, in 1969. Streetyards are
neighborhood commons shared by pedestrians and cars.
Pedestrians have the right-of-way over the entire street.

Drivers are guests on the streetyard and their speed
and movement is restricted by physical barriers, bends in the
route, textured pavement, social practice, and law. Compared
with standard residential streets, studies indicate that there
are over 20 percent fewer accidents and over 50 percent
fewer severe accidents in shared streets (Southworth and
Ben-Joseph 1997: 118).

The shared pedestrian space recaptured from the
automobile is often designed and used for children's play,
informal meetings between neighbors, and neighborhood
celebrations. This shared realm immediately accessible from
homes allows children a place for spontaneous play and
interaction. From his studies in multiple countries, the architectural researcher Jan Gehl concluded that "even very small
outdoor areas placed directly in front of houses can have far
greater and substantially more faceted use than larger recreational areas that are more difficult to reach" (Gehl 1996: 193).
The keys to making successful front-door public spaces are
designing for "Easy access in and out; Good places to stay
directly in front of the house; and something to do, something
to work with, directly in front of the houses" (Gehl 1996: 186).

Streetyards are designed to reduce automobile speed
and traffic. Design methods include (1) making the traffic
lane a one-way route with tight bends in it, (2) placing angled
parking along the route so that parking maneuvers reduce
the free flow of the traffic lane, (3) designing sidewalk corners
with tight radii to reduce turning speeds, and (4) constrict-
ing the actual and perceived width of the driving lane with
street trees and other features.

Moreover, to make a successful streetyard the design
language of the automobile street is replaced with the language of a plaza or pedestrian walkway. Thus parking stalls
are not marked but, rather, suggested by the placement of
trees. Curbs are often eliminated and the traffic lane loosely
defined by bollards, parked cars, lampposts, etc., and pavements other than asphalt are used.

Similarly, along commercial streets street plazas may
be designed to allow vehicular access to shops, but also to
create a vibrant street scene. Pike Place Market in Seattle,
Washington, provides a prime example of a street plaza. On
normal days the brick street is shared among drivers, trucks
unloading goods, parked cars, pedestrians, and workers
pushing carts. During festivals the street is closed to vehicles
and filled with people.

C. Great Sidewalks

Along many streets the traffic lane may not be shared. Yet a
vibrant pedestrian life is also part of the street. The following
set of patterns addresses the typical condition in which the
automobile and the pedestrian have separate zones in the
street. Unfortunately, in the twentieth-century rush to accommodate the car, the sidewalk has often been compromised.

The Uses of the Sidewalk
How can we design great multiuse sidewalks?

First and foremost, great sidewalks are wide and commodious.
The 2.5 to 6 feet of sidewalk width required by many zoning
codes is inadequate. For pedestrians or wheelchair users to
pass each other, each person requires approximately 30 inches of sidewalk width. Thus two couples passing each other
require about 10 feet of clear walkway. However, next to a
building and the curb there is a friction zone in which people
normally do not walk. Also parking meters, lampposts, newspaper racks, sidewalk cafés, flowerpots, bus stops, fireplugs,
queues for movies, and other uses require space. Fig. 14.6 illustrates an approach to accommodating these various uses.

Sidewalks are not simply drive lanes for pedestrians, and
pedestrians should not be thought of as simply another vehicular mode. People stop and talk, listen to street musicians, buy
hot dogs, leaflet for politicians, and simply hang out. A great
sidewalk provides a pleasant environment for these uses. To

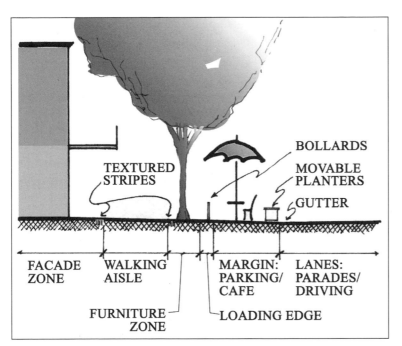

Figure 14.6.
Diagram of sidewalk zones. Redrawn from Mark Childs, Parking Spaces *(New York: McGraw-Hill, 1999).*

help transform walking into strolling, window-shopping, or promenading, designers should temper the microclimate; provide amenities such as access to restrooms, drinking fountains, and benches; and create a coherent but complex environment.

Ceilings are often critical in tempering the sidewalk microclimate. Arcades, awnings, and tree canopies can provide shelter from intense sun and wind and moderate the tribulations of precipitation. Tree canopies and awnings can also filter, shape, and play with sunlight. The design of the pavement can also be critical in moderating the effects of the weather. Sidewalks should be well drained and have slip-resistant surfaces. Gutters should be placed and designed to avoid creating places where vehicles splash pedestrians.

Beyond a pleasant microclimate, sidewalk amenities include (1) basic support services, such as drinking fountains and access to restrooms; (2) seating areas; (3) an engaging line of façades; (4) newsstands and other vendors; (5) access to transportation, such as bus shelters and parking spaces; (6) kiosks and other information devices; and (7) engaging artwork (see chapter 15). A study by the Federal Highway Administration supports the intuition that the provision of

amenities increases the use of the sidewalk (Federal Highway Administration 1978).

Finally, the complex set of parts—various building façades, the sidewalk pavement, newsstands and kiosks, the tree canopy, pedestrian and traffic lampposts, etc.—must become a coherent place. Simple metrics such as maintaining the line of buildings next to the sidewalk, keeping a clear walking aisle, and establishing a rhythm of street trees have traditionally provided a counterpoint to the complexity of multiple store windows and the life of the street. Other elements, such as a shared cornice line or a predominant building material, that allow both collective agreement and individual expression can help produce a complex coherence.

Sidewalk Seating
If sidewalks are also our public living rooms, where can we sit and chat?

The stoop (residential stairs on the sidewalk) is, in some places, the locus of neighborhood culture (see, for example,

Figure 14.7. *Card game on a sidewalk in New York City, 1999.*

Hubbell, *On the Stoop,* 1993; Hiner and Hanes, *Growing Up in America,* 1985; or Ferretti and Darvin, *The Great American Book of Sidewalk, Stoop, Dirt, Curb and Alley Games,* 1975). The barbershop bench also was a cultural fixture, and the café has colonized sidewalks in cities and small towns. Clearly, despite anti-loitering laws, providing places to sit in public is an important function of the sidewalk.

Fear of undesirable loiterers has led many cities to remove seating from the sidewalk or to make benches on which it is difficult to sleep. Homelessness and poverty are not cured, reduced, or mitigated by eliminating places to sit, but the full life of the sidewalk is certainly damaged. The elderly find it hard to rest, parents with small children must trudge on, and the chances for chance meetings are greatly reduced. The great sidewalk has generous places to sit.

Just as in the square, sidewalk seating may be formal (a bench) or informal (the ledge of the building). Empty chairs or benches look empty, while stairs and ledges do not call attention to times of low usage. A generous design approach would be to make every possible element of the sidewalk—lampposts, bollards, building edges, steps, planters, newspaper racks, etc.—into places to sit or lean, *and* to provide formal seating at a minimum of every three hundred feet (see Gehl 1996: 164).

Sidewalk seating must be placed and designed in relationship to both the flow of pedestrians and of automobiles. On narrow streets with few cars, people may effectively talk and otherwise interact across the street, but more typically the street presents a barrier and prime interactions are between sitters and people on the sidewalk and in the parking lane.

For people-watching, the prime view is up and down the sidewalk, or better yet at a corner that provides views up and down two sidewalks. Since people come from multiple directions, good seats for people-watching face the sidewalk so that the watchers may easily look both ways. Group seating, however, typically should face up and down the sidewalk and provide some protection at the back of the seats.

It is nearly impossible to sit comfortably next to a moving lane of traffic. There must be layers of protection. Frequently, sitting areas are next to the buildings separated from traffic by the walking aisle, street trees and furniture, and a row of parked cars. However, with careful design of layers, it is also possible to place comfortable seating on the streetside of the sidewalk.

The layers of protection must be carefully built to provide physical and psychological protection. A line of parallel-parked cars provides a barrier to the wind, noise, smell, and splashes of traffic and presents a six-foot wall of metal to potential out-of-control cars. Its only apparent hazard is the opening of passenger doors. Angled parking does provide more space between moving traffic and the sidewalk than parallel parking, but is more psychologically intrusive. Not only do cars parked at an angle hang over onto the sidewalk, but also, as they arrive they come directly at people on the sidewalk. Jersey barriers, bollards, a line of trees, planters, and other street furniture can provide additional layers of protection.

Bus-Stop Shelters

Bus stops are critical parts of both the bus system and the sidewalk. They present an elemental architectural issue—how to provide simple but delightful shelter?

Bus shelters can be a kind of architectural haiku. They are small, typically freestanding, simple structures that provide temporary shelter and hopefully a bit of delight in the streetscape.

There seem to be two basic strategies about the character of bus shelters: (a) they are part of the bus system and thus similar throughout town, or (b) they are part of the street and thus different on different streets. Seattle has attempted mixing these strategies by creating a standard design within which artwork panels created by the local community are placed.

No matter the symbolic emphasis, shelters should be recognizable as bus stops and provide basic information about the bus system. The technology exists to have a reader board that tells riders when the next bus will arrive, and even to send a signal to cell phones in the area a few minutes before the bus pulls in. Moreover, the shelters should be understood as a critical part of transit service, and be designed to transform impatient and uncomfortable waiting into a pleasant interlude.

To provide a pleasant wait, shelters may be associated with other uses. For example, a newspaper and coffee stand adjacent to a bus stop could benefit from the traffic and provide a service to the bus users. This association may also help reduce crime at the bus stop. "Placing a bus stop in front of surface parking lots, vacant buildings, or other dead space isolates the people waiting for the bus. As our data showed, most serious crimes tend to occur at desolate settings with low levels of activity" (Loukaitou-Sideris 1999: 406).

Bus shelters are transfer nodes and, like their larger cousins, the airport or ferry terminal, they represent the transportation system and should be pleasant and safe. Like larger terminals, they also house dramas of leave-taking, arrival, and the meeting of strangers. Perhaps the haiku of bus shelters should speak to both shelter and threshold.

Excursion

THE ART AND ARCHITECTURE OF COLLABORATION

David and Deborah Rutherford

Throughout history, architects and artists have grappled with the problems and potential of working together. They have tried varied ways of working together to include art in architectural projects, including the following relationships.

Placed Art

The most independent relationship of art and architecture is "placed art," in which architecture tolerates the art or provides a site for its placement but the enhancement of either by the other is not a goal. Rather, they coexist. "Art on the plaza" or "plop art," exemplified by the heroic general astride his horse in the middle of a square, performs an independent function as memorial, but it often neither reacts to nor influences the site, which, in turn, simply shelters the sculpture. An Andy Warhol oversized caricature in the same space may change the space significantly, and a Richard Serra sculpture of steel slabs placed in a plaza to purposefully impede the pedestrian becomes art that actually modifies perception of the place, but all three examples stand in the space created by the architecture rather than making a connection to the architecture.

"Placed art" may sometimes have a social agenda or benefit. For example, "Waiting for the Interurban" in Seattle, although not noted for its aesthetic qualities, is a beloved and frequently community-decorated piece of urban art that functions as a community landmark. Still, it remains a piece of "placed art."

Artist as Artisan/Enhancer

Artists and artisans throughout history have been commissioned to decorate an architectural space or to create an architectural element within the space—such as railings, lighting, furniture, or an entryway—that enhances the architecture. A sensitive eye to both the art and the architecture is essential to the success of the type of work. This mutually reinforcing expression has the potential to augment both the art and the architecture, and to give increased meaning to both disciplines within a given space.

Artist as Contributor

As a contributor, or a cooperative participant, an individual artist's voice is recognized and expressed but not necessarily related to the architecture. Participants support each other's ideas and work toward a common goal, but the final results still retain individual artistic and design statements. The artist is involved in finding opportunities for art and is invited to design a piece that is specific to the project. This

Figure E3. *"Circle game" on the Orrery at Southpark Community Center, Seattle, Washington. Designed by Ginny Ruffner and ARC. Courtesy of ARC Architects.*

In our experience there has been a vast difference between the placement of art within and around an environment and substantive early involvement of artists in the planning stages of environments. The collaborative process often gives the spaces themselves a richness that makes later embellishments unnecessary. More options are available if the artist is aboard early, before the architect begins to design, particularly if integration of the disciplines is a goal.

What follows is a description of a successful collaborative process between an architect and an artist. It describes a challenging, rewarding, but often frustrating process that—if successful—can result in a significantly enhanced project that is better than the sum of its parts.

A Real Collaboration

At South Park Community Center in southwest Seattle, our challenge was to replace a dearly loved community recreation center with a new facility that the community could embrace as theirs. The design team decided that the best way to do that was to ask the community who they were and what they wanted. There ensued a series of very active community meetings that helped the whole team frame their ideas.

The artist on the project, Ginny Ruffner, joined the design team at the onset, before pencil was laid to paper, and participated in both the design and construction process. She is a glass artist, but after listening to the community felt that glass was inappropriate for this project. As a creative problem solver, she perpetually asked "why not" as well as "why" and challenged both the architect and the community to be visionary.

Used to sketching her concepts, she drew her own building elevations to gain our attention. She solicited the neighborhood for input, organized interactive workshops, and kept the community involved while the architect and engineers were putting together the contract documents.

During construction she worked on-site with kids from the neighborhood, enlisting them to help place bronze castings for the concrete walkways and helping them locate their handprint tiles in the bathroom. The result was a wonderfully interactive environment where kids and adults could interact with both the art and architecture.

involvement is not supervised by the architect, but still comes under his approval. Artists are usually selected for their style, with the expectation that they will work within a particular range of possible solutions.

Collaborators

In a true collaborative process, the artist is an equal participant in the design. The intent is to have the art influence the architecture and the architecture influence the art in the conceptual stages. The process of creating the project together guides the direction the design takes. The artist helps strategize during the process and helps implement the product. In this situation, the team's voice is stronger than the individual's voice, and there is a fusion of the artist's and architect's ideas so that the individual contributions are not readily apparent. The quality of the ideas rather than authorship is important.

The archway at the entry to the site is a fun, quirky, colorful, inviting gateway announcing entry to a public place. People are curious: What is this gate? What awaits on the other side? Once through the gate, a seductively entertaining walkway engages you in games on your way to the building. A linear calendar in the pavement invites you to find your birthday and compare it to birthdays of famous people as well as holidays and local historic events. Miniature bronze animals cast in the walkway encourage the kids to find the largest or the scariest or imitate the roar of a lion or the walk of a monkey. At the entrance to the building itself, an orrery (a model of the solar system) is cast into the pavement. It includes the signs of the zodiac and multicolored stones and has its own teaching and game qualities. The walkway is often full of hunched-over figures enthusiastically discovering, writing down clues, inventing new games, and wondering.

Inside the building, more embedded items encourage interaction. Tiles created from the handprints of neighborhood kids and local major-league athletes line the bathroom. Ten years later these same kids use the center and compare their childhood handprints to their now grown hands, witnessing the passing of time; people can put their own hand in the print from Fred Brown, former Seattle Sonics basketball star, or Debbie Armstrong, a local Olympic skier, and see and feel the differences of people. Throughout the building and the site, this art allows for the community (especially the kids) to be a part of the center. It is theirs because they played a role in its creation.

Artist's Impact

Ginny's process challenged the entire design team to "see" beyond concepts and to "think outside the box." Her fanciful, impractical building elevations encouraged us all to consider the building as a place for the amusement, growth, and education of a community. Ginny helped the community "own" the building through her inclusion of kids and adults in the design and construction process. Her participation and her art added vitality not only to the process of design, but also to the product, and that product continues as a vital community center today. We learned an important lesson—in order to be vital, the product must evolve from the process.

Lessons Learned

Although the options and potential for artist/architect involvement are growing and evolving, each project should strive to find its own dynamic. Nothing is more stale than yesterday's project recycled as the "how to" formula, and no one process should serve as "the model" for collaboration. However, difficulties as well as opportunities are inherent in collaborative projects, and after twenty years of working with artists on both public and private projects we have observations to share that may help you to determine whether this process will work for you and is right for your project.

Collaboration Is Not for Everyone

Almost everyone agrees that the strongest requirements for team members are persistence, patience, and a collective willingness to put in extra, often unpaid, time—collaboration is a time-consuming process. Additionally, a positive and curious attitude is almost mandatory, as well as the ability to be flexible, open-minded, and accessible.

Teamwork

"Team" will mean different things to different people. Architects are used to pooling skills with engineers, landscape architects, and consultants, and "collaborating" with owners' needs and program requirements, but the team concept is often new to artists who are used to producing work solo in their studios. Differences in working methods as well as in role definition should be recognized and addressed at the onset of a project. Architects, engineers, and landscape architects share a common language that artists must learn: the language of blueprints, schedules, and budgets. Whereas architects must finalize plans early and follow schedules for various phases of the design process, artists are used to changing and evolving their work as they go, and, if responsible for their own fabrication, do not even have to commit until the artwork is being constructed. The artist working on a collaborative team must commit early enough to integrate the work with the design of the team. While encouraged initially to let the imagination run wild, the artist as team member often faces the problem of having not too few, but too many ideas. Artists must learn that late changes in the architectural world create complications and cost money, and that

Design Team Considerations

Different Working Methods

- Architects have budgets and timelines / Artists often create without a budget or a timeline.
- Architects are used to collaboration and compromise / Artists are typically used to solo situations where their decisions are their own.

Building Teams

- Bring the team together early—establish communication, roles, and responsibilities.
- Artists should attend team meetings.
- Share correspondence with artist—keep them in the communication loop.
- As a member of the team, the artist should be held to schedule and budget.
- Make clear the expectations—what is needed and when.
- Establish the process for constructing and installing the artist's work.
- Coordinate the building and art construction schedules.
- Avoid putting the artwork on the critical path of building construction.
- The strongest requirements for team members are persistence, patience, and a collective willingness to put in extra, often unpaid, time. A positive and curious attitude is almost mandatory.
- Design-team artists should: Not be married to a specific medium; think about process as much or more than product; think about the whole project rather than focus on where their art can fit into the project.
- Design team architects should: Avoid being territorial; think conceptually.
- Let the artists run their hands over every surface.
- It is up to the team to define *their* concept of collaboration at the beginning of the process.

Delights

- Unexpected things happen.
- Relationships grow.
- Artists ask hard questions.

Drawbacks

- Time—It does take more time.
- Money—It can cost more but it doesn't have to. Contractors often have a pricey reaction to the word *artist* when bidding. It helps to clarify roles, timetables, and responsibilities long before bidding begins.

Figure E4. *Design Team Considerations.*

as architects are finalizing their plans artists are losing options for the integration of theirs.

We favor early briefing and frequent updates, so that the artist understands the budget restrictions and scheduling details that the project must meet.

Communication—"Lumps and Bumps"

There are inevitable bumps in the road as the team members try to figure out the style and language of working together, but maintaining good and consistent communication can minimize these. The intent of the project and the design process should be clearly defined for everyone. An information chain should be established with clear contacts. All team members should be informed of changes and developments in a timely way, and clear and consistent documentation is important throughout the project.

Every instance of artists and architects working together will be different, because of the unique makeup of each design team. Every collaborative effort must face its own challenges and find its own dynamic. There is no recipe for success, and to ensure the vitality of a project the sense of experimentation needs to be kept high. It is hard work and not for everyone. You must be equipped to ask, "Is a collaborative approach appropriate for *this* project?"

David Rutherford is a founding partner of ARC Architects, Seattle, Washington, focusing on publicly funded projects dealing with Special Populations. He was the project manager on one of the first Design Team Artist projects in the country—the Viewlands Hoffman electrical Substation for Seattle City Light in 1976 (with artists Buster Simpson, Andrew Keating, and Sherry Markovitz). Dave has served on the Seattle Arts Commission as chair of the Art in Public Places Committee and as chair of the commission. He has also served on the Seattle Design Commission.

Deborah Rutherford received her Master of Fine Arts degree from the University of Washington and has participated on several Design Team Artist projects both as an artist and as a project manager for the Washington State Arts Commission. Her work has been exhibited in galleries and juried shows. She has won both awards and commissions for large-scale textile installations.

THE ARCHITECTURAL ROLES
OF PUBLIC ART

*Those who have enough enthusiasm and faith in good causes should be convinced
that our own era can create works of beauty and worth.*

—*Camillo Sitte*, The Art of Building Cities, 2

It took five days for the text of the Declaration of Independence to reach New York [City], but on July 9, 1776, New Yorkers celebrated the occasion by marching to Bowling Green, site of the city's first and only work of public art. It was an equestrian statue of George III imported from London six years earlier. . . . The crowd toppled the statue and, not yet satisfied, hacked it to bits. . . . [Portions were] melted down by patriots, and with grim efficiency *George III* was transformed into bullets" (Gilmartin 1995: 3). Public art in the United States has always had a complex life, balancing many roles.

In addition to their role as social, political, experiential, and/or formal "speech," public artworks may play a number of different architectural roles within a civic place. They may help shape social space by creating stages and houses, alcoves and halls, inside and out. They may provide iconographic identity and speak of the *genius loci*. Artwork may provide shelter, shape acoustic space, or temper the character of light. Public art may serve as landmarks, entrances, pathways, or other wayfinding devices. Furthermore, artwork can evoke a sense of creative play and create playgrounds. All of these roles may, in response to the site, help create a distinct and engaging place.

The influential art critic Lucy Lippard wrote, "Public art suggests an architectural scale and milieu" (Lippard 1997: 265), and "a place-specific public art. This would be an art that reveals new depths of a place to engage the viewer or inhabitant. . . . It should become . . . part of, or a criticism of, the built and/or daily environment, making places mean more to those who live or spend time there" (1997: 263). Removed from the physical context and self-selecting audiences of the museum, public art must live within civic places and the public realm.

Public art can be a critical ingredient of urban and civic-place design. Pope Sixtus V's transformation of Rome in the sixteenth century depended in large part on the careful siting of obelisks to establish termini for future streets (Kostof 1995: 498). Similarly, Baron Haussmann's reshaping of Paris was anchored by a set of monuments and monumental buildings that served as foci for the new boulevards (Kostof 1992: 266–73). Bernard Tschumi's Parc de la Villette project in Paris plays with admixing public art and urbanism. Tschumi placed a number of "follies" throughout the park to create "event places" within the structure of the park (Tschumi 2000).

A number of urban-design theorists and commentators have included monuments and other public art as central components of urban design. Camillo Sitte devotes a chapter of *The Art of Building Cities* (1945 [1889]) to the placement of monuments. Obelisks, monumental arches, statuary, and other works of public art are so completely integrated into Hegemann and Peets's *American Vitruvius* (1988 [1922]) as to make it undeniable that public monuments are included in their broader term *civic art*. A number of the patterns in *A Pattern Language,* such as "Main Gateways," "Paths and Goals," and "Something Roughly in the Middle," provide support and reasons for public art (Alexander et al. 1977). For example, the Main Gateways pattern—"Mark every boundary in the city which has important human meaning . . . by great gateways where the major entering paths cross the boundary"—could be fulfilled with public art. San Francisco's Chinatown gates are an example.

A strong understanding of public art's potential to enliven urban form may be critical for cities and towns in this age of tourism, equity migrants, and suburban dominance. Public art may promote dialog by providing an excuse for strangers to talk to each other, or a gameboard for people to play with each other. By interacting with the wind or framing views, public art may help make the climate and the landscape more legible and anchor us in place. Public art may help compose or structure a city or district, provide keys for wayfinding, or help make the functioning of the city legible.

A. Dialog

The urban researcher William H. Whyte coined the term *triangulation,* i.e., the situation in which an object or event provides the excuse or subject matter for strangers to talk with one another (Whyte 1980). His research specifically mentions street performers and some kinds of sculpture as having this effect.

Dialog does not have to be verbal face-to-face conversation. We use our dress and body language to make social and political statements (see Sennett 1977); we seek appropriate

stages from which to reach our audience; we leave written messages for each other; and we converse by creating artworks.

However, to help make a good city, it is my belief that public art must also evoke a sense of sanguinity. It may embody serious social commentary, but I hold, it will be much more successful and enduring if it does not do so in an implacable manner, but rather suspends the commentary within a sense of play or empathy.

Campfires and Snowmen
How can sculptural art foster dialog between strangers?

Think of your artwork as creating a ring of people (like people around a campfire) and place this ring in a comfortable spot with places where people can sit, and near the flow of pedestrians.

Like a campfire, artwork that is animated captures attention. Anticipating and enjoying an artwork's movements provides an immediate excuse for strangers to talk. The inducement to conviviality and play is even stronger if the artwork can be played with, either through direct controls or by moving oneself in response to the artwork (e.g., changing the angle from which you look at a hologram). Adults and children in the field of water jets at the Olympic Rings Fountain in Atlanta's Centennial Olympic Park play with the water and with each other.

In his classic study of European plazas, *The Art of Building Cities,* Camillo Sitte observed and promoted a pattern for placing artworks: "It may be surprising to say that one of [children's] favorite games can teach us the principles of good monument location. As a matter of fact, the snowmen with which they amuse themselves . . . are located in exactly the same manner as fountains and monuments were according to ancient practices. . . . Consider the snow-covered plaza of a town. Here and there are snow paths—natural thoroughfares. . . . snowmen are built [between the paths]. It was at such points, similarly dispersed from traffic, that the ancient communities set up their fountains and monuments" (Sitte 1945 [1889]: 14). This pattern of placement gives space for an audience and is near the flow of pedestrians so that passers-by may become engaged.

Figure 15.1. *The Wall Street Bull is a prime site for souvenir photographs, New York City, 1999.*

Numinous Presence

How can figural sculpture evoke an active persona in the minds of a community? Which figures will the community ignore and with which will it play?

In his book *The Uses Of Images*, the art historian E. H. Gombrich suggests that one of the roles of outdoor sculpture is its animate presence—that it somehow becomes a part of our lives, a focus for a cultural force. He discusses the statue of the goose girl of Göttingen (Germany), the Statue of Liberty, the Little Mermaid of Copenhagen, and the Pasquino. During the Middle Ages in Rome, the Pasquino was a fragment of a Roman work that in its broken form looked like a court jester. "It had become the habit or tradition to affix to this statue satirical verses about topical issues as if it was Pasquino who spoke, and the genre of such satires became known as Pasquinades" (Gombrich 1999: 144).

The question of how a work may become a numinous presence awaits vigorous study and debate. I suggest a few considerations. First, the works should be accessible, either in a simple physical sense or, more difficultly, in a conceptual sense (the Little Mermaid in the harbor is in her appropriate place but not readily physically accessible). They need to be accessible so that we may interact with them by giving them political poems to announce, dressing them up on holidays, or having them inhabit our dreams. Second, they need to belong to the city and not be primarily the voice of the artist. T. S. Eliot wrote that a poet must be aware of the "mind of his own country" and value this mind over his own private mind. "The emotion of art is impersonal. And the poet cannot reach this impersonality without surrendering himself wholly to the work to be done. And he is not likely to know what is to be done unless he lives in what is not merely the present, but the present moment of the past, unless he is conscious, not of what is dead, but of what is already living" (Eliot 1920: 51 and 59).

Time Marks

How and where should we mark cyclical, mythic, or historic time in our towns?

A sense of belonging to a place involves orientation within the seasons, history, and foundational stories of the place. Festivals and gardens often mark the seasons and the cycle of time. Monuments and buildings are typically used to mark historic time. Mythic time is the conceptual time in which the stories of fundamental types in the worldview of a people are told. Mythic stories may be boldly portrayed—for example, the Saint Louis Arch reinforces the story of manifest destiny—or they may be ingrained into the culture of building. Suburban tract homes, for example, often have vestigial porches used solely to evoke a sense of home.

Tourism and the symbolic economy make the history of a place an important economic resource. The subtle manipulations and unabashed hucksterism engendered by the tourist economy confounds the political and social battles inherent in defining history. How does the marketing of history affect our conceptions of history?

Public art may reinforce, challenge, undermine, or assist

the evolution of a community's sense of time. It is in this light, perhaps, that the political nature of public art can best be seen. For which (or whose) heroes should we cast bronzes? How do we mark winter solstice? Which buildings have historical significance? Should public art challenge and confront the dominant paradigms and myths of a community, or should it seek to make manifest notes of harmony? How can memorials speak not only to the past, but also leave opportunities for future honor? In London, England, the Memorial to Heroic Sacrifice is a wall of plaques honoring people who lost their lives saving others. Perhaps the most powerful part of this wall is the set of blank plaques waiting and available.

Chapter 4, "Writing the Syllabus," discusses ways to engage the community in planning an urban commons. But times change. New people join a community. Long-term residents change their views, and new stories arise. How can a design give place for new stories? How can we promote a living dialog and at the same time preserve past voices?

Can memorials, rather than reaching for permanence through indestructibility, aim for perpetuity through periodic renewal? Shakespeare, although perhaps a biased advocate of verse, made the argument for memory through renewal in his sonnets:

> Not marble, nor the gilded monuments
> Of princes, shall outlive this powerful rhyme;
> But you shall shine more bright in these conténts
> Than unswept stone, besmeared with sluttish time.
> When wasteful war shall statues overturn,
> And broils root out the work of masonry . . .

As architects our work is cast in physical form, not words, but we can design in ways that are renewed through time. Rather than casting bronze, might we plant a grove or begin a mosaic to which others may add? Should we honor poets by painting and repainting their poems on a wall? Should renewal ceremonies be part of public art projects? Of course, all materials do wear. Perhaps the bronze horse that needs repair every hundred years simply represents a pace of renewal longer than a lifetime. The question for the designer of a memorial is, then, What is the appropriate pace of dialog and renewal?

On Stage

Can we create soapboxes and stages from which people will speak and around which people will gather? Can the artwork encourage thoughtful, funny, and significant speech?

In the United States, the soapbox is a custom fallen greatly out of favor. Yet what could better epitomize participatory democracy than a citizen speaking in public to fellow citizens about the issues of the day?

Can sculptural or performance art help reestablish this tradition? Can the artwork provide a vehicle that invites and inspires citizens to speak with eloquence? Creating places for street performers (a.k.a. buskers) may be a start. Good street stages need to be near a pedestrian crossroads, but in a sub-space with a radius of about fifteen to twenty-five feet from the performer to accommodate the stage and the audience. Many buskers prefer to have a wall or other backdrop, but some prefer theater-in-the-round. Sculptural and architectural artwork that provides props, or creates a stage, may also invite a renaissance. Should we provide bronze soapboxes to induce politicians to come from behind the TV cameras into the crowds? Should we create a traditional bronze horse in the center of the square on which individuals could mount so that they may take on the role of honored hero?

The Writing on the Wall

Can artwork provide vehicles for dialog through public text?

Public text need not be exclusively carved in granite. U.S. embassies ought to have chalkboards on the outside to demonstrate a commitment to freedom of speech.

The rise and persistence of graffiti, while a complex phenomena, certainly suggests a strong desire for graphic public speech. That graffiti is often perceived as, or actually is, threatening to public order could indicate that there are insufficient venues for public speech.

Street kiosks give permission and opportunity to the long practice of posting handbills (see "Kiosks," chapter 13). Perhaps the design of kiosks could, like electronic chat rooms, have themes—a kiosk in front of the music hall could cater to musical notices, another could specialize in poetry.

The electronic web provides new opportunities for text and other media in civic squares. Could people email messages to a reader board along Denver's Sixteenth Street Mall? Could the plazas of sister cities have electronic portals to each other? Could ATMs host a poet's work? Could the sound track to an outdoor movie be broadcast to people's cell phones? Could artworks and memorials record people's comments and replay them?

Open-Source Artwork
Most artworks are monologues—a single artist speaking once to the audience. How, where, and when can artworks be more like dinner-table conversations with multiple authors speaking over a long period of time?

In Post Alley, below Pike Place Market in Seattle, a brick wall is covered with faces and designs made of bubble gum. Created over the years by people waiting in line for the theater, the gum wall is not formally a great work. It is, however, a delight. The gum wall is a kind of game; open to all players and open to inventive moves. It is an evolving conversation about whimsy.

Other examples of collective but undirected artworks include: living Christmas trees decorated by various groups along the median of the freeway, graffiti yards, and the memorials of teddy bears, flowers, and other items that were created at Columbine High School, in Oklahoma City, near ground zero in New York City, and elsewhere.

These works each (1) have a framework (e.g., a brick wall, a strip of land, a cyclone fence) that offers a large canvas and gives some order, (2) are typically made of small increments of inexpensive materials, and (3) allow people to act individually in a manner that adds to others' actions.

Other clues about how open source artwork could function may be gleaned from the internet. For example, Wikipedia is an effort to create a collectively written and edited encyclopedia (www.wikipedia.com). Anyone may add to and edit the text. Skeptics may believe this will lead to babble, but the success of the Linux operating system and other wiki-like projects points to the potential merit of the experiment. Wikipedia has some noteworthy mechanisms to focus the work. The projects' main page clearly defines what its purpose is (an encyclopedia), and what it is not (a chat room, dictionary etc). It suggests appropriate places to engage in these other activities. Commonly followed policies (or norms) and rules to consider are posted, and talk pages are used to discuss the work before modifying the body of the text.

B. Anchoring
To bring forth the genius loci *of a settlement, we must understand and express the underlying structure of the landscape.*

Sky Light
How can we shape light and shadow, color the sun, trace the stars, align with moonrise, and frame the heavens to shape space?

In pattern no. 135, "Tapestry of Light and Dark," Alexander and his coauthors observe that people orient to and move toward light, and suggest that buildings should be structured around this characteristic. This holds true for outdoor rooms as well. The important places should be more luminous than the surrounding support spaces. Squares should draw people into them from the adjacent streets. The field of a square—an ice rink, stage, or pond, for example—should be brighter than the edges when the field is active.

This tapestry can be complex, subtle, and dynamic. Perhaps at night the edges of a square should be brighter than the center, and in the day a canopy of trees lets the edges be shadier than the field. Perhaps some places should be less lit than the streets during the day to help make a quiet oasis that looks out on the bustle of the street. Artworks acting as luminous landmarks create lines or edges of light, or are volumes of radiance can help structure the balance of light in a square.

Likewise, the lights of the sky are not simply light. Rather moonlight, the full light of day, sunrise, moonless starlight, even the traces of artificial satellites evoke different meanings. The sky is the ceiling of civic squares and courtyards. Artworks may frame, shape, and make manifest the character of the lights of the sky.

Figure 15.2. *A whirligig by Jackie Williams, Budaghers, New Mexico, 2003.*

Windthings

Wind helps us define place and season. It provides movement, energy, and mood. If we play with the wind can we strengthen a common sense of place?

Along the Front Range in Colorado, it seems that the summer thunderstorms blow in at 3 P.M. and blow out at 4. Could one build a storm clock? On the beaches of the Gulf of Mexico, the force of hurricanes is almost unimaginable in the calm of early spring, but physical reminders such as seawalls or weather vanes that require one-hundred-mph winds to move may quicken our memory.

Playing with the wind can also help animate a place and suggest moods. A lazy breeze flirting with a streamer sets a different scene than a brisk morning wind holding streamers rigid. Whirligigs and mobiles are four-dimensional sculptures playing with tempo, time, and gesture as well as plastic form. The sound of the wind can be shaped. Doug Hallis's *A Sound Garden* is a complex of wind-activated organ pipes on windmill-like towers in a Seattle park. Wind can be crafted to improve the microclimate, and wind scoops, wind fences, windmills that activate fountains and other devices offer opportunities for public art and public comfort.

Artwork that makes present the wind, or, perhaps, records its whims, can deepen our perception of place and season.

City Water

How should we continue the deep tradition of gathering and delighting in water?

Water is life, and can be displayed to reflect many of life's conditions. Still water may be somber, and jets playful. Water can suggest connection to other waters—the ocean, mountain lakes, the River Styx. Water plays with light, cools the air, whispers and rushes, seasons the taste and smell of the breeze, quenches thirsts, and washes away sins. Importantly for the creation of civic squares, clean water attracts people, and provides opportunities for strangers to commune or play together.

The following projects suggest a range of ways city water may help build convivial places.

"When the bus stopped at Seventy-second Street, Stuart jumped out and hurried across to the sailboat pond in Central Park. Over the pond the west wind blew, and into the teeth of the west wind sailed the sloops and schooners, their rails well down, their wet decks gleaming. The owners, boys and grown men, raced around the cement shores . . ." Thus begins Stuart Little's sailboat race (White 1945: 30). The sailboat pond is a wet central field edged by a frame of cement shores where the spectators gather. The citizen-operated fountains, water wheels, and other waterworks that inhabited the pools of the Seattle Science Center likewise provided a field of play.

Waterworks, of course, may also provide landmarks or focal points, and even create civic rooms. Many of the Savannah squares feature a fountain, giving each square a distinct landmark. The urban focal point of Fountain Square in Cincinnati, Ohio, is the Tyler Davidson Fountain. New York's Paley Park and Seattle's Waterfall Park are small urban rooms created around large water features.

Figure 15.3. *Playing at the fountain, 2002.*

A much more subtle approach is to highlight the infrastructure of urban water. For example, as part of "Growing Vine Street" Buster Simpson created a miniature garden made by a set of water traps in a downspout (fig. 8.5). Drinking fountains, street gutters and grates, water meters, and even the sewer system (Paris's is legendary) offer opportunities.

C. Structuring

In *Good City Form*, Kevin Lynch presented a set of criteria by which to evaluate the quality of a settlement. One of the criteria he offers is "sense"—"the degree to which the settlement can be clearly perceived and mentally differentiated and structured in time and space by its residents and the degree to which that mental structure connects with their values and concepts—the match between environment, our sensory and mental capabilities, and our cultural constructs" (1981: 118). In his book *Wayfinding in Architecture,* Romedi Passini discusses a particular aspect of "sense," that is, how physical design can provide spatial orientation.

The Yellow Brick Road
How can paths orient and lead us in everyday and profound ways?

The color, material, and pattern of a path or street can help separate it from other routes and provide a legible structure to a district. How could we pave or otherwise mark parade routes, the street from the courthouse square to the railroad depot, and other important routes with distinctive and appropriate materials?

Within a single town's network of paths one can easily get lost, particularly if, as is typical, all the streets are made with the same materials in similar ways. Paving or otherwise distinctively marking (a colonnade of Maypoles? A trellis of kites?) the main organizing paths—maybe a ring road, or the main cross streets—can help make sense of a web of streets, provide visual boundaries or centers to districts, and add fun.

Marking the festive, historic, and/or spiritual routes of a town can help orient us in other ways. Countless people have followed a painted line through the streets of Boston that marks the Freedom Trail. The parade decorations of innumerable towns rival the scale of Christo's work, and provide an orientation to festivity. Paths through museums and memorials have been used to help structure a narrative, and the proverbial garden path has led to many things. Certainly this genre can evolve.

Meet Me at the Brass Pig
What makes a good place for a rendezvous?

At Pike Place Market in Seattle there is a large brass piggybank. In addition to being a rather remarkable fundraiser, it serves as a meeting place—"I'll see you at the pig at 10"—because it is located just within the edge of the market, it has ample space around it for hanging out, a shed roof offers

Figure 15.4. *Rachel the Pig, by Georgia Gerber, at Seattle's Pike Place Market (c. 1998) serves as an icon, a meeting place, and a fundraising device.*

shelter, there are interesting things to watch as you wait, and the pig is a distinctive figure. What this meeting ground lacks is places to sit.

The grand steps to M.I.T. or Columbia University Library and the bleacher-like base of the statues in London's Piccadilly Square are also well-used meeting places. Again they are distinctive places with activities to watch as you wait. They also offer stadium seating and in good weather they become destinations in themselves.

Ideally the rendezvous point will provide aids to orientation. The Pike Place Market pig sits below a clock, and at an elbow of the street so that one can look down both branches of Pike Place.

Artwork may improve a meeting grounds by providing a missing ingredient—a distinctive feature, seating, shelter, things to watch as you wait, or orientation devices.

Towers and Columns

How should we, as designers and community members, create towers that aid in wayfinding, make sense of the structure of the town, and speak to the nature of the square, the town, and the landscape?

Standing distinctly on the skyline or against the horizon of buildings, towers help us find our routes and make our conceptual maps of a place. They may also structure symbolic and spiritual maps. These landmarks anchor squares and help them become central places, places that structure the town.

The Eiffel Tower is perhaps the classic landmark. It is tall and distinctive and thus helps orient people within Paris. As a wayfinding aid, its symmetry is problematic—you cannot readily tell if you are looking at the north, south, east, or west face of the tower. The tower was hotly contested when it was built because as such a dominant landmark it usurped for itself the right to symbolize Paris (Barthes 1979).

In their book *Urban Design: Ornament and Decoration,* Cliff Moughtin, Taner Oc, and Steven Tiesdell (1995) suggest a classification of landmarks. First, they can be divided into natural and constructed landmarks. Constructed landmarks they divide into buildings (or parts of buildings) and civic furniture, and civic furniture they further divide into individual artworks and repetitive elements such as lampposts. Public artwork intentionally serving as a landmark may of course fit into any of these categories.

Freestanding towers, columns, obelisks, and large statues fit into the individual civic furniture/artwork category. I discuss lampposts, parking meters, bollards, and other "repetitive" civic fixtures in chapter 13.

As singular works, landmarks are placed and sized to be seen on the scale of the city and landscape. San Francisco's Coit Tower atop Telegraph Hill commands much of the bay and the northeastern quadrant of the city. The glass towers of New England's Holocaust Memorial in Boston, designed by Stanley Saitowitz, frame an edge to the City Hall plaza, and are visible down multiple street axes. The church spires of the small towns of Quebec and New England and the grain elevators of the prairie towns give a précis from afar of the activities and places we will find at their feet. Often the spires hold the actual doors to the buildings they mark, but even if they do not house the main doorway they serve the role of marking entrance. In a way, their power is not of mystery but of familiarity—a power adopted by the Golden Arches. Yet, unlike chain stores, these markers may vary within the pattern, offering not near-uniformity, but family resemblance. The question for the designer is how to discover and express both the uniqueness of a place and its alliance with others.

Strong landmarks are also designed to be engaging at the scale of the individual. Coit Tower has rooms and murals in its base. Boston's Holocaust Memorial has the identity numbers of victims etched into the glass walls of the towers. After these landmarks attract you to their vicinity, they reward close attention.

Legible Infrastructure
Can we use the repetition and collective form of infrastructure to build a set of places and artworks that express the structure of a settlement?

The infrastructure of a settlement often creates a similar urban situation in multiple parts of the town (for example, electrical substations). Moreover, infrastructure typically provides a common resource and thus reflects the collective nature of a settlement.

Currently, we tend to design our infrastructure to maximize a single goal. Waterworks, for example, are constructed simply to provide an ample supply of clean water at a minimal price. The classic fountains of Rome, on the other hand, fulfill multiple urban roles. They are a public utility (they provide water), provide public space in the city (the fountains have piazzas and piazzettas encircling them), and, through their artwork, serve as places to celebrate the aqueduct that feeds them, its builders, and the gods.

Expressing infrastructure (the underlying structure) can help make a settlement legible both in its construction and its relationship to its resources. Sewer lines, for example, typically follow drainage sheds, and could illustrate our dependence on natural systems to clean our wastes. For

example, perhaps we could build "outfall gardens" where we return sewer water to our rivers, lakes, and oceans.

In the 1988 Public Art Master Plan for Phoenix, Arizona, William R. Morrish, Catherine R. Brown, and Grover Mouton proposed a comprehensive link between public art, urban design, and infrastructure. "In the public works sense infrastructure provides a city's residents with warmth (heat), security (street lights), and comfort (water, electricity). We identified a parallel structure system—a 'cultural infrastructure'—that we thought was as important to residents' sense of security, comfort and belonging. . . . This 'cultural infrastructure' was compromised of at least three types of structural systems: historic urban patterns, the urban terrain, and . . . the public cognitive map" (Brown and Morrish 1992: 12).

The historic urban patterns include the traces of all the cultures that have shaped a town. In Phoenix, it included sixteen-hundred-year-old canals built by the Hohokam Indians. The urban terrain includes topography and environmental systems. The public cognitive map, a concept developed by Kevin Lynch (see Lynch 1960), is akin to those tourist-oriented cartoon maps that show landmarks, districts, boundaries, and major roads in exaggerated detail and size. The public cognitive map is the conceptual structure, the sum of the residents' internal maps, of the town. The Phoenix Public Art Master Plan, based on these three components of "cultural infrastructure," serves to guide the design of public works and public art so that they work together to intensify Phoenix's sense of place. Freeway bridges over city streets, for example, may serve as gateways between neighborhoods.

Power substations, wells and water tanks, cell-phone towers, parking meters, manhole covers, parking garages, telephone switching boxes, storm drains, lampposts, bollards, stop signs, telephone poles, and ten thousand other aspects of infrastructure provide opportunities for artwork and urban commons that express the collective nature of our towns as well as variation within the commonality. This cultural infrastructure can reinforce a sense of convivial belonging by making palpable the environmental structure, urban patterns, and our mental maps.

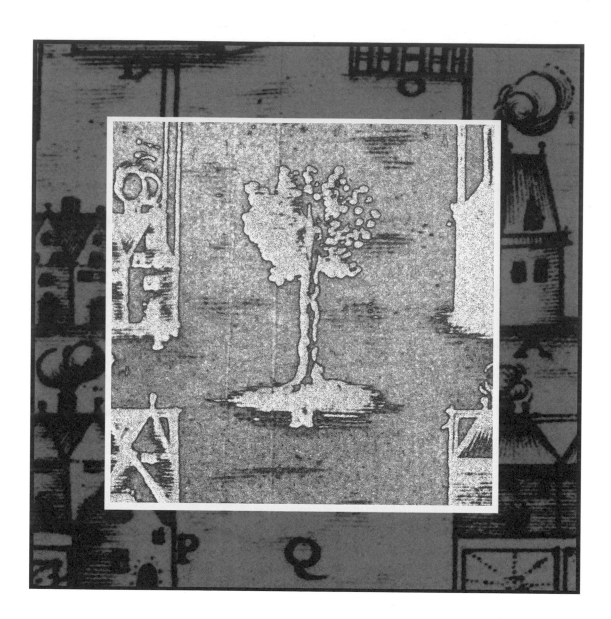

CODA

Stop Making Sense

The Tao that can be told is not the eternal Tao.
The name that can be named is not the eternal name.
The nameless is the beginning of heaven and earth.
The named is the mother of ten thousand things.
Ever desire less, one can see the mystery.
Ever desiring, one can see the manifestations.
These two spring from the same source but differ in name;
this appears as darkness.
Darkness within darkness.
The gate to all mystery.

—*Lao Tsu*, Tao Te Ching

The queries of this book are an attempt to raise and analyze significant questions that face the planners, designers, and managers of an urban commons. They are phrased as questions to suggest that the answers may change from place to place and time to time. The questions themselves, however, are not complete and the set of appropriate questions also changes from situation to situation. Moreover, designing is not simply a matter of adding together architectural answers to a set of questions. The whole must be more than the sum of the parts. There is a limit to analysis.

The complementary task to analysis is synthesis—knitting together, making whole, and creating a higher truth. Synthesis is not an imposition of form, but the emergence of coherence from the forces at play. Strong squares are synthetic wholes. They knit together the structure and infrastructure of the city. They intermingle a sense of the town and the land. They are the places we gather and assemble. They are built places that support conviviality.

ACKNOWLEDGMENTS

This book rests on the foundations built by countless architects, artists, philosophers, ditch diggers, poets, city officials, patrons, and citizens who have contributed to the civic commons. I owe particular debts or gratitude to:

My wife and children—Elaine, Emily and Quinault

✠

The writers of the excursions—Ted Harrison, Stanley Crawford, Marilys Nepomechie, Andrew Stone, Alf Simon, David and Deborah Rutherford

✠

Contributors of images—Devin Cannady, Joel Condon, Rick Martinez, John Reps, Buster Simpson

✠

My cabinet of readers and advisors—Elaine Thomas, Dorothy Thomas, Alf Simon, Andy Pressman, Mark Savage, Rocky Piro, Jennifer Chamberlin, students in my Civic Space and Public Art seminar

✠

The anonymous reviewers and my editor, Luther Wilson

✠

The editor of my previous book, Wendy Lochner, for her continuing critical advice

✠

The University of New Mexico community, particularly Andy Pressman and Baker Morrow,

✠

and the host of librarians and curators that preserve and make available our heritage.

BIBLIOGRAPHY

Adams, Don, and Arlene Goldbard. 2001. *Creative Community: The Art of Cultural Development.* New York: Rockefeller Foundation Creativity and Cultural Division.

Alexander, Christopher, Sara Ishikawa, Murray Silverstein, with Max Jacobson and Ingrid Fiksdahl-King. 1977. *A Pattern Language.* New York: Oxford University Press.

Alexander, Christopher, Hajo Neis, Artemis Anninou, and Ingrid King. 1987. *A New Theory of Urban Design.* New York: Oxford University Press.

Altman, Irwin, and E. H. Zube. 1989. *Public Places and Spaces.* New York: Plenum Press.

American Water Works Association. "Water Systems: Guidelines for Rainwater Catchment and Filtration." Denver: American Water Works Association.

Arendt, Randall. 1999. *Crossroads, Hamlet, Village, Town.* American Planning Association. Planning Advisory Service Report Number 487/488.

Arens E., P. McNall, R. Gonzalez, L. Berglund, and L. Zeren. 1980. "A New Bioclimatic Chart for Passive Solar Design." In *Proceedings of the Fifth National Passive Solar Conference.* Newark, Del.: American Section of the International Solar Energy Society.

Axelrod, Robert. 1984. *The Evolution of Cooperation.* New York: Basic Books.

———. 1997. *The Complexity of Cooperation.* Princeton, N.J.: Princeton University Press.

Barthes, Roland. 1979. *The Eiffel Tower and Other Mythologies.* Translated by Richard Howard. New York: Hill and Wang.

Berry, Susan and Sharman Apt Russell. 1986. *Built to Last.* Santa Fe: New Mexico Historic Preservation Division.

Biggar, H. P., ed. 1922. *The Works of Samuel de Champlain.* Toronto: Champlain Society.

Brand, Stewart. 1994. *How Buildings Learn.* New York: Viking Press.

———. 1999. *The Clock of the Long Now.* New York: Basic Books.

Breslin, J. William, and Jeffrey Z. Rubin, eds. 1991. *Negotiation Theory and Practice.* Cambridge, Mass.: The Program on Negotiation at Harvard University.

Brown, Catherine R., and William Morrish. 1992. "Making a Public Art Master Plan." In *Stodola Public Art Works: The Arizona Models,* by Betsy Jarrett. Phoenix, Ariz.: The Phoenix Arts Commission.

Brown, G. Z., and Mark DeKay. 2001. *Sun, Wind and Light.* New York: John Wiley and Sons.

Chelminski, Rudy. 2001. "Cold Comfort." *Smithsonian* 32, no. 9 (December): 63–70.

Childs, Mark. 1996a. "The Living End." *Planning* 62, no. 5 (May): 14–15.

———. 1996b. "The Incarnations of Central Avenue." *The Journal of Urban Design* 1, no. 3: 281–98.

———. 1999. *Parking Spaces.* New York: McGraw-Hill.

———. 2000. "Community Markets in the American City." *Designer/Builder* 7, no. 1 (May): 5–7.

———. 2001. "Civic Ecosystems." *Journal of Urban Design* 6, no. 1 (February): 55–72.

Childs, Mark, and Emily R. Childs. 2000. "Measuring Middle School Students' Preferences for Urban Form—Techniques for Visual Dialogues." Charleston: International Making Cities Livable Conference.

Cooper, Clare. 1974. "Children's Play Behaviour in a Low-Rise Inner City Housing Development." *Environmental Design Research Association* 5, no. 12: 197–211.

Correll, M. R., J. H. Lillydahl, and L. D. Singell. 1978. "The Effects of Greenbelts on Residential Property Values: Some Findings on the Political Economy of Open Space." *Land Economics* 54, no. 2: 207–17.

Cosner, Lewis. 1956. *The Functions of Social Conflict.* New York: Free Press.

Crawford, Stanley. 1988. *Mayordomo.* Albuquerque: University of New Mexico Press.

Crouch, Dora P., Daniel J. Garr, and Axel I. Mundigo. 1982. *Spanish City Planning in North America.* Cambridge, Mass.: MIT Press.

Crow, W. J. and J. L. Bull. 1975. *Robbery Deterrence: An Applied Behavioral Science Demonstration— Final Report.* La Jolla, Calif.: Western Behavior Sciences Institute.

Crowe, Timothy D. 2000. *Crime Prevention through Environmental Design,* 2d ed. Boston: Butterworth-Heinemann.

Davis, Howard. 1999. *The Culture of Building.* New York: Oxford University Press.

Dennis, Michael. 1986. *Court and Garden.* Cambridge, Mass.: MIT Press.

Dowie, Mark. 2003. "In Law We Trust." *Orion* (July/ August): 19–25.

Durrell, Lawrence. 1955. *The Tree of Idleness.* New York: Faber and Faber.

———. 1957. *Bitter Lemons.* New York: Faber and Faber.

Eck, John. 1997. "Preventing Crime at Places." In *Preventing Crime: What Works, What Doesn't, What's Promising.* A Report to the United States Congress. College Park: University of Maryland. NCJ 165366.

Edwards, Kathy and Esmé Howard. 1997. "Monument Avenue: The Architecture of Consensus in the New South, 1880–1930." In *Shaping Communities,* ed. Carter L. Hudgins and Elizabeth C. Cromley. Knoxville: University of Tennessee Press.

Eliot, T. S. 1920. *The Sacred Wood.* London: Methuen and Co.

Ellickson, Robert C. and A. Dan Tarlock, 1981. *Land-Use Controls: Cases and Materials.* Boston: Little, Brown and Company.

Emanuel, Steven L. 1994 [1979]. *Torts,* 5th ed. Larchmont, N.Y.: Emanuel Law Outlines.

Eran, Ben-Joseph. 1995. *Livability and Safety of Suburban Street Patterns: A Comparative Study.* Berkeley: Institute of Urban and Regional Development, University of California, Working Paper 641.

Faulkner, William. 1951. *Requiem for a Nun.* New York: Random House.

Favro, Diane. 1994. "The Street Triumphant: The Urban Impact of Roman Triumphal Parades." In *Streets: Critical Perspective on Public Space,* ed. Zeynep Celik, Diane Favro, and Richard Ingersoll. Berkeley: University of California Press.

Federal Highway Administration (FHWA). 1978. *A Pedestrian Planning Procedures Manual.* Report No. FHWA-RD-79–47.

Feyerabend, Paul. 1975. *Against Method.* London: Humanities Press.

Forbes, S. Russell. 1899. *The Aqueducts, Fountains and Springs of Ancient Rome.* Rome: Via Della Croce.

Francaviglia, Richard V. 1996. *Main Street Revisited.* Iowa City: University of Iowa Press.

Franck, Karen A., and Lynn Paxson. 1989. "Women and Urban Public Space." In *Public Places and Spaces,* ed. Irwin Altman and Ervin H. Zube. New York: Plenum Press.

Galbraith, John Kenneth. 1958. *The Affluent Society*. Boston: Houghton Mifflin.

Gard, Robert. 1999 [1954]. *Grassroots Theater*. Madison: University of Wisconsin Press.

Gehl, Jan. 1996. *Life Between Buildings*. Bogtrykkeriet, Skive: Arkitektens Forlag.

Gehl, Jan, and Lars Gemzøe. 2001. *New City Spaces*. Copenhagen: The Danish Architectural Press.

Gilmartin, Gregory F. 1995. *Shaping the City: New York and the Municipal Art Society*. New York: Clarkson Potter.

Goebbels, Joseph. 1929. *Michael*. Quoted in Elizabeth M. Wilkinson and L. A. Willoughby (1982), *On the Aesthetic Education of Man,* p. cxlii. New York: Oxford University Press.

Goffman, Erving. 1959. *The Presentation of Self in Everyday Life*. Garden City, N.Y.: Doubleday Anchor.

———. 1963. *Behavior in Public Places*. New York: Free Press of Glencoe.

———. 1971. *Relations in Public*. New York: Basic Books.

———. 1983. "The Interaction Order." *American Sociological Review* 48 (February): 1–17.

Gombrich, E. H. 1999. *The Uses of Images*. London: Phaidon Press.

Gribben, Arthur. 1992. *Holy Wells and Sacred Water Sources in Britain and Ireland: An Annotated Bibliography*. London: Garland Publishing.

Grimm, Jacob. 1883. "The Elements." In *Teutonic Mythology,* translated by J. S. Stallybrass. London: George Bell and Sons.

Habermas, Jürgen. 1989. *The Structural Transformation of the Public Sphere*. Translated by Thomas Burger. Cambridge, Mass.: MIT Press.

Hall, Edward. 1966. *The Hidden Dimension*. Garden City: N.Y.: Doubleday.

Hall, Sir Peter. 1998. *Cities in Civilization*. New York: Pantheon Books.

Hamilton, Mark. 1995. *Nineteenth Century Mormon Architecture and City Planning*. New York: Oxford University Press.

Handelman, Don. 1990. *Models and Mirrors: Towards an Anthropology of Public Events*. Cambridge, England: Cambridge University Press.

Hardin, Garrett. 1968. "The Tragedy of the Commons." *Science* (new series) 162, no. 3859 (Dec. 13): 1243–48.

Harries, Karsten. 1997. *The Ethical Function of Architecture*. Cambridge, Mass.: MIT Press.

Hayden, Dolores. 1995. *The Power of Place*. Cambridge, Mass.: MIT Press.

Heath, Kingston. 1997. "False-Front Architecture on Montana's Urban Frontier." In *Images of An American Land,* Thomas Carter. Albuquerque: University of New Mexico Press.

Hegemann, Werner and Elbert Peets. 1988 [1922]. *The American Vitruvius: An Architects' Handbook of Civic Art*. New York: Princeton Architectural Press. Originally published in 1922 by the Architectural Book Publishing Company, New York.

Hildebrand, Grant. 1999. *Origins of Architectural Pleasure*. Berkeley: University of California Press.

Hoffman, Donald D. 1998. *Visual Intelligence*. New York: W. W. Norton.

Hubbard, William. 1980. *Complicity and Conviction*. Cambridge, Mass.: MIT Press.

Illich, Ivan. 1973. *Tools for Conviviality*. New York: Harper and Row.

Itoh, Teiji. 1980. *Space and Illusion in the Japanese Garden*. New York: Weatherhill/Tankosha.

Jackson, J. B. 1985. "Urban Circumstances." *Design Quarterly* 128: 5–31.

Jacobs, Allan. 1993. *Great Streets*. Cambridge, Mass.: MIT Press.

Jacobs, Allan, Elizabeth MacDonald, and Yodar Rofé. 2001. *The Boulevard Book.* Cambridge, Mass.: MIT Press.

Jacobs, Jane. 1961. *The Death and Life of Great American Cities.* New York: Vintage Books.

Je, Hae-Seong. 1986. "Urban Residential Streets." Ph.D. diss. in Architecture. University of Pennsylvania.

Joardan, S. D. and J. W. Neill. 1978. "The Subtle Differences in Configurations of Small Public Spaces." *Landscape Architecture* 68, no. 11:487–91.

Kagan, Richard L. 2000. *Urban Images of the Hispanic World 1493–1793.* New Haven, Conn.: Yale University Press.

Kaplan, Rachel, and Stephen Kaplan 1989. *The Experience of Nature.* Cambridge, England: Cambridge University Press.

Kaplan, Rachel, Stephen Kaplan, and Robert L. Ryan. 1998. *With People in Mind.* Washington, D.C.: Island Press.

Kocpsell T., L. McCloskey, Wolf M. A. V. Moudon, D. Buchner, J. Kraus, and M. Patterson. 2002. "Crosswalk Markings and the Risk of Pedestrian-Motor Vehicle Collisions in Older Pedestrians." *Journal of the American Medical Association* 288, no. 17: 2136–44.

Köhler, Wolfgang. 1929. *Gestalt Psychology.* New York: Horace Liveright.

Kostof, Spiro. 1992. *The City Assembled.* London: Thames and Hudson.

———. 1995. *A History of Architecture.* New York: Oxford University Press.

Lam, W. F. 1998. *Governing Irrigation Systems in Nepal: Institutions, Infrastructure, and Collective Action.* Oakland, Calif.: Institute for Contemporary Studies Press.

Lee, Antoinette J. 2000. *Architects to the Nation.* Oxford, England: Oxford University Press.

Lippard, Lucy. 1997. *The Lure of the Local.* New York: New Press.

Lofland, Lyn H. 1998. *The Public Realm.* Hawthorne, N.Y.: Aldine De Gruyter.

Loomis, Dana, Stephen W. Marshall, Susanne H. Wolf, Carol W. Runyan, and John D. Butts. 2002. "Effectiveness of Safety Measures Recommended for Prevention of Workplace Homicide." *Journal of the American Medical Association* 287, no. 8 (Feb. 27): 1011–17.

Loukaitou-Sideris, Anastasia. 1999. "Hot Spots of Bus Stop Crime." *Journal of the American Planning Association* 65, no. 4 (autumn): 395–411.

Lynch, Kevin. 1960. *The Image of the City.* Cambridge, Mass.: MIT Press.

———. 1971. *Site Planning,* 2d ed. Cambridge, Mass.: MIT Press.

———. 1981. *Good City Form.* Cambridge, Mass.: MIT Press.

Lyndon, Donlyn and Charles W. Moore. 1994. *Chambers for a Memory Palace.* Cambridge, Mass.: MIT Press.

Manning, Frank E. 1983. *The Celebration of Society.* Bowling Green, Ohio: Bowling Green University Press.

Marcus, Clare Cooper and Carolyn Francis. 1998. *People Places.* New York: John Wiley.

Maslow, Abraham. 1970. *Motivation and Personality,* 2d ed. New York: Harper and Row.

Mayo, J. 1979. "Suburban Neighboring and the Cul-de-Sac Street." *Journal of Architectural Research* 7, no. 1.

McShane, Clay. 1994. *Down the Asphalt Path.* New York: Columbia University Press.

Mead, Margaret and Rhoda Metraux. 1980. *Aspects of the Present.* New York: Morrow.

Milne, A. A. 1928. *The House at Pooh Corner.* New York: E. P. Dutton and Company.

Moudon, Anne Vernez. 1986. *Built for Change.* Cambridge, Mass.: MIT Press.

Moughtin, Cliff, Taner Oc, and Steven Tiesdell. 1995. *Urban Design: Ornament and Decoration.* Oxford: Butterworth Architecture.

Nabokov, Peter, and Robert Easton. 1989. *Native American Architecture*. New York: Oxford University Press.

Neeson, J. M. 1993. *Commoners: Common Right, Enclosure and Social Change in England, 1700–1820*. Cambridge, England: Cambridge University Press.

Newman, Oscar. 1972. *Defensible Space*. New York: Macmillan.

———. 1995. "Defensible Space—A New Physical Planning Tool for Urban Revitalization." *Journal of the American Planning Association* 61, no. 2: 149–55.

Norberg-Schulz, Christian. 1979. *Genius Loci*. New York: Rizzoli.

———. 1984. *The Concept of Dwelling*. New York: Electra/Rizzoli.

———. 1986. *Architecture: Meaning and Place*. New York: Electra/Rizzoli.

Oldenburg, Ray. 1989. *The Great Good Place*. New York: Marlowe and Company.

Orr, David. 2002. *The Nature of Design*. New York: Oxford University Press.

Orwell, George. 1981. *A Collection of Essays*. San Diego: Harcourt Brace Jovanovich.

Ostrom, Elinor. 1990. *Governing the Commons*. Cambridge, England: Cambridge University Press.

Passini, Romedi. 1992. *Wayfinding in Architecture*. New York: Van Nostrand Reinhold.

Pevsner, N. 1955. *The Englishness of English Art*. London: British Broadcasting Corporation.

Poyner, Barry. 1983. *Design against Crime*. London: Butterworths.

Preiser, Wolfgang F. E. and Elaine Ostroff, eds. 2001. *Universal Design Handbook*. New York: McGraw-Hill.

Price, Edward T. 1968. "The Central Courthouse Square in the American County Seat." *Geographical Review* 58, no. 1: 29–60.

Price, V. B. 1997. "Epilogue." In *Anasazi Architecture*. Edited by Baker H. Morrow and V. B. Price. Albuquerque: University of New Mexico Press.

Project for Public Spaces (PPS). 2000. *How to Turn a Place Around*. New York: Project for Public Spaces.

Putnam, Robert D. 2000. *Bowling Alone*. Touchstone Books.

Reps, John W. 1965. *The Making of Urban America*. Princeton, N.J.: Princeton University Press.

Rich, Adrienne. 1978. *The Dream of a Common Language: Poems 1974–1977*. New York: W. W. Norton.

Riger, S., and M. T. Gordon. 1981. "The Fear of Rape." *Journal of Social Issues* 37: 71–93.

Robinson, Charles Mulford. 1903. *Modern Civic Art*. New York: The Knickerbocker Press.

Roddier, Mireille. 2003. *Lavoirs: Washhouses of Rural France*. New York: Princeton Architectural Press.

Rossi, Aldo. 1982. *The Architecture of the City*. Translated by Diane Ghirardo and Joan Ockman. Cambridge, Mass.: MIT Press.

Roy, Pam. 2002. Presentation at the School of Architecture and Planning. University of New Mexico, Albuquerque. March 7.

Rudofsky, Bernard. 1964. *Architecture without Architects*. Garden City, N.Y.: Doubleday.

Rykwert, Joseph. 1982. *The Necessity of Artifice*. New York: Rizzoli.

Sabean, David. 1984. *Power in the Blood: Popular Culture and Village Discourse in Early Modern Germany*. Cambridge, England: Cambridge University Press.

Sanoff, H. 2000. *Community Planning Methods in Design and Planning*. New York: John Wiley.

Sanoff, H., and J. Dickerson. 1971. "Mapping Children's Behavior in a Residential Setting." *Journal of Architectural Education* 25, no. 4: 100–103.

Senkevitch, Anatole. 1979. *The Architecture and Settlements of Russian America.* Washington, D.C.: Kennan Institute for Advanced Russian Studies.

Sennett, Richard. 1977. *The Fall of Public Man.* New York: Alfred A. Knopf.

———. 1990. *The Conscience of the Eye.* New York: Alfred A. Knopf.

Simon, Alfred. 2002. "Mixing Water and Culture: Making the Canal Landscape in Phoenix." Ph.D. diss., Arizona State University.

Sitte, Camillo. 1945 [1889]. *The Art of Building Cities.* Translated by Charles T. Stewart. New York: Reinhold Publishing Company.

Smith, Adam. 1976 [1776]. *The Wealth of Nations.* Oxford: Clarendon Press.

Smith, Morris. 1980–1981. Personal communications.

Sorkin, Michael. 1992. *Variations on a Theme Park.* New York: Hill and Wang.

Southworth, Michael, and Eran Ben-Joseph. 1997. *Streets and the Shaping of Towns and Cities.* New York: McGraw-Hill.

Stevenson, John. 1998. "The Mediation of the Public Sphere: Ideological Origins, Practical Possibilities." In *The Production of Public Space,* ed. Andrew Light and Jonathan M. Smith, 189–206. Lanham, Md.: Rowan and Littlefield.

Stone, Gregory. 1954. "City Shoppers and Urban Identification: Observations on the Social Psychology of City Life." *American Journal of Sociology* 60, no. 1 (July): 36–45.

Susskind, Lawrence, Sarah McKuaran, and Jennifer Thomas-Larmer, eds. 1999. *The Consensus Building Handbook.* Thousand Oaks, Pa.: Sage Publications.

Swentzell, Rina. 1997. "An Understated Sacredness." In *Anasazi Architecture.* Edited by Baker H. Morrow and V. B. Price. Albuquerque: University of New Mexico Press.

Tien, J. M., V. F. O'Donnell, A. Barnett, and P. B. Mirchandani. 1979. *Phase I Report: Street Lighting Projects.* Washington, D.C.: U.S. Government Printing Office.

Tschumi, Bernard. 2000. *Event-cities 2.* Cambridge, Mass.: MIT Press.

Turner, P. V. 1984. *Campus, An American Planning Tradition.* Architectural History Foundation. Cambridge, Mass.: MIT Press.

Underhill, Paco. 1999. *Why We Buy.* New York: Simon and Schuster.

Urban Land Institute (ULI). 1982. *Parking Requirements for Shopping Centers.* Washington, D.C.: ULI.

———. 1999. *Shopping Center Development Handbook,* 3d ed. Washington, D.C.: ULI.

Van Vleet, Russell. 1983. "An Examination of the Home Range of City and Suburban Teenagers." *Environment and Behavior* 15: 567–88.

Vance, James E., Jr. 1990. *The Continuing City.* Baltimore: Johns Hopkins University Press.

Veselka, Robert E. 2000. *The Courthouse Square in Texas.* Edited by Kenneth E. Foote. Austin: University of Texas Press.

Wandersman, A. 1981. "A Framework of Participation in Community Organizations." *Journal of Applied Behavioral Science* 17: 27–58.

Warner, Sam Bass. 1962. *Streetcar Suburbs.* Cambridge, Mass.: Harvard University Press.

Webb, Michael. 1990. *The City Square: A Historical Evolution.* New York: Whitney Library of Design.

Weiss, M. A. 1987. *The Rise of the Community Builders.* New York: Columbia University Press.

West, Cornell. 1992. "Learning to Talk of Race." *New York Times Magazine,* 2 August 1992, 24–26.

White, E. B. 1945. *Stuart Little.* New York: Harper and Row.

Whyte, William H. 1980. *The Social Life of Small Urban Spaces*. Washington, D.C.: The Conservation Foundation.

———. 1988. *City: Rediscovering the Center*. Garden City, N.Y.: Doubleday.

Wilhelm, Richard. 1950. *The I Ching*. Translated by Cary F. Baynes. Princeton, N.J.: Princeton University Press.

Wilson, Chris. 1997. *The Myth of Santa Fe*. Albuquerque: University of New Mexico Press.

Wilson, J. Q., and G. L. Kelling. 1982. "Broken Windows: The Police and Neighborhood Safety." *Atlantic Monthly* 249, no. 3: 29–38.

Wilson, William H. 1989. *The City Beautiful Movement*. Baltimore: Johns Hopkins University Press.

Wood, Joseph S. 1997. *The New England Village*. Baltimore: Johns Hopkins University Press.

Wooley, Helen, Christopher Spencer, Jessica Dunn, and Gwyn Rowley. "The Child as Citizen." *Journal of Urban Design* 4, no. 3: 255–82.

Wright, Robert R., and Susan Webber Wright. 1985. *Land Use in a Nutshell*. St. Paul, Minn.: West Publishing Company.

Zucher, Paul. 1959. *Town and Square*. New York: Columbia University Press.

Zukin, Sharon. 1991. *Landscapes of Power*. Berkeley: University of California Press.

INDEX

Italics = figure, **Bold** = definition, or main discussion